Mid Coast Hospital
Healthline
373-6585

200 Kid-Tested Ways to Lower the Fat in Your Child's Favorite Foods

200 Kid-Tested Ways to Lower the Fat in Your Child's Favorite Foods © 1993 by Elaine Moquette-Magee, M.P.H., R.D.

Library of Congress Cataloging-in-Publication Data
Moquette-Magee, Elaine.
200 kid-tested ways to lower the fat in your child's
favorite foods: how to make the
brand name and homemade foods your kids love   m o r e
healthful and delicious /
Elaine Moquette-Magee.
      p.   cm.
Includes index
ISBN 1-56561-034-2 : $12.95
1. Children—Nutrition. 2. Low-fat diet—Recipes. I. Title.
II. Title: Two hundred kid-tested ways to lower the fat in
your child's favorite foods.
RJ206.M82 1993
641.5'63'083—dc20   93-21046
                                                CIP

Edited by: Lisa Bartels Rabb
Cover and Interior Design: Terry Dugan
Production Coordinator: Claire Lewis
Printed in the United States of America

10   9   8   7   6   5   4   3   2   1
Published by: CHRONIMED Publishing
P.O. Box 47945
Minneapolis, MN 55447-9727

Table of Contents

Dedication

This book is dedicated to my two miracles, Devon and Lauren. Nothing in this world compares with the joy I feel watching you both grow up. Being a mother may be life's ultimate lesson in giving, but it's also life's grandest reward.

Acknowledgments

I would first like to thank my personal guinea pigs (Devon, Lauren, and husband Dennis) who tried many of the products and recipes contained in this book. (My daughter Devon loved helping me research the tips on pizza and fast food!) I would also like to thank my two major employers during this project, Lynda Trelut at Nob Hill Supermarkets in California and Lorelei DiSogra with Dole Food Products. Much of my research and writing while working for them "fed" into this book.

Foreword

Parents today do not want or need another nutrition lesson. Most of you already know what needs to be done, nutritionally speaking. What parents do need help in is figuring out how to cut the fat in their child's diet, without them noticing, and how to make lower-fat versions of the popular foods their children ask for. And of course, we all want to do this without sacrificing any important nutrients our children need to grow. What parents really want to know is:

- Which breakfast cereals are best for my kids?

- Is all fast food fat food? And what's the best fast-food chain to go to?

- Are the new "light" hotdogs light enough to make them okay for my kids?

- What are the 10 best and worst "children's" frozen meals or snacks?

- How can I make the best of the "school lunch" situation?

- What are some snack foods I can have around the house for when my children come home from school?

- Are there any "goodies" (cookies, crackers, chips) I can feel good about putting in my child's lunch box?

- Is it better to go out for pizza or for burgers after my son's little league game?

- Is any one pizza chain better than the others in terms of fat?

- Which of the heavily advertised kids' food products are particularly bad fat offenders?

These questions (and many, many more) will be answered in the pages of this book. I call this a "bathroom book" because you can flip through it, find a particular tip that interests you, and read through the page or two in just a few minutes.

Elaine Moquette-Magee

Introduction:
Looking at the Problem

Children today have never been fatter and less fit. Most will have a "family history" of heart disease or cancer (the No. 1 and No. 2 killers in this country).

The number of children with high blood pressure has risen in recent years, and 5 percent of our children from age one to 19 already have elevated or "at risk" serum cholesterol —200 milligrams per deciliter (mg./dl.) and above—before they even learn how to spell cholesterol. Twenty-five percent have serum cholesterol values of roughly 170 mg./dl. or more, which is considered "borderline" for children.

When it comes to concerns about food and diet, consumer surveys show fat is the nutrient people are *most* concerned about today. Although Americans have made some diet changes (eating less red meat, butter, eggs, and whole milk), the typical children's diet is still horribly high in fat. How can that be? Because we're also getting more fat in our diet from margarine, cooking oils, and convenience food products, including crackers, cookies, and ice cream. Most of the food products advertised on children's TV programs are mainly sugar held together with fat. Many of our school lunches even flunk out in the fat department.

The final concern that cannot be ignored is that today's parents are busy, busy, busy! Both probably punch time cards and then split their "after work" hours between little league games and dance classes, homework, and bath time. Precious little time is left for worrying about what to feed the hungry troops. Most of us have limited time and energy for figuring out a balanced nutrition plan for our kids.

Well, that's what the rest of this book is all about: How to feed a low-fat diet to the world's toughest food critics—our children—and get away with it!

The Pyramid:

A New Look for Nutrition

The Pyramid: New Look for Nutrition

Kids today may score high in finger dexterity tests (because of all the video games they play), and they may know more about computers than kids did 20 years ago. But when it comes to exercise, obesity, or their diets, many kids are flunking out.

According to several researchers, the main culprit behind the serious lack of fitness in our youth today is television. Forget an occasional show or two a couple of evenings a week. It's more like several hours after school every day and then again after dinner. It seems to me the actual physical activity of playing baseball or basketball has been replaced with video and hand-held sports games.

One researcher, studying over 1,000 children, found that kids who watched 4 hours of television a day were 4 times as likely to have high serum cholesterol as the kids who watched less than 2 hours a day.

The consequences of this modern sedentary childhood don't stop at lack of muscle tone either. Over the past 20 years obesity (being more than 20 percent above the ideal weight for your height and frame size) among children between the ages of 6 and 11 has increased by 54 percent, and for 15 to 17 years olds, the rate of obesity is 39 percent higher. This adds up to a grand total of 20 million obese children currently in the United States.

What probably frightens me the most as a registered dietitian is the thought of these kids being put on strict or "fad" diets. After all, that's how most parents deal with their own weight problems, even though that kind of weight loss is usually temporary. But the tendency toward obesity in our children (and adults for that matter) is usually a direct result of a lifestyle short on physical activity and exercise and tall on fat and sugar calories. One source estimates that 75 percent of American children's daily food fare contains too much fat, and about one-fifth of the total calories come from refined sugar.

So isn't it logical for the answer to be a healthier diet (low in fat and sugar) and an increase in exercise? Not only is the alternative—"dieting"—likely to be ineffective, it's downright dangerous in children—physically and emotionally. Dieting can interfere with a child's growth and can encourage eating disorders, not to mention affecting their alertness in school. Child psychologists have documented that although diets or parental pressures to diet are temporary, they can cause permanent emotional scars on children.

Instead of policing the *quantity* of food our children eat, experts suggest paying attention instead to the *quality*. Choose foods lower in fat and added sugar; discourage sweets and high-fat snacks and desserts; encourage fruits, vegetables, low-fat dairy products, and grains. Sound familiar? This is the way the whole family should be eating!

Food Guide Pyramid
Suggested Daily Servings

Key

• Fat (naturally occurring and added)

▼ Sugars (added)

These symbols show that fat and added sugars come mostly from fats, oils, and sweets, but can be part of, or added to foods from the other food groups as well.

Fats, Oils & Sweets
Use Sparingly

Milk, Yogurt & Cheese Group
2-3 Servings

Meat, Fish, Dry Beans, Eggs & Nut Group
2-3 Servings

Vegetable Group
3-5 Servings

Fruit Group
2-4 Servings

Bread, Cereal, Rice & Pasta Group
6-11 Servings

The Eating Right Pyramid

The Eating Right Pyramid is an illustration designed to educate Americans on what's in a healthful diet.

In the 1920s, a government-released food guide listed sugar as a food group. Twenty years later, an eight-food group plan was used with eggs and butter and margarine having their own grouping. The Basic Four Food Groups were introduced in the '50s. Finally, in April of 1992, this new pyramid-shaped guide was born. The pyramid visually emphasizes breads, cereals and grains, and fruits and vegetables.

With the Eating Right Pyramid, the largest portions of the pyramid (the bottom) represent the food groups we should eat more of (grains, fruits, and vegetables). And the smallest portions of the pyramid (the top) represent the food groups we should eat less of (meats, dairy products, and added fats and sugars).

Important concepts to keep in mind with this eating plan are:

- *Moderation*. Avoid too much fat, saturated fat, cholesterol, and sugar.

- *Proportionality*. Eat appropriate amounts of food from the major food groups.

- *Variety*. Eat a selection of foods from each of the the major food groups.

How the Pyramid Came To Be

The Human Nutrition Information Service (branch of U.S. Department of Agriculture [USDA] responsible for education on nutrition) decided to develop a teaching tool that would promote the 1990 Dietary Guidelines more aggressively.

Focus groups of adults showed that the pyramid, when compared with hundreds of other graphic representations, communicated the guidelines most clearly. The pyramid was then sent to 30 university and federal nutritionists who determined it was accurate and useful. A year later, the pyramid was tested on school children and low-income adults.

How does the new food pyramid differ from the Basic Four Food Groups?

- The Basic Four was pictured as a pie, which visually implies all pieces have equal value.

- The pyramid groups fruits and vegetables separately, so there are five food categories instead of four.

- In the Eating Right Pyramid, the number of servings recommended per day for breads and cereals increases from four to a minimum of six. The recommended number of servings for fruits and vegetables goes up from four a day to a minimum of five. The serving recommendations for dairy products and the meats remained the same—two servings of each a day.

Meeting Nutrient Needs on a Low-Fat Diet

Some parents hesitate feeding their children low-fat foods because they fear the kids won't get enough vitamins, minerals, and protein for healthy growth. In my experience, when children are given a moderately low-fat diet, especially one that doesn't exclude any of the food groups, the only difference is the fat, not the vitamins and minerals.

Why? Because the best sources for many vitamins and minerals are fruits, vegetables, and grains. Even with meat, milk, and other dairy products, lower fat choices tend to be richer in essential nutrients.

If you lower the fat in your child's diet, will you also lower the amount of vital nutrients he or she gets? That's one of those questions best answered with a few more questions

- How low is the fat in the diet?
- Is any food group being eliminated to achieve this low-fat diet?
- Is your child getting the minimum number of servings recommended each day?

If the answers to those three questions are "moderately low in fat," "no," and "yes," your child should be much better off with a low-fat diet than the typical high-fat American diet.

These are the key nutrients your child needs to support healthy growth:

- protein
- calcium, phosphorus, iron, and zinc
- vitamins A, C, B_6, folic acid, B_{12}

Fiber is also an important nutrient at any age, and we all need an adequate calorie intake to support our health.

Using the new food pyramid, let's compare various low- and high-fat choices for key nutrients. One of the best standards to use is the recommended daily allowance (RDA). But keep in mind that the RDAs are set above what most individuals need in order to ensure that even the biggest people in the population (who usually have the highest requirements) will be covered.

Higher-Fat Diet	**Lower-Fat Option.**
(Not all choices are high fat.)	

2 servings milk/dairy group:

1 cup whole milk	1 cup 1 percent low-fat milk
1 1/2 oz. cheddar cheese	1 1/2 oz. reduced-fat cheese
	(5 gm. of fat per oz.)

2 servings meat/meat alternatives group:

3 oz. regular ground beef, cooked	3 oz. ground sirloin, cooked
3 oz. chicken thigh roasted with skin	1 chicken breast without skin

3 servings vegetable group:

1 small serving McDonald's french fries	3/4 cup broccoli (=1 1/2 servings)
1/2 cup yellow corn	3/4 cup carrots (=1 1/2 servings)
1/2 cup potato salad	

At least 2 servings fruits:

3/4 cup orange juice	3/4 cup orange juice
1 apple	1 apple
1 banana	1 banana

6 servings bread, grains, and cereal group:

1 oz. Nature Valley Granola®	1 oz. Wheaties®
1 fried corn tortilla	1 steamed corn tortilla
1 biscuit from mix	1 slice whole wheat bread
1/2 cup macaroni, cooked	1/2 cup macaroni, cooked
1/2 cup rice, cooked	1/2 cup rice, cooked
1 slice whole wheat bread	1 slice whole wheat bread

Let's Compare:

	Higher-Fat Choices	Lower-Fat Choices
Calories	2207	1484
Fiber	26 gm.	28 gm.
Protein	95 gm. (146%*)	99 gm. (152 %*)
Fat	91 gm.	26 gm.
Saturated Fat	35 gm.	11 gm.
Cholesterol	335 mg.	183 mg.
Calcium	830 mg. (83%*)	952 mg. (95% *)
Phosphorus	1439 mg. (144%*)	1463 (146%*)
Iron†	12 mg. (67-120%*)	16 mg. (89-160%*)
Zinc	13 mg. (87%*)	13 mg. (87%*)
Vitamin A	372 RE (37%*)	3705 RE (370%*)**
Vitamin C††	138 mg. (230%*)	223 mg. (372%*)
Vitamin B$_6$	2 mg. (100%*)	3.2 mg. (160%*)
Vitamin B$_{12}$	4.2 mcg. (70%*)	5.5 mcg. (92%*)
Folic acid	239 mcg. (60%*)	340 mcg. (85%*)

The USRDA (United States recommended daily allowance) for ages 4 years through adults was used for comparison purposes.

* *Percentage of recommended daily allowance.*
† *The RDA for iron is higher for menstruating women (18 mg.) than for nonmenstruating girls and women and boys and men (10 mg.).*
** *This value is extremely high because a serving of carrots and broccoli were selected for the vegetable group, and these two vegetables are extremely good sources of carotene (vitamin A).*
†† *The RDA was calculated for nonsmokers, ages 4 year through adults (60 mg.). The RDA for smokers is now 80 mg. per day.*

Most of you probably know by now that much of the saturated fat and cholesterol in the typical American diet, and a handsome portion of the total fat, comes directly from the milk/dairy and meat groups. So let's look specifically at the differences in the key nutrients in higher and lower fat choices.

Higher-Fat Choices	Lower-Fat Choices
2 servings milk/dairy group:	
I cup whole milk	I cup 1% low-fat milk
I 1/2 ounces cheddar cheese	I 1/2 oz. reduced-fat cheese
	(5 gm. of fat per ounce)
2 servings meat/meat alternatives group:	
3 oz. regular ground beef, cooked	3 oz. ground sirloin, cooked
3 oz. chicken thigh roasted with skin	I chicken breast, without skin

Let's Compare:

	Higher Fat	Lower Fat
Calories	799 gm.	534 gm.
Protein	64 gm.	72 gm.
Fat	54 gm.	19.5 gm.
Saturated Fat	25 gm.	10 gm.
Cholesterol	249 mg.	181 mg.
Riboflavin (B$_2$)	0.90 mg.	0.91mg.
Vitamin B$_{12}$	3.9 mcg.	4 mcg.
Calcium	617 mg.	644 mg.
Iron	12 mg.	16 mg.

The following list of key nutrients is based primarily on those required during the growing years.

Vitamin A—This vitamin affects DNA and ultimately the type and amount of protein synthesized by the cells, affecting growth and health of cartilage, bone and body coverings and linings.

Sources: The fruit and vegetable groups contain a number of foods that are great sources. The carotene-containing deep orange and dark green vegetables have the highest vitamin A content.

Vitamin B$_6$—Many reactions involved in protein metabolism require B$_6$. It makes sense then that the amount of B$_6$ needed is in direct proportion to the amount of protein in the diet.

Sources: Meats and meat alternatives are generally good sources. The body does not generally use B$_6$ from plant sources as well as it does from animal sources.

Folic Acid and B$_{12}$—Each of these is involved in DNA and RNA metabolism. Since DNA and RNA direct cell division, these vitamins are especially vital during periods of growth.

Sources: Folic acid is found in fruits and vegetables, legumes, and some grain products. B$_{12}$ is found in meat and other animal products.

Vitamin C—Vitamin C is needed for the formation of collagen, the substance required for making the framework of bone, healthy skin, muscle, and scar tissue.

Sources: Many common fruits and vegetables have a high vitamin C content, but citrus fruits, broccoli, cabbage, cantaloupe, cauliflower, green peppers, and strawberries are excellent sources.

Iron*—Iron is a component of many enzymes. It is also part of blood protein (hemoglobin) and muscle protein (myoglobin), both of which bind with and carry oxygen.

Sources: Meat, fish, and poultry are excellent sources. Significant amounts are found in eggs, legumes, nuts, whole grains, enriched cereal products, and leafy vegetables.

Zinc*—Zinc is a part of 70 enzyme systems in the body. If a diet is deficient in zinc, various symptoms can occur, including a failure to grow.

Sources: The best diet sources are seafood, red meats, nuts and legumes.

Calcium and Phosphorus—These two minerals are important during growth because they contribute to the body structure and have many other functions as well. They are the minerals that appear in the greatest amounts in the body. Ninety-nine percent of the body's calcium and 85 percent of the phosphorus are found in the bones and teeth.

Sources: Both can be found in milk and milk products, but phosphorus can also be found in meat sources.

* A 1986 national survey of nutrition in American children found that the average intakes of children ages 1 to 5 years met the RDA for all nutrients except iron and zinc.

Kids and Cholesterol

Everything you ever wanted to know about serum (blood) cholesterol and the early development of atherosclerosis (fatty deposits in the lining of the arteries) in children is covered in a recent summary report by the National Cholesterol Education Program.

According to this report:
- Autopsy studies on children and teens have strongly suggested that the atherosclerotic process begins in childhood.
- Elevated serum (blood) cholesterol levels early in life play a role in the development of adult atherosclerosis.
- Children and teens with high serum cholesterol are more likely than the general population to have high levels as adults.

But the news does get better. We can't do much about hereditary cholesterol problems and heart disease risk, but we can do a lot about our eating habits. It probably comes as no surprise that diet is the primary treatment for high cholesterol in children. And, according to this national study, lowering serum cholesterol in children and teens is indeed beneficial.

The report provides these suggestions for healthier eating.
- Reduce saturated fat intake to less than 10 percent of total calories.
- On average, reduce total fat intake to no more than 30 percent of total calories.
- Keep dietary cholesterol below 300 mg. per day.
- Eat a wide variety of foods.

- Make sure you have enough calories to support growth and development and reach desirable body weight.

Note: These recommendations refer to an AVERAGE over a period of several days.

How far does the average American child have to go to meet these diet recommendations? Apparently not far. According to the preliminary data from the USDA 1987-88 Nationwide Food Consumption Survey, the average cholesterol intake for children is already under 300 mg. per day.

The percentage of calories from fat and saturated fat share a slightly different scenario. The average intake of saturated fat is 14 percent, so it needs to be reduced by at least one-third to meet the recommendation of less than 10 percent. And children, on average, are getting about 36 percent of their calories from fat, which needs to be lowered to 30 percent or less.

Where is All This Fat Coming From?

What's the major source of fat in the American diet? If you guessed meat and dairy products, sorry, but no cigar. One government survey confirms that when you add up all the fats and oils used in cooking and on the table, they win the fat race.

If you really want to know where to point the fat finger, take a look at the list that follows. It shows the amount of fat each food category contributes after food "mixtures" are analyzed by ingredients.

	Ranking	Percent contribution to total fat in the American diet
1.)	Fats and oils (shortenings, oils, butter, margarine, mayonnaise, salad dressings, fatty sauces, nondairy sour cream, etc.)	30
2.)	Meat, fish, poultry	26
3.)	Milk and milk products (cream, sour cream, all types of cheese, etc.)	19
4.)	Grain products (breads and other baked goods, cereals, pastas, biscuit mix, etc.)	9
5.)	White potatoes (plain potatoes, French fries, potato chips, potato soup)	5
6.)	Legumes, nuts, seeds (beans, peas, soybean-derived products, nuts, peanut butter, coconut milk and cream, seeds)	4
7.)	Eggs	4
8.)	Sugars, sweets (candy and chocolate)	1
9.)	Other vegetables (olives and some fat added to commercial vegetables)	1

TIP #1 / KNOW WHO YOU'RE DEALING WITH—THE WORLD'S TOUGHEST FOOD CRITICS.

How do you feed a low-fat diet to kids—the world's toughest food critics? The answer may depend on the personal profile of your particular little person(s).

The child who is interested in fitness and health might be impressed by knowing how much fat various foods contain. These prize pupils, whom I call "Eager To Pleasers," may need little convincing to switch to lower-fat milk, reduced-fat cheese and cold cuts, low-fat and fat-free crackers, etc.

On the other hand, some kids criticize and question just about everything. These Picky Pauls and Sarcastic Sallys instantly think anything with a "lite" label is "gross" or "disgusting." I affectionately call this group the "Gladsome Gluttons."

If you happen to have an Eager To Pleaser, simply including him or her in your fat-fighting activities might be all you need to do.

If you share your home with one or more Gladsome Gluttons, though, you have your work cut out for you.

So, the first key to lowering fat is to know who you are dealing with—whether it's a Gladsome Glutton or an Eager To Pleaser. Then you can adjust your actions accordingly.

TIP #2 / DON'T DENY THEM THEIR FAVORITES.

The second key concept to feeding a low-fat diet is to **do it without denying your kids their favorite foods.** Sound impossible? That's what this book is all about. We'll give you lots of ideas for modifying your kids favorite foods to cut the fat.

TIP #3 / YOU DON'T HAVE TO TELL THEM IT'S GOOD FOR THEM.

Sometimes what they don't know won't hurt them—and just might help them. So don't feel you need to explain your new recipes or lower-fat meals.

I confess I have trouble keeping quiet about my low-fat meals. I usually want people to know that the food they're eating is part of a lower-fat, healthful diet. I need to help disprove the common myth that if it tastes good it must be bad for you. Contrary to popular belief, healthful foods can taste great!

So go ahead and quietly serve the lower-fat recipes and food products described in this book. Then sit back and collect the compliments. No one has to be the wiser.

TIP #4 / EAT AT THE BOTTOM OF THE FOOD PYRAMID.

Getting kids to eat from the bottom of the new food pyramid (which basically means eating more breads, grains, and cereals and more fruits and vegetables) is the challenge of the decade. Doing so will increase complex carbohydrates, which will usually bring a multitude of fiber, vitamins, and minerals with them, while decreasing the amount of fat, cholesterol, and empty calories.

Actually most kids already like the bread and cereals group. They just don't realize it. Kids think of cheese when they think of macaroni and cheese. But the macaroni is actually the primary ingredient. Kids think about meat when they think of hamburgers, but I haven't met a burger yet that didn't come with a bun. And pizza, probably the most popular kid food, contains cheese and tomato sauce, but all of that sits on a nice, thick layer of bready crust—and the thicker the better.

The new food pyramid recommends 6 to 11 servings per day for breads and cereals.

That may sound a little intimidating, but you might be surprised how fast these carbohydrate-rich servings add up. A sandwich at lunch counts as two servings, since a serving is one slice. And with an ounce of hot or cold cereal at breakfast and a cup of cooked rice or pasta, or 2 bread servings with dinner, you're up to 5—just one serving shy of the minimum.

As a nation, we would be health wise to be heavier-handed with the rice and other grains, noodles, breads, and cereals and go lighter on the dairy products, meats, eggs, and nuts.

And, of course, while maximizing bread and grain servings, we should be minimizing the cheese sauces and butters we cover them with.

Another thing we can do is choose as many whole-grain options as possible. Personally, I prefer my rice and pasta white and enriched but, without exception, I buy whole-grain hot and cold cereals and whole-grain bread. It might well be the other way around for you and your family.

And lastly, there are many more interesting ways to meet your bread/cereals/grain servings than you might think. Clear broth soups (preferably low sodium) with noodles and rice are a warm way to get a serving, while cold pasta salads, like macaroni or Italian pasta salads (preferably with lower-fat dressings), are a cool way. Bagels, English muffins, and cinnamon-raisin breads can be a nice accompaniment to many a boring breakfast entree. To beat the breakfast cereal blahs, rotate your cold cereal choices and don't forget your plentiful hot cereal options, especially during the winter.

Don't forget that some of the fancier rolls, such as croissants, biscuits, and cinnamon rolls have quite a bit more fat added to them. Here are some comparisons:

- Two slices of raisin bread have 133 calories and 1.4 gm. of fat, compared with a cinnamon roll, which might contain at least 300 calories and over 10 gm. of fat.

- An English muffin, with 140 calories and 1 gm. of fat is a better choice than a biscuit with around 300 calories and 10 gm. of fat.

- A dinner roll (93 calories and 2 gm. of fat) beats a crescent roll or small croissant (240 calories and 12 gm. of fat).

- A blueberry bagel (180 calories and 1 gm. of fat) is a smarter choice than a blueberry muffin (with 270 calories and 10 gm. of fat)

Bread products that are most similar in texture to an actual loaf of bread—such as a bagel, hamburger bun, or dinner roll—are also generally the lowest in fat.

Bread is also a great way to get some of the 20 to 30 gm. of fiber the National Cancer Institute recommends we get every day. Look for "100 percent whole-wheat" or "100 percent whole-grain" when selecting bread, bagels, or English muffins. If there's a "wheat" or whole-grain bread that's not 100 percent whole wheat but you just love, enjoy it. Some whole wheat is better than none. What about days when you can't resist picking up a loaf of warm sourdough or French bread? Well, just eat a few more beans that day to make up for the fiber you won't be getting from your bread.

TIP #5 / FIND MORE FIBER.

Most parents today are expert jugglers. Between getting the kids to school and getting themselves to work and managing all the other activities they're involved in, who has time to calculate whether they're getting the recommended 20 to 30 gm. of dietary fiber every day?

Your body benefits most when fiber is spread out each day. But with a daily goal of at least 20 gm. of fiber, who wants to mess around with one measly gram of fiber here and another gram there. A breakfast cereal, for example, needs to contain at least 5 gm. of fiber per serving to impress me.

Fiber comes to us naturally in fruits, vegetables, legumes, nuts and seeds, and, of course, whole grains and their products. But I'll warn you right now, the grams of fiber the legume group (beans and peas) contributes are pretty hard to beat. Only a few dried fruits even come close!

By capitalizing on the distinguished high-fiber foods listed here and choosing at least one per meal, you're well on the way to meeting your fiber needs.

	Fiber (gm.)	Calories
Legumes, I cup cooked		
Pinto beans	19.5	235
Refried	20	270
Kidney beans, canned	19	208
Navy beans	16	259
Lima beans, fresh	16	208
Black beans	15.4	227
Lima beans, canned	14.5	164
Blackeyed peas, frozen	14	224
Baked (white) beans	14	235
Blackeyed peas, fresh	12	160
Garbonzo beans	11	269
Lentils	10	231
Baby lima beans, frozen	8.0	94
Soybeans	6.0	298

Nuts and Seeds, 1/4 cup * *CAUTION: These foods are usually a good source of fat as well as a good source of fiber (except pumpkin seeds and chestnuts).*

Pumpkin seeds	5.7	71
Chestnuts, roasted	4.6	88
Almonds, dried	4.4	210
Peanuts, dry roasted	3.2	211
Sunflower seeds, dried	2.5	205
Peanut butter, 2 Tbsp.	2.4	188

Whole Grains and Their Products

Bread: 2 slices	Fiber (gm.)	Calories
100 percent whole wheat	4.2	140
Pumpernickel	3.8	160
Rye	3.4	130
Roman Meal®	7.4	147

Hot Cereals: 1 cup cooked

Corn grits	4.5	145
Oatmeal	4.1	145
Whole wheat cereal	3.9	150
Cream of Wheat®	3.4	140
Wheatena®	3.3	135
Ralston®	3.3	134
Farina®	3.2	116
Malt-O-Meal®	3.0	122

Cold Cereals: (with 5 gm. of fiber or more per serving)

Bran Chex®	13.5	234
Fruit and Fibre®	11.0	269
Most®	9.7	262
Shredded Wheat 'n Bran®	9.0	202
Shredded Wheat with Oat Bran®	9.0	224
Kellogg's 40% Bran Flakes®	8.0	190
Frosted Mini-Wheats® (8 biscuits)	7.0	224
Common Sense Oat Bran®	6.0	200
Muesli Almond/Date®	6.0	280
Post Raisin Bran®	6.0	120

GRAINS:
I cup cooked

	Fiber (gm.)	Calories
Bulgar	10.6	151
Barley	4.5	193
Whole-wheat spaghetti noodles	4.5	174
Wild rice	4	166
Brown rice	3.3	217
BRAN: 1/4 cup		
Oat bran	4.1	33
Wheat bran	3.8	33
Wheat germ	3	90
OTHER:		
Popcorn, 3 cups popped	3.9	30
Bran muffin, small (wheat or oat)	2.8	135
Corn tortilla, 1	2.4	87

FRUITS:
(with 2 gm. or more of fiber per serving)

Dried fig, 1	2.1	48
Mango slices, 1 cup	5.8	108
Guava, 1	5.3	45
Papaya, 1	5.2	117
Pear, 1	4.6	98
Blackberries, 1/2 cup	4-4.8	75-95
Dried prunes, 5	4.1	100
Orange, 1	3.1	60
Apple with skin, 1	3	80
Peaches, 1 cup	3	109
Prune juice, 1 cup	2.8	173
Nectarine, 1	2.7	67
Boysenberries, 1/2 cup	2.6	66
Raisins, 1/4 cup	2.1	109
Strawberries/raspberries 1/2 cup	2	22-30
Applesauce, 1/2 cup	2	53

VEGETABLES: (with 2.5 gm. or more of fiber per 1/2 cup cooked)	Fiber (gm.)	Calories
Potato with skin, 1	4.7	220
Succotash	4.5	100
Corn, from fresh	4.3	45
Sweet potato, baked or boiled	3.5-4.5	120-160
Green peas, frozen	3.6	63
Turnip greens, frozen	3.5	24
Corn, frozen	3.4	34
Brussels sprouts	3.4	30
Winter squash (acorn, butternut, Hubbard)	3	50
Eggplant cubes	3	23
Carrots from fresh/frozen.	2.7	13-18
Broccoli from frozen	2.7	51
Spinach from frozen	2.5	27
Broccoli from fresh	2.4	22

TIP #6 / PUMP THE IRON.

Iron probably is one of the most sexist minerals around. Iron deficiency, while almost nonexistent in men, runs rampant in the female gender. I'm afraid when it comes to "pumping iron," women just can't win for losing. Even though their bodies are usually smaller than men's, their RDA for iron is quite a bit higher, because they lose some iron every month through menstruation. And yet their diet intake of iron is usually lower than men's because they tend to eat fewer calories overall and, in particular, smaller portions of meat, fish, and poultry—the richest sources of iron.

The RDA for men ages 25 to 50 and for women after menopause is 10 mg., compared with 15 mg. for women ages 19 to 50, and 30 mg. for those pregnant or nursing. At first glance, 10, 15, and 30 mg. certainly doesn't sound that intimidating. But once you learn that a serving of one of the best food sources of iron (3 ounces of lean beef) contributes a meager 2 mg. toward the 10, 15, or 30 mg. goal, iron starts earning a little respect.

Iron is an essential component of hemoglobin in the blood—the substance that carries oxygen from the lungs to the body tissues. Iron also is a component of myoglobin, which stores oxygen in muscle tissue for use during future muscle contractions. And that's not all. Iron is also a part of several enzymes and important proteins that the body needs to run its best.

How do Americans weigh in when it comes to pumping their all-important iron? Well, for American women, iron is considered the most common nutrient deficiency. The groups at highest risk for deficiency are infants, adolescents, and women between puberty and menopause, pregnant women especially. That pretty much covers half the population!

Since the majority of body iron is in the hemoglobin, iron-deficiency anemia usually results in a reduction in the size and number of red blood cells, which means there are fewer cells in the blood to pick up oxygen. That's why some of the most common symptoms of iron deficiency are decreased energy and endurance and a pale complexion. Recent evidence also suggests (although a cause-and-effect relationship has not yet been established) that iron deficiency may decrease our resistance to infection.

The good news is iron can be found in a wide variety of foods. The bad news is almost none of these foods have impressive amounts of iron. While it's true the meat, fish, and poultry group enjoys the reputation of being "the best" iron food source, it's not because they outrun all the other foods with their hefty iron content. It's actually because these animal products contain heme iron, which the body absorbs better than it does non-heme iron, the type of iron found in plant foods.

Listed below are some assorted sources of iron.

Meat/Fish/Poultry	Serving size	Iron (mg.)
Beef, cooked:		
Ground sirloin,		
extra lean	3 oz.	2
Steak, lean	3 oz.	2
Roast beef, lean	3 oz.	1.7
Lamb, cooked:		
Leg of lamb or cutlet, lean	3 oz.	1.8
Pork, cooked:		
Center loin	3 oz.	0.8

Turkey/Chicken, cooked:	Serving size	Iron (mg.)
Dark meat	3 oz.	2
Light meat	3 oz.	1.2
Chicken half breast	1, skinless	0.9
Chicken thigh	1, skinless	0.7

Fish, cooked:

Clam meat, steamed	3 oz.	23
Clams, canned, drained	1/4 cup	11
Eastern oysters, steamed	3 oz.	11
Oysters, canned, drained	3 oz.	5.7
Shrimp	3 1/2 oz.	3
Tuna, light, canned in water	6 1/2 oz. can	2.4
Eggs	1 whole	0.7 (mostly in yolk)
Hot dog	1 2 oz. frank	0.8

Beans, legumes:

Regular style tofu	1/2 cup	6.6
Soybeans, cooked from dry	1/2 cup	4.4
Lentils, cooked	1/2 cup	3.3
Garbonzo/chickpeas, cooked	1/2 cup	2.4
Kidney or white beans, canned	1/2 cup	1.6
Lima beans, cooked	1/2 cup	1.5
Black-eyed peas, cooked	1/2 cup	0.9

Fruits:

Mango slices	1 cup	2.1
Raspberries, frozen	1 cup	1.6
Strawberries, frozen	1 cup	1.1
Raspberries, fresh	1 cup	0.7
Strawberries, fresh	1 cup	0.6
Apricots, fresh	3 whole	0.6

Dried Fruits:

Dried apricots	5 whole (10 halves)	1.6
Raisins/currants	1/4 cup	1.2
Dried prunes	5 whole	1

Fruit Juices:	Serving size	Iron (mg.)
Prune juice	1 cup	3
Orange juice,		
canned/unsweetened	1 cup	1.1
(in refrigerated cartons)		0.4
Grape juice, from frozen	1 cup	0.8
Grape juice, bottled	1 cup	0.6
Pineapple juice	1 cup	0.7

Vegetables:

Potato, microwaved	1 whole	3.5
Spinach, cooked from fresh	1/2 cup	3.2
Spinach, raw leaves	2 cups	3
Chard, cooked	1/2 cup	2
Spinach, frozen, and cooked	1/2 cup	1.45
Peas, frozen and cooked	1/2 cup	1.25
Romaine lettuce, raw	2 cups chopped	1.2
Brussels sprouts, cooked	1/2 cup	0.9
Cabbage (bok choy), cooked	1/2 cup	0.9
Broccoli, cooked	1/2 cup	0.65
Asparagus, cooked	1/2 cup	0.6

Hot Cereals, cooked:

Cream of Wheat®	1 cup	10.5
Malt-O-Meal®	1 cup	9.5
Oatmeal, instant/fortified	1 cup from packet	6
Oatmeal, prepared from oats	1 cup	1.6
Grits, enriched	1 cup	1.6
Roman meal, Wheatena	1 cup	1.5

Cold Cereals:

Wheaties®	1 oz.	4.5
Kellogg's Cornflakes®	1 oz.	1.8
Grapenuts®	1 oz.	1.2
Shredded Wheat®	1 oz.	1.2

* Most ready-to-eat cereals are fortified with iron (usually about 25 percent of the USRDA, about 2.5 to 3.8 mg. per ounce).

Bread Products:	Serving size	Iron (mg.)
Submarine (hoagie) roll	I	3.8
Whole-wheat bread	2 slices	2.4
Bagel (plain)	I whole	2.1
English muffin	I whole	1.7
Pancakes from recipe/mix	3, 4-inch dia.	1.5-2.1
Waffles from recipe/mix	1, 7-inch dia.	1.2-1.5
Muffins from recipe/mix	I	1-1.5
Enriched breads	2 slices	1.4
(white, raisin bread,		
wheat, light rye, oatmeal)		
Hamburger/hot-dog bun	I	1.25
Tortillas, enriched	2, 6-inch corn or 8-inch flour	1.2

Other Grain Products:

White rice, enriched,		
cooked	I cup	2.3
Pasta noodles,		
enriched, cooked	I cup	2
Bulgar, cooked	I cup	1.8
Barley, cooked	I cup	1.6
Stove Top Stuffing® mix	1/2 cup	1.2
Brown rice, cooked	I cup	0.8

Note: Organ meats (liver, kidney, and heart) are considered good sources of iron. But these foods may also be possible sources of environmental contaminants and toxins and are definitely high in fat and cholesterol.

When it comes to iron there's an old saying: "Don't count your milligrams before they're absorbed." A milligram "eaten" isn't necessarily a milligram "used." The percentage of iron actually absorbed into the bloodstream depends on two things: the food source of that iron and whether any iron absorption "enhancers" or "inhibitors" have also been eaten at the meal.

If "enhancers" are present, a higher percentage of the iron will usually be absorbed. But it can also work the other way. If any "inhibitors" are eaten at the same time, a lower percentage of the iron will be absorbed. So, obviously, to get the greatest bang for our buck we should avoid foods that inhibit absorption while capitalizing on those that enhance it. The major inhibitors are antacids, bran, phytates (which are found in grains and leafy green vegetables), calcium phosphate, and tannic acid/polyphenols in tea. Drinking coffee before a meal also may inhibit iron absorption.

On the other hand, there appear to be only two iron "enhancers." The first is vitamin C. If a vitamin-C-rich food or beverage is part of the meal, more of the iron present will be absorbed. That gives you yet another reason to have orange juice with breakfast and to include vitamin-C-rich fruits and vegetables with lunch or dinner (such as kiwi, citrus fruits, strawberries, potatoes, and dark leafy green vegetables). You may have noticed that leafy green vegetables contain both the "inhibitor" phytates and the "enhancer" vitamin C. That probably makes them a wash when it comes to iron.

The second enhancer is animal protein found in meat, fish, and poultry. Even if the amount is quite small, animal proteins apparently increase the availability of the iron from non-animal foods. For example, the iron in the little bit of beef in a stir-fry will increase the amount of iron absorbed from the rice or vegetables in the same dish. Or the iron from the chicken breast in your burrito or enchilada will help increase the amount of iron absorbed from your Mexican beans. And the beef in chili con carne will enhance the absorption of iron from the beans in the chili.

TIP #7. BUILD THOSE BONES.

Most people start becoming concerned about calcium when the threat of osteoporosis looms. And although we're finding out that getting enough calcium can be helpful for preventing osteoporotic bone fractures, probably the most pivotal time to invest in (and ingest) calcium is when your bones are still forming!

Almost all (99 percent) of our bodies' calcium is stored in our bones and teeth. And since we know we can fit all of our teeth in one hand, obviously a bunch must be in our bones. The human skeleton is commonly thought of as tough and permanent, but bone is actually living tissue. Whenever the amount of calcium in our diet is less than our body needs to keep up a relatively constant supply of calcium in the bloodstream, the body can make up the difference by withdrawing calcium from bones.

What could be so urgent that the bones actually sacrifice themselves to keep the supply of serum calcium plentiful? Well, calcium helps the heart (and other muscles) contract—a much more immediate need than strong bones.

In general, most women barely get half of their recommended daily allowance of calcium. For women between ages 11 and 24, 1200 mg. a day is recommended. After age 24, 800 mg. per day is recommended unless the woman is pregnant or nursing. What kind of help do experts offer American women who don't make the calcium cut?

- Get as much calcium as you can from food, then use calcium supplements only to fill in the gaps. (Anyone who has had calcium-containing kidney stones should check first with a physician).

- Supplementation much higher than the RDA is *not*, I repeat *not*, recommended, mainly because excessive calcium can interfere with the absorption of other important minerals, including iron and zinc.

Speaking of absorption, only 30 to 50 percent of calcium eaten is usually absorbed from the intestines. So the actual amount absorbed can look quite different from what went in. Unfortunately, for every factor that enhances calcium absorption, there are several that inhibit it.

The two known calcium absorption enhancers are vitamin D (in milk and milk products) and stomach acidity, which peaks after a meal. That's one more reason why it's wise to get as much calcium as possible from food rather than supplements.

Now for the bad news. Alcohol, protein, sodium, caffeine, and possibly phosphorus can influence absorption of calcium. Drinking excessive amounts of alcohol can inhibit calcium absorption. A high-protein diet (when amounts are twice what the body needs) seems to promote the loss of calcium through the urine. Sodium and caffeine apparently can also have this effect. And then there's the one factor you can do absolutely nothing about—age. As a body ages, its ability to absorb calcium tends to weaken.

More studies need to be done before anything definitive can be said, but there is the possibility that too much phosphorus in our diet can cause calcium to be excreted from the body. If this is true, the finger then points to carbonated beverages, such as soda pop, which contains phosphoric acid.

A study reported in the July 1989 *Journal of Orthopedic Research* surveyed 2600 female former athletes. Those who drank carbonated beverages showed a 2.28 greater rate of bone fractures after age 40 than those who didn't drink soda. I would imagine they had to look pretty hard to find women who don't drink diet soda. But the most scientifically impressive finding was that researchers found a significant relationship between the amount of soda consumed and the number of fractures in women over age 40.

The following foods are some of calcium's hardest hitters, with 1 serving contributing 150 to 250 mg. of calcium.

	Calcium (mg.)	Calories	Fat (gm.)
Yogurt, plain, nonfat, 1 cup	451	126	0.4
Yogurt, plain, low-fat, 1 cup	414	143	3.5
Yogurt, flavored, 1 cup	344	231	3
Oatmeal, homemade (1/2 cup oats, 1 cup 1% low-fat milk)	333	260	5
Milk, nonfat, 1 cup	316	90	0.6
Milk, 1 percent low-fat, 1 cup	312	104	2.4
Milk, 2% low-fat, 1 cup	296	121	5
Milk, whole, 1 cup	291	149	8
Spinach, boiled/drained, 1 cup	277	53	0.4
Pudding, instant, vanilla 1 cup	258	300	8
Frozen yogurt, 1 cup	240	220	3.5
Cheese pizza, 1 slice	220	290	9
Mozzarella, part skim, 1 oz. (low moisture)	207	79	5

	Calcium (mg.)	Calories	Fat (gm.)
Sockeye salmon, 3-oz. can	203	130	6
Macaroni & cheese, 1 cup	200	230	10
Turnip greens, cooked from fresh, 1 cup	197	29	0.3
Evaporated skim milk, 1/4 cup	184	50	N/A
Pink salmon with bones (canned), 3 oz.	181	118	5
Waffle, 1, from mix	179	206	8
Ice milk, vanilla, 1 cup	176	183	5.5
Tapioca pudding, 1 cup (homemade)	173	220	8
Ricotta cheese, 1/4 cup (part-skim)	167	85	5
Instant oatmeal, 1 packet (fortified)	160	105	4

The following foods are also worth mentioning, with one serving contributing between 50 and 150 mg. of calcium.

Hot cocoa, 6 oz.
Tofu, 1/2 cup
Beans, 1 cup cooked
Life® cereal, 1 ounce
Cream of Wheat® or Maypo®, 1/2 cup cooked
Blackstrap molasses, 1 Tbsp.

TIP #8 / WATCH THE ADDITIVES.

Start reading the ingredient labels on your child's favorite packaged or processed foods and you're bound to run into quite a few multi-syllabic scientific names. Many of these hard-to-pronounce words, representing additives, preservatives, and coloring agents, sound mighty scary.

Tetrazine (yellow dye No. 5), for example, sounds like a prescription drug for acne. And the ubiquitous preservative butylated hydroxytoluene (BHT), as far as you know, could be an ingredient in your kitchen cleanser.

But just because you can't pronounce some of these product ingredients doesn't necessarily mean they're potentially toxic or bad for you and your family. Beta carotene and ascorbic acid, referring to vitamins A and C, respectively, are both commonly used additives. Beta carotene is a natural yellow coloring, and ascorbic acid is an antioxidant/preservative. And let's not forget that, healthwise, some of the worst offenders are words we're quite familiar with, such as sugar, hydrogenated vegetable oil, and salt, to name just a few.

So what's a cautious parent to do? Well, the Citizens' Commission on School Nutrition (a national committee of allied experts that released a report on school nutrition in late 1990) reviewed the more controversial food additives.

With children in mind, they made what I would call a "just-to-be-on-the-safe-side" list of suggestions for food additives they believe should be limited whenever possible in children's meals.

The list includes several artificial sweeteners:

- *Acesulfame-K:* The commission believes this agent needs to be fully tested for cancer-causing effects before it can be considered totally safe.

- *Aspartame (NutraSweet®):* In 1984, the American Academy of Pediatrics' Commission on Genetics and Environmental Hazards expressed concern about aspartame in diets of young children and pregnant women. Now, nearly ten years later, the Citizens' Commission on School Nutrition concluded it may cause occasional behavioral reaction and also needs to be more fully tested for cancer-causing effects before it can be considered totally safe for children.

- *Saccharin:* As already listed on warning labels, saccharin is thought to increase the risk of cancer in animals.

Also on the list are two well-known sodium sources:

- *MSG (monosodium glutamate):* The report states that "in susceptible individuals, MSG can cause headache, muscle tension, and other symptoms."

- *Sodium nitrite:* Mainly found in cooked sausage, cured pork, and dried beef, this substance can react with other chemicals to form cancer-causing nitrosamines, according to the commission's report. Of greatest concern is bacon, which tends to contain the greatest amounts of nitrosamines.

No list like this would be complete without a preservative or two. The commission listed *BHA* and *BHT* because "they have caused cancer in several animal studies." Although the commision admits these preservatives probably pose a "slight" cancer risk, a well-known consumer nutrition advocacy agency, the Center for Science in the Public Interest, believes they should be avoided when possible.

Another preservative on the list is *sulfites*. In sensitive individuals (particularly asthmatics) sulfites can cause serious allergic reactions. Approximately 5 to 10 percent of asthmatics are probably sulfite sensitive. The commission warned that sulfites are widely used in golden raisins and dehydrated potato flakes. California is one of the states that has banned the use of sulfites by restaurants.

Of course, *caffeine* is a culprit for children. The commission states, "It is a mild stimulant and is considered mildly addictive." If you're thinking, "Kids don't drink coffee," remember caffeine is also found in many soft drinks as well as tea leaves, kola beans, and to a lesser degree in cocoa (in other words, chocolate).

Yellow dye #5 was also listed because it can cause occasional allergic reactions. The FDA estimated between 47,000 and 94,000 people are sensitive to the dye. (These people also tend to be sensitive to aspirin.) The dye has already been banned in Sweden and Norway. Don't get ready to kiss all your favorite yellow foods goodbye, though. There are many natural ways to color food yellow. Beta carotene (vitamin A), turmeric, and annatto (from a South American tree) are alternatives to yellow dye #5.

Favorite Foods That Measure Up

Life without lasagna? A party without pizza? A Friday without french fries and hamburgers? Unimaginable! If your kids are breathing and have a pulse, chances are they love food in general. But we all have a handful of favorite foods we dream about—foods we just can't imagine going without.

Most red-blooded American kids seem to list the same favorite foods over and over again. After surveying several classrooms of third graders in Northern California, my suspicions were confirmed. Pizza, hamburgers, tacos, and spaghetti top the list.

With a few minor adjustments, these foods actually help you meet the RDA for major nutrients like protein, iron, vitamins, and calcium—without causing too much damage in the fat and cholesterol categories.

TIP #9 / LET 'EM EAT PASTA.

A large restaurant portion of the most popular pasta—spaghetti with meat sauce—usually consists of a king-sized bed of noodles (2 cups) covered comfortably with about 1 1/2 cups of meat sauce. This calculates to more than 800 calories, 33 percent from fat (depending on how much oil and what type of meat is added), and about 150 mg. cholesterol. It also contains 38 grams of protein, which is almost 136 percent of the RDA for children between 7 to 10 years of age, 61 percent of the RDA for vitamin A, 85 percent of thiamin, 77 percent of niacin, and over 70 percent of vitamins C and E, and almost 90 percent RDA for iron.

TIP #10 / MAKE IT MEXICAN.

Whether it's "Fresh Mex," Southwestern style, or from a small, family-run restaurant, Mexican food continues to tantalize American taste buds. Tacos, in particular, are often mentioned as a favorite food. Some people are a little more detailed with their taco specifications than others, choosing "soft chicken tacos," "spicy beef," etc. Just saying "soft" when you order or make tacos saves you almost 50 calories and at least 4 gms. of fat per pair over fried tacos. Two soft chicken tacos, one of my personal favorites, add up to about 300 calories, 35 percent from fat (12 gm. of fat), and 90 mg. cholesterol. They also come with 31 grams of protein, which is 110 percent of the RDA for a child between 7 and 10 years of age, 64 percent of the RDA for niacin, about 31 percent of the RDA for vitamins B_6 and B_{12}, and 2 mg. of high-quality iron (20% of RDA for 7- to 10-year-olds).

TIP #11 / MODIFY THE BURGER AND FRIES.

What could be more American! And, depending on where you're getting your burger and fries, what could be more greasy? If you make your burger and fries at home using ground sirloin (about 13 percent fat—half that of regular ground beef) and bake your potato strips (raw or microwaved potatoes cut into your favorite style with half a teaspoon of oil per potato spread on the baking sheet) I'd be hard pressed to find anything bad to say about your meal. If you're ordering your burger out, you can save calories and fat simply by ordering it without all the "extras" (bacon, cheese, creamy sauces, guacamole). Instead, dress your burger up with onions, pickles, tomatoes, lettuce, catsup, mustard, or barbecue sauce.

If you make the sirloin burger and baked french fries version mentioned above, you are now talking about a meal that totals about 577 calories, 23 percent from fat (14.5 grams of fat), and 74 mg. of cholesterol. Your daily protein total will increase by 32 gms., which is more than 110 percent of the RDA for a child between 7 and 10 years of age, and you will also get 6 gms. of fiber, 141 percent of the RDA for vitamin B_{12}, over 65 percent of the RDAs (for a child 7 to 10 years of age) for niacin and vitamin B_6. About half of the RDA for thiamin, vitamin C, and zinc, and almost a fourth of the RDA of several other essential vitamins and minerals will be in each serving.

TIP #12 / IF IT'S STEAK, KEEP IT SMALL.

Quite a few people would like nothing better than to sink their bicuspids into a nice juicy steak. Obviously, this favorite is going to score pretty high in the protein and iron departments. But if you're concerned about also scoring high in fat, calories, and cholesterol, there are a few tips you may want to take to the steak house.

A sirloin or London broil steak is going to be much leaner (and lower in fat and calories) than your average T-bone or prime rib. But if you just gotta have the latter two, try to trim the visible fat off and order your steak without added fats and fancy sauces. A 4-ounce grilled or broiled sirloin steak has just over 220 calories, 37 percent from fat (9 gms. of fat), and 100 mg. of cholesterol. It also has 34 gms. of protein, which is 121 percent of the RDA for a child 7 to 10 years of age, more than 220 percent of the RDA for vitamin B_{12}, 39 percent the RDA for niacin, about a third of the RDA for riboflavin (40 percent RDA for a child 7 to 10 years of age), vitamin B_6, 4 mg. of high-quality iron, and a plentiful supply of other essential minerals (73 percent of RDA for zinc, 76 percent of selenium, 34 percent phosphorus).

TIP #13 / GRILL THAT SEAFOOD.

Savory shrimp sizzling on the grill. Softly smoked salmon with herbs, pink to perfection. These could bring this seafood lover to her knees. If getting more iron is your ambition, you're better off with fish that comes with its own shell. Shellfish on average seems to have much more iron than the other types of fish. The trick with all types of seafood is to grill it without added fats and to resist the temptation to coat it in crumbs and submerge it in a deep vat of fat. Enjoying 10 grilled shrimp instead of fried will save you more than 40 calories and 8 gms. of fat. This rather large pile of shrimp will add up to about 140 calories, 1.5 gm. of fat (10 percent calories from fat), but 250 mg. of cholesterol. You will also be getting 30 gms. of protein (which is 107 percent of the RDA for a child between 7 and 10 years of age), 96 percent of the RDA for vitamin B_{12}, more than 200 percent the RDA for selenium, over a third of the RDA for vitamin E and niacin, and 4.5 mg. of high-quality iron (45 percent RDA for a child between 7 and 10 years of age).

Low-Fat Foods
Kids Love
to Hate:

Fruits
and
Vegetables

Low-Fat Foods Kids Love to Hate

Fruits and Vegetables

"Eat your vegetables!" It's sound parental advice, but is it being followed, even by the adults giving it? You probably will guess some children aren't eating enough fruits and vegetables, but unfortunately it's more accurate to say that some children aren't eating any at all!

According to preliminary results of a new survey from California, 20 percent of the population eat no fruit on an average day and 27 percent eat no vegetables or salad. And the California Department of Health Services folks were even giving Californians the benefit of the doubt by conducting their survey during the summer months when gorgeous fresh produce is plentiful.

TIP #14 / SIGN ON FOR "FIVE A DAY."

The national "Five a Day" for Better Health program is jointly sponsored by the National Cancer Institute (NCI) and the Produce for Better Health Foundation (PBHF). The program has a simple message for Americans: Eat five or more servings of fruits and vegetables each day for better health. The goal of the program is to meet one of the nation's Year 2000 health objectives by increasing average fruit and vegetable consumption to at least five servings a day.

The "Five-a-Day" for Better Health program is the largest ever industry/government joint nutrition education program and the first nationwide health promotion program focusing specifically on the importance of fruits and vegetables in Americans' diets.

In 1991, the PBHF and NCI conducted a national baseline telephone survey of 2,837 Americans 18 years of age and over. The survey found that Americans are unclear about how many daily servings of fruits and vegetables they really need for good health. Two-thirds of the respondents believed two or fewer servings each day is sufficient. Only 8 percent of those surveyed knew they should be eating five or more servings a day of fruits and vegetables.

Research has shown that eating more fruits and vegetables may help prevent certain cancers. Studies by the U.S. Department of Agriculture, the Department of Health and Human Services, and the National Academy of Sciences have concluded that dietary changes could play a vital role in improving the health of many Americans.

All these studies show that diets low in total fat or saturated fat and cholesterol and including plenty of whole-grain breads and cereals and fruits and vegetables decrease the risk of heart disease and may help reduce the risk of cancer.

What Are People Currently Eating?

In July of 1992, 22 percent of the respondents of a national telephone baseline survey conducted by NCI answered "five or more" to the question, "How many servings of fruits and vegetables do you think a person should eat each day for good health?" Twenty-seven percent thought they should eat three servings each day and 30 percent thought they should eat two or few servings each day.

Typically, most Americans ate only three and a half servings a day, with only 23 percent eating five servings or more of fruits and vegetables. Forty-two percent ate two servings or less.

Data from the second National Health and Nutrition Examination Survey conducted from 1976 to 1980, showed that when subjects were asked to recall what they had eaten in the past 24 hours, only 9 percent met the guidelines for both fruits and vegetables, and 11 percent ate neither a fruit nor a vegetables. Forty-five percent ate no fruit and 27 percent ate no vegetables.

An Important Message From the National Cancer Institute.

Did you know that most fruits and vegetables contain no cholesterol and are naturally low in fat and sodium? They are also a good source of fiber, vitamins, and minerals. Studies have shown that fruits and vegetables may help reduce your risk of cancer. They are low in fat and are rich sources of vitamin A, vitamin C, and fiber.

Did you know that eating **five servings of fruits and vegetables every day** is one of the most important choices you can make to help maintain your health? To help you remember **five**—and to help improve your health—here are **five important points to remember:**

TIP #15 / SERVE AT LEAST FIVE SERVINGS OF FRUITS AND VEGETABLES EVERY DAY.

Contrary to popular belief children do like many different fruits and vegetables. A healthy variety should be served each day. Be creative.

TIP #16./ PROVIDE AT LEAST ONE SELECTION RICH IN VITAMIN A.

These are such as carrots, tomatoes, tangerines, winter squash, apricots, sweet potatoes, peaches, nectarines, dark green leaf lettuce, and cantaloupe.

TIP #17 / EAT AT LEAST ONE SELECTION RICH IN VITAMIN C.

Food rich in vitamin C are bananas, bell peppers, broccoli, cabbage, cantaloupe, cauliflower, grapefruit, honeydew, kiwi, oranges, peaches, pineapples, plums, potatoes, straw-berries and other berries, tangerines, and tomatoes.

TIP #18 / INCLUDE HIGH-FIBER EVERY DAY.

Fiber-rich foods are apples, bananas, broccoli, grapefruit, green beans, kiwi, nectarines, oranges, pears, potatoes, and strawberries,etc.

TIP #19 / DON'T FORGET THE CABBAGE.

Several times a week, give your family **cabbage family (cruciferous) vegetables,** such as broccoli, Brussels sprouts, bok choy, cabbage, cauliflower, and various greens like mustard, turnip, beet greens, kale, and Swiss chard.

New FDA Nutrition Labeling for Fruits and Vegetables

The new government rules indicate seven acceptable health claims that can be promoted on packaging or in advertising. Three of these directly name fruits and vegetables! They are:

- Fiber-containing grain products, fruits, and vegetables are associated with a reduced risk of certain types of cancer.
- Fiber-containing grain products, fruits, and vegetables are associated with a reduced risk of coronary heart disease.
- Fruits and vegetables that are good sources of vitamins A or C or fiber are related to a possible reduction in the risk of some types of cancer.

TIP #20 / CHOOSE FOOD OVER PILLS.

The link for nutrients, such as vitamin C, in the prevention of certain diseases is not as strong as the link between foods like fruits and vegetables and certain diseases. That's because the fruits and vegetables contain more than just vitamin C. Other compounds, naturally occurring in produce, may play an additional role in preventing disease.

According to many researchers, these agents have both complementary AND overlapping anticarcinogenic functions. It seems rather unlikely then that any one substance in fruits and vegetables is responsible for the decrease in risk for some cancers, but rather it is the "whole package" of special compounds in fruits and vegetables that are particularly beneficial to our health.

TIP #21 / GIVE 'EM THE BEST.

If you had to tell someone to eat the same five fruits and vegetables every day, which would they be?

I can only tell you which three I try to eat every day (and I'll warn you right away former President Bush isn't going to like my first selection): broccoli, carrots, and orange juice.

Broccoli is a cruciferous vegetable and a good source of fiber, vitamin A, and vitamin C. Carrots are a superb source of beta-carotene, which converts to vitamin A. I've made it a habit to start my morning with a glass of orange juice, which is loaded with vitamin C.

However, it's still important to eat many types of fruits and vegetables, since they provide other important vitamins and minerals. For example, a recent study published in the *British Medical Journal* (Aug. 8, 1992) suggests that fruit and vegetables containing other forms of carotene, besides beta-carotene (like spinach, sweet potatoes and winter squash), could be helpful in protecting against the development of cataracts by preventing damage to proteins in the eye.

TIP #22 / THE FRUIT AND VEGETABLE PAYOFF.

The earlier you start your kids eating more fruits and vegetables, the easier it is. It just becomes a way of life; they don't know the difference. Try to start while the kids still appreciate eating foods plain and unsauced. That's usually between the ages of one and two.

If we all can stick with it, there are three immediate *health rewards* to eating more fruits and vegetables:

- The amount of fiber increases, often by as much as 10 gm.
- We eat more of the many important vitamins and minerals, such as vitamins A and C and folic acid.
- We usually reduce the amount of fats we eat.

Here are a few helpful hints to help parents get their children to eat more fruits and vegetables (without resorting to bribery, trickery, or high-fat cheese sauce).

TIP #23 / LIBERATE THE FRUIT BOWL.

Take a few minutes to slice, peel, and/or chop fruit from your fruit bowl and refrigerator crisper to make a simple fruit salad. Drizzle with vitamin C rich fruit juice like orange or pineapple to keep the fruit from browning, then cover the container well.

Fruit that would otherwise sit in the fruit bowl rotting becomes irresistibly colorful, cool, and convenient when it is chopped, mixed with other fruit, and chilled.

TIP #24 / SERVE IT RAW.

Raw vegetables are sometimes more appealing to kids than their stronger flavored, cooked counterparts. Serve raw cauliflower and broccoli florets. Use spinach leaves for salads, or make a low-fat coleslaw using raw shredded cabbage and a reduced-calorie dressing.

TIP #25 / MAKE IT A DRINK.

Most kids love fruit juice and cold creamy drinks. Make a fruit "soda" by mixing 100% fruit juice with sparkling mineral water or club soda. Try adding a fruit to blender drinks. Bananas, canned or fresh peaches, pears, or crushed pineapple work great.

TIP #26 / PUT IT IN A SALAD.

For many children, salads are a great way to work in a serving or two of fruits and vegetables. Some kids might like grated carrots or tomato wedges, while others might enjoy adding raisins or orange segments to a standard lettuce salad.

TIP #27 / MIX IT IN THEIR FAVORITE FOODS.

Some kids might not mind grated carrots if it's in their tacos, or pineapple, zucchini or tomato if it's on their pizza. Or chopped apples or raisins if it's in their tuna or chicken salad sandwich, or broccoli or green beans if it's in their macaroni & cheese—it's worth a try!

TIP #28 / ADD VEGETABLES TO SOUP.

Many commercial soups already come with vegetables. But if your child loves soup, why not slip in another serving yourself. Just add your leftover chopped, cooked vegetables while you're heating up the soup.

TIP #29 / SNEAK IT IN THEIR PACK AS A SNACK.

Stocking your child's backpack or school bag with some quick fruit or vegetable snacks might just do the trick when your child is hungry in between meals or after school. Try adding baby carrots, assorted dried fruits, or even whole fruits that travel well, such as bananas or apples.

TIP #30 / MAKE FRUITS AND VEGETABLES FUN TO EAT.

- Make corn on the cob wheels (by cutting cooked corn on the cobs widthwise into 1-inch thick disks).
- Fill celery sticks with peanut butter and sprinkle with raisins.
- Make melon balls by using a melon ball scoop for cantaloupe and other melons.
- Dip fruits in low-fat yogurt. Dip vegetables in lower-fat cheeses or reduced-calorie ranch dressing.
- Play games with fruits and vegetables, such as:

  —who can spit more of their watermelon seeds or cherry pits into bowls placed on the backyard grass.

  —who can stack up the most baby carrots without the whole pile tumbling down.
- Try counting exercises (teaching counting or times tables) with small boxes of raisins.

TIP #31 / LET THE SMALL HANDS HELP IN THE KITCHEN.

As early as you can, get your kids to participate in the shopping for and preparation of fruits and vegetables. This helps teach kids that fruits and vegetables are not the enemy. Fruits and vegetables can be fun, colorful, tasty, and healthful.

TIP #32 / PAIR IT WITH PEANUT BUTTER.

Peanut butter is extremely high in fat so remember to spread it thin.

TIP #33 / TRY AN OVEN FRY FOR FRUITS AND VEGETABLES.

Just dipping vegetables in non- or reduced-fat mayonnaise and then rolling them in Italian seasoned bread crumbs and baking on a lightly greased baking sheet (in a 375-degree oven) changes the most boring vegetables into tasty treats! For sweet or white potatoes, skip the mayonnaise and bread crumbs and just bake pieces on a lightly greased baking sheet until lightly browned.

- Make sweet potato or yam french fries by slicing them into fries (as you would a potato) and baking them on a lightly greased baking sheet (400 degrees F. for 15 minutes).

TIP #34 / WHEN ALL ELSE FAILS, THERE'S ALWAYS (LOW-FAT) CHEESE SAUCE.

But let's at least make the sauce lower in fat. Page 122 gives an excellent recipe for low-fat Three-Cheese Sauce.

TIP #35 / CHANGE YOUR HABITS.

If we're supposed to eat five servings of fruits and vegetables a day, and we usually eat three meals a day, we really need to eat a fruit or vegetable at every meal plus two more servings throughout the day, like fruit or fruit juice as a snack and fruit with dessert.

Remember, one serving is equal to a piece of fruit, 6 oz. of fruit or vegetable juice, 1/2 cup of cooked vegetables, 1 cup of leafy salad greens, or 1/4 cup of dried fruit.

I suggest five specific food habits to work 5 servings into your child's day (try this for a week and see how it goes):

Drink juice at breakfast

Eat a fruit or vegetable salad with lunch

Have a big serving of vegetables with dinner

Snack on fruits and vegetables

Enjoy fruit for (or with) dessert

Here are some other suggestions:

TIP #36 / BEGIN WITH BREAKFAST.

- Chop apples, bananas, strawberries, or peaches into your child's bowl of hot or cold cereal.
- Top their pancakes, waffles, or french toast with sliced fruit or berries.
- They can also have fruit on the side and on the go.

TIP #37 / LOOK FOR LUNCH IN ALL THE RIGHT PLACES.

Some tips for people and children who often eat lunch out include the following:

- Tuck dried fruits like raisins, apricots, prunes, apples, pears, etc., into your child's lunchbox or backpack.
- Serve or send along a fruit salad with the sandwiches.

- Order vegetables on the lunch pizza
- Choose a three-bean or potato salad to fill out your vegetable quota. Of course, the lower in fat they are, the better.

TIP #38 / INCLUDE FRUIT AND VEGETABLE SNACKS.

- Freeze banana slices and serve them right out of the freezer.
- Always have a medley of dried fruit handy for a quick, sweet snack.
- Fruit goes great with reduced-fat cheese for a picnic or snack.
- Fruit can be dipped in tasty low-fat yogurt.
- Vegetable sticks (zucchini, carrot, celery) right out of the refrigerator (stored in a bit of water) make a cold, crisp snack when served with a reduced-fat dip or salad dressing.
- Oven-baked lower-fat frozen french fries hit the spot on a cold afternoon.
- Serve vegetable soup as a snack.
- Make a vegetable fondue for a group snack using the Three-Cheese Sauce recipe on page 122.

TIP #39 / DO IT AT DINNER.

- Fruit can be used for garnish on the dinner plate. It's amazing how fast orange slices or a small bunch of grapes goes when it is on your plate with other food.
- Fruit salads go well with many dinner entrees.
- A slice of melon is a welcome refresher on a summer dinner plate.
- Add vegetables to your dinner entree when possible. Just mix them right in to the lasagna, casseroles, spaghetti, macaroni and cheese, stir-fry, etc.

TIP #40 / HIDE IT, IF NECESSARY.

Sometimes parents have a better chance of getting children to eat a fruit or vegetable if it's hiding in a favorite food. For example, most kids love pizza. They're not likely to complain about the pineapple chunks and Canadian bacon sitting on top. Here are some other ways to work fruits and vegetables into their favorite foods:

- Add chunks of zucchini, eggplant, or yellow squash to the spaghetti sauce.
- Get your kids in the habit of adding lots of fresh tomato when fixing hamburgers and hot dogs.
- Arrange banana, apple, or peach slices on pancakes once you've poured the batter in the pan.
- Serve waffles with fresh or frozen raspberries, sliced strawberries, or peach slices.

- Add chopped bell pepper or grated carrots or zucchini while browning beef for tacos. Serve the tacos with plenty of tomatoes.
- Add broccoli florets to macaroni and cheese—whether from a box or homemade.
- Add peas or broccoli florets to packaged side dishes such as Stove Top Stuffing®, scalloped potatoes, or rice or noodle dishes.

TIP #41 / ENCOURAGE FRUIT JUICE INSTEAD OF SODA.

Mix up some flavor and fun with 100 percent fruit juice. The kids may even like it better than the usual soda or flavored drinks.

- Instead of punch, mix 100 percent cherry or raspberry juice with pineapple juice.
- Instead of orange drink, mix 100 percent orange juice with sparkling mineral water or club soda.
- Instead of grape drink, mix 100 percent grape juice with sparkling mineral water or club soda.
- For a treat, offer the kids sparkling apple cider. Opening the champagne-like bottle is half the fun.
- Make a citrus cooler by mixing orange juice with sugar-free lemonade.

TIP #42 / DRESS UP THE FINGER FOODS.

Kids love to eat with their hands, no matter what their age. Finger foods can be a fun way for kids to get their "five-a-day." Try these ideas:

- Serve pineapple (canned in juice) with lunch or as a tasty snack.
- Cut jicama into fun shapes, like hearts and diamonds, or into sticks.
- Give them asparagus spears, lightly cooked and cooled.
- Fix an antipasto platter with bell pepper rings, broccoli florets, baby carrots, and light salami. Serve with a reduced-calorie vinaigrette dressing.
- Make a "five-a-day" fondue. Serve broccoli and cauliflower florets with a lower-fat cheese sauce. Heat a spreadable cheese with no more than 5 gm. of fat per ounce until it is liquid and smooth.

TIP #43 / GRILL THE FRUITS AND VEGGIES.

After the meat is taken off the grill, why waste the hot coals? Many fruits and vegetables grill great! Older kids will get a kick out of stringing fruit or vegetables on skewers to make colorful kabobs. Fruits and soft vegetables won't need any precooking, but firm vegetables, such as sweet potatoes, will benefit from steam or microwave cooking before hitting the grill.

Most vegetables just need to be cleaned and maybe brushed oh-so-lightly with olive or vegetable oil. Cook vegetables over medium coals and turn occasionally.

Here are some specific ideas:

- Grill peach halves or pineapple spears with a lower-fat marinade, reduced-calorie vinaigrette, balsamic vinegar, or fruit nectars or a quick raspberry sauce. (Melt no- or low-sugar raspberry preserves in pan.)

- Vegetables like whole mushrooms, cherry tomatoes, bell peppers and onion wedges, and zucchini coins make great veggie kabobs. A basting can be made by mixing vegetable juice with lemon juice and thyme.

- Onions: Slice onions 1/2 inch thick. Grill until tender (15 to 20 minutes), turning occasionally.

- Corn: Pull back husks, leaving them attached to base and remove silk. Fold husks back around corn; tie at end and soak in cold water 1 to 2 hours. Remove and grill 20 to 30 minutes.

- Squash (yellow and zucchini): Cut small squash in half lengthwise. Grill 8 to 12 minutes.

- Bell Peppers: Cut peppers in half lengthwise; remove seeds. Grill 12 to 15 minutes.

- Potatoes: Cook small red or white potatoes until barely tender when tested with fork. Rinse in cold water to stop cooking; drain well. Thread potatoes on skewers. Grill 10 to 15 minutes.

- Tomatoes: Slice tomatoes 1/2 to 3/4 inch thick. Grill until heated through, 3 to 5 minutes.

TIP #44 / SURPRISE THEM WITH NEW FOODS.

Many kids like trying new things, especially if there is something unusual about it, like a silly shape or strange color or texture. The following are funny looking fruits and vegetables your child may enjoy trying.

—kiwi coins or kiwi halves

—jicama sticks

—pineapple spears

—green cauliflower

—miniature corn cobs (also called baby corn),

found in cans in the oriental food section

—spaghetti squash

Note: For preparing spaghetti squash in the microwave, cut squash in half horizontally, then place, cut side up, in 9 X 13-inch microwave safe dish with 1/4 cup water. Cover and cook on high for 5 minutes. Rotate and cook 15 minutes more. Scoop out strands of squash with a fork.

TIP #45 / TURN OFF THE TV AND PLAY WITH FRUITS AND VEGETABLES.

Let your kids play in the kitchen—safely, of course. Here are some suggestions for making fruits and vegetables more fun.

- Use fruit slices and shapes to write words in gelatin. (Prepare gelatin according to directions on box. Pour into 9" x 12" pan. The kids can arrange fruit (banana, peach, or pear slices) in the gelatin. Refrigerate gelatin until completely solid.

- Open individual packets of a medley of dried fruit or small boxes of raisins. Help your child arrange the fruit pieces in groups of threes. Count how many groups of three and practice using your three's times tables to add them up. Rearrange the fruit pieces in groups of four, then five, and repeat the counting exercises. Did they end up with the same number of pieces each time?

- Make a "Five-a-Day" pizza. Kids can make their own pizza using assorted vegetable toppings (such as summer squash, mushrooms, onions, eggplant, broccoli florets, fresh tomato, and pineapple. For crusts, individual-sized prepared pizza crusts (such as Boboli)® can be used or a larger prepared crust can be cut into fourths for each child to decorate. The new lower-fat biscuits in cans (in the refrigerator section of your grocery store) can also be used to make mini-pizzas.

- Create dip sticks. You and your child can prepare several types of dips and dippers. Some possible dips are vanilla low-fat yogurt, reduced-calorie ranch dressing, and catsup. Some possible dip sticks are apple or pear wedges, melon cut into thick sticks, jicama, carrots, summer squash, or celery cut into sticks, and blanched green beans or asparagus spears. Encourage your child to experiment by dipping their dippers in a variety of dips.

- Try a Magical Fry Maker. Using a fry-cutting hand tool (that you press down onto the vegetable), you and your child can make fries from a variety of vegetables besides white potatoes. Sweet potatoes, yams and summer squash all work well. Older children can learn to use the tool on their own. Then spread 1 to 2 teaspoons of vegetable oil on a nonstick cookie sheet. Arrange the assorted fries in the pan and bake in a 400 degree oven for about 10 minutes. Flip the fries and bake until lightly brown and tender. (Cooking time will vary by the type of vegetable. Summer squash will cook quicker than the potatoes, so you may want to keep them separate on the cookie sheet so they can be removed earlier. White potatoes require the longest cooking time, so you may want to partially pre-cook them).

- Make Applesauce. September—prime harvest time for apples—is a great time to teach your child how to make applesauce. Flavors can be added using spices like freshly ground cinnamon and cloves instead of sugar.

TIP #46 / IDEAS FOR
"FIVE-A-DAY" FUN.

- Make "Five-a-Day" juice pops using 100 percent fruit juice and fruit puree.

- Have a ball with "Five-a-Day." Using seedless wedges of cantaloupe, honeydew and/or watermelon, help your child use a melon ball tool to scoop out balls of melon. The multicolored balls can be made in preparation for a family party or picnic.

- Freeze melon balls or 1-inch cubes of melon for up to 2 hours. Then whirl them in a blender or food processor to make fresh melon smoothies.

- Let the kids make cool, fruity blender shakes. Use peach slices, cinnamon, low-fat granola and low-fat or nonfat frozen yogurt or ice-milk to whip up Peach Cobbler Sundaes. Use sliced strawberries, crushed pineapple and vanilla or strawberry frozen yogurt to make Strawberry Aloha Shakes.

- Make fruity snow using a standard homemade sorbet recipe. For St. Patrick's Day, use kiwi puree. On Halloween, use peach puree. For Christmas or Valentines Day, use strawberry or raspberry puree.

- Turn a small basket of fresh berries into a mouth-watering topping for cool, low-fat frozen yogurt or ice-milk. Just spoon about 2 cups of fresh berries or sliced strawberries into a medium nonstick saucepan. Sprinkle 1 tablespoon each of cornstarch and sugar over the top and gently stir. Pour in 1/2 cup of fruit juice and heat over medium heat, stirring gently, until the mixture bubbles and thickens slightly.

TIP #47 / ENCOURAGE THE SALAD BAR, KID STYLE.

Some children really like salads—believe it or not. Salads are a great way to sneak in some more fruit or vegetable servings. Remember, the darker colored types of greens contain more nutrients than the light ones. This chart might spark some ideas.

Item	Calories	Fiber grams	Vit.A mg.	Vit.C mg.	Folic Acid mcg.	Potassium mg.
Broccoli 1/4 cup	6	0.6	34	21	16	72
Carrots 1/4 cup	12	0.9	774	3	4	89
Cauliflower 1/4 cup	6	6	0.5	18	17	89
Cucumber 4 slices	2	2	0.8	0.8	2	24
Green pepper 1/4 cup	7	0.4	16	22	6	44
Lettuce 3/4 cup Looseleaf	8	0.6	80	8	21	110
Orange pieces 1/4 cup	21	1	10	24	14	81
Pineapple 1 slice	35	0.6	2	6	3	71

Item	Calories	Fiber grams	Vit.A mg.	Vit.C mg.	Folic Acid mcg.	Potassium mg.
Raisins						
1 Tbsp.	31	0.5	0.1	0.3	0.3	77
Spinach	9	1.4	282	12	81	234

Three-bean salad
(1 Tbsp. garbanzo beans, 1 Tbsp. kidney beans, 1 Tbsp.
green beans, 1 tsp. vinaigrette

	55	1	4	.7	29	81

Tomato

1/4 whole	7	4	19	6	5	68

Basic Salad
Looseleaf lettuce, tomato, cucumber, carrots

	28	13	874	17	32	291

Hearty Salad
Spinach, broccoli, cauliflower, beans

	76	4	321	51	142	475

Tropical Salad
Looseleaf lettuce, pineapple, raisins

	74	1.7	82	13	24	258

TIP #48 / DRESS UP YOUR SUMMER FRUIT DESSERTS.

On a warm summer night—when the air is thick, sticky, and still, chocolate chip cookies hot from the oven just don't cut it like cool and creamy ice cream. But you can't have ice cream for dessert every night. (Believe me, I've tried).

Summer is the perfect time to try out fresh fruit desserts. Many of our favorites come chilled and sweet as can be. In fact, since many of our favorite fruits are their ripest and sweetest during the summer months, a bowl of fresh fruit, sporting nothing but a spoon can be the perfect prelude to a peaceful summer's slumber.

Here are some more ways to get part of your "Five-a-Day" with low-fat fruity summer desserts:

- Some of our favorite warm winter desserts can be served chilled, including pies, crisps, and cobblers.
- Add color by topping puddings or custard tarts with kiwi, strawberries, peaches, or other fresh fruit.
- Add fruit to traditional cool summer desserts, such as frozen yogurt or ice milk. Fruit goes great with angel food cake.
- Whip up a fruit smoothie by mixing fresh fruit and juice or milk in a blender or food processor with some low-fat yogurt or ice milk.
- Make a Pina Colada shake by mixing crushed pineapple and juice with vanilla ice milk or frozen yogurt, and top with toasted flaked coconut.

- Make a Cantaloupe Cooler by mixing chopped soft cantaloupe with sherbet or vanilla low-fat frozen yogurt or ice milk.

- Make colorful fruit kabobs for your next barbecue or party by stringing fresh fruit onto bamboo skewers.

- Make a quick fruit parfait by layering fresh fruit with low-fat granola or vanilla wafers (or similar low-fat cookies) and low-fat frozen yogurt.

- Try partially dipping fresh strawberries, orange segments, or peach slices in melted chocolate.

- Make fruit squares by adding fresh fruit chunks and fruit juice to unflavored gelatin.

TIP #49 / REPLACE FATS WITH FRUITS AND VEGETABLES.

If there were a popularity contest between the fruit group and vegetable group, I would put my money on fruit. Somehow fruit manages to rise above the "eat it because it's good for you" stereotype. You may even have read an article or two suggesting applesauce and other fruit purees and juices as replacements for fat in baked goods.

It may be a little more challenging, but vegetables, too, can act as a tasteful fat replacement in an interesting range of recipes. If you thought you were stretching your culinary limits when you added applesauce to spice cake or prune puree to brownies, hold onto your apron. You are about to see vegetables in a whole new "lite!"

What about adding mashed potatoes to cream soups and sauces, or peas to lower-fat guacamole, or carrot puree to zucchini bread? If you think about it, we already make breads, cakes, and even pies with vegetables (pumpkin pie or bread, zucchini bread, carrot cake, etc.) So why not use vegetable purees as fat replacements too?

The mistake most people make when attempting to lighten their recipes is concentrating on one side of the fat equation—taking the fat out. But in most cases, when you take some or all of the fat out, you have to add something else in its place to compensate for the loss in moisture, liquid volume, and of course, flavor.

The key to veggie fat replacement is finding appropriately colored and textured vegetables to add to your dishes. Green peas, for example, can easily replace half of the avocado in guacamole. Yellow peas work well in yellowish dishes, such as corn bread or in the yolk mixture in deviled eggs. For a rich, orange-brown color, look to your sweet potatoes or canned pumpkin for possibilities.

Keep an open mind, then read the following suggested uses for vegetables in place of fat:

- Instead of bulking up your pasta sauce with lots of fatty olive oil, try adding baby carrot puree, roasted red pepper puree, or mashed potatoes.

- In nut breads or cakes like carrot cake or zucchini bread, vegetable purees or juices, such as carrot juice or pumpkin puree, can replace some of the fat normally called for.

TIP #50 / SAVE THOSE VITAMINS AND MINERALS.

Generally, vitamins (such as vitamins A, C, and folic acid) are weaker and more likely to be destroyed than minerals (such as iron or potassium). And vitamins and minerals in fresh vegetables tend to be weaker than the vitamins and minerals in fresh fruits and meats.

We can lose some of the vitamin A (and carotenes), vitamin C, and folic acid in fruits and vegetables when they are in contact with air, light, and heat. We can also lose some of these vitamins simply because time passes. And since vitamin C and folic acid can dissolve in water, some are lost in the cooking water.

Specific Tips:

• *Vegetables can lose three to four times more vitamin C at room temperature than when refrigerated.*

What can you do? Store vegetables in the refrigerator or freezer and remove them just before cooking.

• *The faster a fruit or vegetable loses its moisture, the more vitamins are lost.*

What can you do? Keep fresh vegetables wrapped as airtight as possible. And keep them in the crisper drawer of your refrigerator.

• *When fresh vegetables are not eaten immediately after they are harvested from the farm, some vitamins will be lost as time passes. Vitamin C and A and other fat-soluble vitamins are particularly vulnerable.*

What can you do? It is important to wrap vegetables up well and eat them as soon as possible.

• *Some of the vitamins that can be lost when in contact with air can be destroyed when fruits and vegetables are cut or chopped and left out for a while. More of the inside of the fruit or vegetables is in contact with the air and oxygen in the room and more vitamins will be destroyed.*

What can you do? Wait as long as possible before cutting fruits and vegetables for a meal, snack, or recipe.

• *The hotter the cooking heat and the longer the fruits or vegetables are being heated, the greater the losses of vitamin A and carotenes, vitamin C, and folic acid.*

What can you do? Use as low a cooking heat as possible. And cook fruits and vegetables for the shortest time possible. Or eat fruit and vegetables raw when possible—but remember to wash them thoroughly first!

• *Vitamins and minerals can dissolve in water while vegetables and fruits are cooking.*

What can you do? It's better to steam, grill, bake, microwave, or stir-fry them.

• *Cooking fruits and vegetables in the microwave is a good way to hold on to as many of the vitamins and minerals as you can, because microwave cooking usually takes less time.*

What more can you do? To hold on to as many of the vitamins and minerals as possible, cook fruits and vegetables in very little cooking water and for as short a time as possible.

TIP #51 / "SHAKE" UP THE SUMMER WITH FRUIT.

What's cold and refreshing, can be whipped up in a minute or two, and helps you get your five servings of fruits and vegetables? FRUIT SHAKES!

To make a fruit shake all you need is a good blender or food processor, one-half cup or so of a creamy base like low-fat or nonfat frozen yogurt or nonfat plain or flavored yogurt, maybe some crushed ice or club soda, and of course, fruit.

Even when fruit is not in season, fruit shakes can be made with frozen fruits, such as peach slices, strawberries, raspberries, and boysenberries.

Here are a few of my favorite shakes:

Lemon Strawberry (or Raspberry) Whip

3/4 cup fresh or frozen sliced strawberries (or raspberries)

1/2 cup nonfat or low-fat lemon yogurt

1/2 cup crushed ice

2 to 4 Tbsp. club soda or mineral water to desired thickness

Put first three ingredients in food processor or blender and blend until smooth. Add club soda or mineral water to desired thickness. Makes 1 serving.

Nutrition analysis per serving: 149 calories, 3 gm. fiber, 5 mg. cholesterol, 67 mg. sodium, 15 percent of calories from protein, 76 percent from carbohydrate, 9 percent from fat (1.5 gm. fat)

Spicy Peach Shake

1/2 cup sliced fresh or frozen peaches

1/2 cup low-fat or nonfat vanilla frozen yogurt or ice milk

2 or 3 pinches ground cinnamon

2 Tbsp. concentrated peach juice

(i.e. Dole 100 percent Juice Orchard® Peach)

Add above ingredients to food processor or blender and blend until smooth. Makes 1 serving.

Nutrition analysis per serving: 205 calories, 1.5 gm. fiber, 15 mg. cholesterol, 69 mg. sodium, 7 percent of calories from protein, 80 percent from carbohydrate, 13 percent from fat (3 gm.fat)

Orange Julia

3/4 cup low- or nonfat vanilla frozen yogurt or ice milk,

slightly softened

1/4 cup concentrated orange juice

1/2 to 3/4 cup sparkling mineral water or club soda

1/2 ripe banana, cut into slices (optional)

In food processor or blender, whip above ingredients together until smooth and frothy. Start with 1/2 cup mineral water, then add more if needed for desired consistency. Pour into glass. Makes one serving.

Nutrition analysis per serving (with sliced banana in parenthesis): 278 (330) calories, 1 gm. (2 gm.) fiber, 92 mg. (93 mg.) sodium, 9 percent (7 percent) of calories from protein, 78 percent (81 percent) from carbohydrate, 13 percent (12 percent) from fat, 4.5 gm. from fat (4.9 gm. fat)

TIP #52 / CREATE FUN AND FANCY FRUIT SALADS.

Every time I take the little bit of time required to cut fruit for a salad, I'm reminded of how easy and rewarding making fruit salad really is.

If you think about it, fruit salad can be a work of art. You basically want the fruit to represent a variety of:

- colors
- shapes
- tastes
- textures

What's exciting about fruit salad made with pear and apple slices with marshmallows and a light nondairy whipped topping (Light Cool Whip®) for dressing? Nothing! There is no eye appeal because all the ingredients are the same color. But combine the sweet softness of peach slices with the tartness and crispiness of apple cubes and plump purple grapes or blueberries, and you have a celebration of many colors, textures, shapes and flavors.

Just adding one exciting fruit can make all the difference in the world. I call these fruits my "garnish group" because they all have strong, unique colors. They include blueberries, strawberries, purple grapes, raspberries, boysenberries, blackberries, fresh or dried cherries, fresh or dried cranberries, and kiwi fruit. Many of these can be bought frozen in the off-season.

Fruit salad is also a fun and fancy way to get a truckload of nutrition with a miniscule amount of fat and calories. Usually when you make a fruit salad, a 1-cup serving contains less than 100 calories and less than 1 gm. of fat (not including the dressing). But what will this 100 calories buy you in vitamins, minerals, and fiber? Plenty!

I analyzed two fruit medleys—one fruit salad made with apple, nectarine, strawberries and grapes, and the other with pear and peach slices and blueberries. A 1-cup serving of the first fruit salad contained more than 3 gm. of fiber, twice the daily requirement for vitamin C, 65 mg. calcium, and 1.7 mg. iron, as well as a good supply of other vitamins and minerals, including folic acid, potassium, and beta-carotene. A cup of the second fruit salad contained almost 4 gm. of fiber, almost a full days' supply of vitamin C, 49 mg. calcium, 1.2 mg. iron, and healthy amounts of other vitamins and minerals.

TIP #53 / DRESS YOUR FRUITS LIGHTLY.

So how do you dress these beautiful, nutritious fruit salads? You want to make sure the dressing color and flavor doesn't overwhelm the fruit. You also want to make sure you aren't polluting your perfectly healthful salad with a rich, fatty dressing.

Just drizzling some fruit juice over the fruit adds lots of vitamin C (which will help preserve the fruits' natural colors and prevent them from browning). Orange and pineapple juice are good examples of this. You can also stir in a flavored yogurt and top with low-fat granola.

If you want to get a little fancier, try mixing Light Cool Whip® or nonfat or light sour cream with a couple of tablespoons of concentrated fruit juice. You can also add a little fanfare to your fruit salad by featuring a modest amount of other ingredients like roasted nuts, miniature marshmallows, shredded coconut, or dried fruit. Obviously adding the coconut and nuts will add some fat and calories, so add them ever so lightly. Try these simple dressings.

Lemon Cream Dressing or Dip

3/4 cup Light Cool Whip®, thawed in refrigerator

2 Tbsp. lemonade concentrate, thawed

4 to 6 cups of fruit salad

In small bowl, blend Cool Whip with lemonade concentrate until smooth. Spoon into fruit salad and toss, add as a dollop on top of each fruit salad serving, or keep as dressing on the side. If you like marshmallows, this dressing goes great with miniature marshmallows stirred into the fruit salad. Makes 4 servings of dressing or dip.

Nutrition analysis per serving: 40 calories, no cholesterol, no sodium, no calories from protein , 71 percent of calories from carbohydrate, 29 percent from fat (1.3 gm. fat)

Cranberry Cocktail Dressing or Dip

1/4 cup nonfat or light sour cream

3 to 4 Tbsp. frozen cranberry juice cocktail, concentrate, thawed

(Use the no-sugar-added varieties, such as Welch's®

Cranberry Raspberry frozen concentrate).

4 to 6 cups of fruit salad.

In small bowl, blend nonfat sour cream with cranberry concentrate until smooth. Spoon into fruit salad and toss, or serve as a side dressing. Makes 4 servings

If you like roasted nuts, this dressing goes great with a sprinkle or two or roasted walnuts or pecans.

Nutrition analysis per serving of dressing (without nuts): 35 calories, 21 mg. sodium, 12 percent of calories from protein, 88 percent from carbohydrate, no fat

TIP #54 / ADD MORE VEGETABLES TO MAIN AND SIDE DISHES.

Here are ideas for dressing up main dishes with vegetables.

Microwave Garden Meatloaf

I lb. ground sirloin
I cup grated carrot
I cup grated crookneck or zucchini squash
2 egg whites
2 oz. cornflake crumbs
1/3 cup chopped onion
I Tbsp. Worcestershire sauce
I Tbsp. prepared mustard
Salt to taste
1/4 tsp. pepper
8 oz. tomato sauce or bottled low-fat spaghetti sauce
4 oz. reduced-fat sharp cheddar cheese, grated (optional)*

Mix the first 10 ingredients thoroughly. Mold into round or square glass loaf pan that has been coated with nonstick spray. Cover with microwave-safe plastic wrap and microwave on high about 20 minutes. Remove from microwave and pour sauce and cheese over meatloaf. Cook 5 more minutes. Makes 4 large servings.

Nutrition analysis per serving: 280 calories, 3 gm. fiber, 76 mg. cholesterol, 631 mg. sodium, 44 percent of calories from protein, 32 percent from carbohydrate, 24 percent from fat (7 gm. of fat), 1030 RE vitamin A, 21 mg. vitamin C, 44 mg. calcium, 46 mg. iron.* Cheese will add 80 calories, 5 gm. fat, 15 mg. cholesterol, 150 mg. sodium, and 200 mg. calcium per serving.

Garden Stuffed Potatoes

2 large (or 3 medium) sized Russet baking potatoes

I or 2 green onions (top and part of green), finely chopped

1/4 cup nonfat or light sour cream

I Tbsp. reduced-fat or nonfat mayonnaise

Pepper to taste

1/2 tsp. parsley flakes

1/2 tsp. Italian herb blend (such as Parsley Patch® Salt-Free

Italian Blend)

2 oz. reduced-fat sharp cheddar cheese, grated

3 Tbsp. grated Parmesan cheese

I clove garlic, minced or 1/4 tsp. garlic powder

I cup cooked, chopped broccoli florets

Microwave or oven bake potatoes until tender (stab a few times with fork before cooking). Meanwhile, in a medium-sized bowl mix the remaining ingredients (except broccoli) together with a fork. Cut potatoes in half and scoop out center, leaving about 1/2 inch of potato around the skin. Add potato and broccoli pieces to mixture. Mix with fork, then spoon into potato halves. Microwave each serving on HIGH for about 2 minutes or broil until lightly brown on top. Makes 2 large servings.

Nutrition analysis per serving: 516 calories, 9 gm. fiber, 26 mg. cholesterol, 419 mg. sodium, 18 percent of calories from protein, 68 percent from carbohydrate, 14 percent from fat (8 gm. fat)

Oven-Fried Zucchini Sticks

> 3 medium-sized zucchini
> 1/4 cup egg substitute or 1 egg
> 2 Tbsp. nonfat or light sour cream
> 1 tsp. lemon juice
> 1/2 cup Italian seasoned bread crumbs
> 2 Tbsp. finely shredded Parmesan cheese
> 2 tsp. oil

Preheat oven to 450 degrees. Cut each zucchini lengthwise in half then each half into 4 strips. In a shallow bowl, blend egg with sour cream and lemon juice. In another shallow bowl, blend bread crumbs with Parmesan cheese. Spread oil on baking sheet with spatula. Dip each zucchini stick in egg mixture and then gently coat with bread crumb mixture. Place on baking sheet and bake 10 minutes. Serve with a low-fat ranch dressing or dip, if desired. Makes 4 servings.

Nutrition analysis per serving: 130 calories, 1 gm. fiber, 3 mg. cholesterol, 587 mg. sodium, 20 percent of calories from protein, 55 percent from carbohydrate, 25 percent from fat (3.5 gm. fat)

TIP #55 / LOWER THE FAT IN YOUR DRESSINGS.

Try these modified recipes for delicious dressings.

Thousand Island Dressing

1/4 cup light or reduced-fat mayonnaise

1/4 cup fat-free mayonnaise

2 Tbsp. catsup

1-2 Tbsp. minced stuffed olives or dill pickles

1 Tbsp. minced onion

2 tsp. parsley flakes

1/2 Tbsp. chopped green pepper (optional)

1/2 hard-cooked egg, chopped (optional)

Combine the above ingredients and serve over salad greens. Makes about 3/4 cup of dressing.

Nutrition analysis per 2 Tbsp. of dressing: 54 calories, 3 mg. cholesterol, 300 mg. sodium, 1 percent calories from protein, 44 percent from carbohydrate, 55 percent from fat (3.4 gm. fat)

Quick Ranch Dip or Dressing

1 packet (1.6 oz.) Good Seasons Lite Ranch® or Hidden

Valley Ranch Reduced-Calorie Ranch Dressing®

3 Tbsp. nonfat sour cream

1 2/3 cups 1 percent milk (reduce to 1 1/2 for dip)

3 Tbsp. reduced-fat or nonfat mayonnaise

Combine all ingredients in a medium-sized bowl. Beat with wire whisk or mixer until smooth and creamy. The dressing will thicken in refrigerator and will stay fresh about for 3 weeks when kept covered in the refrigerator. Makes 2 cups.

Nutrition analysis per 1/4 cup serving (using Good Seasons® packet): 51 calories, 5 mg. cholesterol, 420 mg. sodium

New Ways
To Fix Your
Kid's
Favorite
Foods

The 3 R's for Cooking with Less Fat: Replace, Reduce, and Remove

These are the three key steps to cutting some or all of the fat from our favorite recipes:

TIP #56 / REPLACE THE FATS.

This involves substituting a lower-fat or nonfat version of an ingredient, such as light or nonfat sour cream, light or nonfat cream cheese for regular, part-skim cheese or turkey light sausage for the fatter versions, or ground sirloin instead of ground chuck.

TIP #57 / REDUCE THE FATS.

This involves cutting back on the amount of fatty ingredient called for in a recipe. For example, you could add 2 Tbsp. of oil to your muffin recipe instead of 1/2 cup, use 6 oz. of light sausage instead of 10, or use 1 or 2 tsp. of oil in a stirfry instead of 1/4 cup, or 4 Tbsp. butter to make biscuits instead of 10.

TIP #58 / REMOVE THE FAT ALTOGETHER.

This might seem drastic to many--but the items involved here are "optional" or "extra" to the flavor appeal of the finished product. This might mean steaming your tortillas instead of frying, not adding nuts to your cookies or banana bread, not dotting your pie crust or filling with butter, leaving out the whipped cream on fruit dessert or cake, or eliminating the avocado and olives from your taco salad.

TIP #59 / ASK THESE QUESTIONS.

Do these suggestions leave you shaking in your apron? Are you wondering how you will know which **"R"** to use, and what fat-free ingredients to add in their place and how much? Well, RELAX. You're holding a book containing lots of recipes, each of which is a perfect example of how to exploit the **3 R's**. Here are some questions to ask yourself when you're staring down at that prospective recipe:

- Is there a "light" or reduced-fat version of any of the fat-containing ingredients in this recipe?
- How much of this cooking fat is really necessary?
- Can I cook this food or dish by baking, broiling, steaming, etc., instead of high-fat frying?
- Can I simmer any of these items (meats, mushrooms, etc.) in chicken broth instead of frying or stir-frying in oil, butter, or margarine?

- How much of this fatty item do I really need for a nice flavor? Can I get away with using less?
- Is there a unique characteristic (like color, flavor, texture) that the fat or fatty ingredient is contributing to this recipe?
- Can some of the fat be taken out and substituted with a nonfat ingredient?
- Can I add a little extra flavor using a nonfat or low-fat ingredient, to help compensate for the loss of flavor from the reduction or elimination of the fat or fatty ingredients?
- How much of the nice "extra" and fancy ingredients do I really need in this recipe? Can I get away with adding less or taking them out completely?

TIP #60 / REPLACE SOME FAT WITH THESE.

Here are some possible replacements for some or all of the fats, oil, shortening, butter, or margarine used in cooking.

- **For baking, some of the fat might be replaced with:**
  —evaporated skim milk
  —nonfat or low-fat yogurt, plain or flavored (lemon or vanilla).
  —light or nonfat cream cheese mixed with evaporated skim milk
  —light sour cream
  —pureed fruit, such as applesauce

—fruit juice or nectars

—nonfat or low-fat cottage cheese whipped in
   a food processor

—nonfat or low-fat ricotta cheese

- **When sauteing or stir-frying meat, fish, or vegetables,** some or all of the fat might be replaced with:
  —low-sodium chicken broth
  —non-alcoholic beer or wine
  —fruit juice

- **For coating meats and fish** before breading, baking, or grilling, fat might be replaced with:
  —nonfat or low-fat plain yogurt
  —lemon or lime juice
  —light or nonfat sour cream
  —fruit purees or fruit juice or nectars
  —low-fat egg substitutes
  —reduced-fat or nonfat margarine

TIP #61 / DON'T FOLLOW THE DIRECTIONS!

Probably one of our first lessons as youngsters learning to cook was to "always follow the directions on the package or recipe." Even as adults we have this innate fear that if we stray from the directions on the box, ever so slightly, the dish will be a complete flop.

Call it blind faith or sheer curiosity, but even as a child, I never let mere words on a package stop me from experimenting a little. Of course, when I became a dietitian, I started experimenting with the ingredients more as a health nut than a thrill seeker. What I soon discovered was that it's okay not to follow the directions sometimes. In fact, with a few nutrition tricks up your sleeve, you can transform most mixes normally calling for eggs, milk, butter, margarine or oil into a lower-fat, but still tasty, treat. Here are the tricks:

Trick #1. One of the simplest ways to lower fat and calories is to add skim or 1% light milk when the directions ask for "milk" (which means "whole milk"). Regardless of whether you're making pancakes or a creamy or cheesy pasta dish from a box, it usually works out just fine.

Trick #2. Believe it or not, you can usually cut the fat by three fourths! To tell you the truth, I didn't believe it either until I tested this out on quite a few dishes. When the directions called for 1/4 cup (4 Tbsp.) margarine or butter, I added only 1 tablespoon. If it called for 2 tablespoons, I added 1/2 tablespoon. I personally tried Noodle Roni's® Parmesano, Savory Classic's® Broccoli Au Gratin and Chicken Flavored Stove Top Stuffing® with results that brought even my husband and children to their knees in disbelief.

When you follow this "cut the fat by 3/4 rule" and replace whole milk with 1 percent milk, the nutrition picture of mixes changes for the better, right before your eyes.

Breakfast Favorites

Here are some specific ideas for lowering fat without anyone noticing.

TIP #62 / DE-FAT YOUR HOMEMADE WAFFLES.

1 egg
2 egg whites
1 cup plus 2 Tbsp. low-fat buttermilk
1 Tbsp. vegetable oil
1 1/2 cups flour
3 tsp. baking powder
2 tsp. sugar
1/2 tsp. salt

Heat waffle iron. Mix eggs with buttermilk and oil. Stir in flour, baking powder, sugar, and salt and mix until blended. When ready, generously coat waffle iron top and bottom with nonstick spray. Pour approximately 1/3 of batter onto hot waffle iron. Close and bake until the steaming stops and waffles are cooked and slightly brown. Makes 3 large waffles.

Nutrition analysis per serving: 355 calories, 1.7 gm. fiber, 74 mg. cholesterol, 838 mg. sodium, 16 percent of calories from protein, 64 percent from carbohydrates, 20 percent from fat (7.5 gm. fat)

TIP #63 / MONKEY WITH PANCAKE AND WAFFLE MIXES.

For many families that box of Bisquick® is an old, faithful friend. If you didn't have something planned for breakfast all you had to do was pull out that box and "voila"—suddenly you had a handful of options to choose from.

Well, recently Bisquick got the nutrition ball rolling by introducing a new reduced-fat Bisquick (with 50 percent less fat to be exact). Even Aunt Jemima® has gotten into the act with a "70 percent less fat than Bisquick" buttermilk mix.

It's always been possible to lighten-up the **incomplete** pancake and waffle mixes because in these cases you're adding most of the fat yourself. The trick here is to add a lot less than is called for in the package directions. Less oil in the mixing bowl, fewer egg yolks to help blend the batter and almost no butter in the pan can mean big savings!

On one bright spring Saturday morning, I decided to test the universally accepted hypothesis that waffles taste better homemade than from a mix.

I proceeded to use real buttermilk, farm fresh eggs, and a touch of the highest quality sugar. And—to my dismay—my family couldn't taste a big difference. (I usually use Reduced-Fat Bisquick.)

What's the difference nutritionally between homemade and reduced-fat Bisquick? Not much. In fact, their nutrition analysis is almost identical.

When I make waffles homemade, I add 1 Tbsp. of oil instead of the 3 they call for. And I use 1 percent fat buttermilk and only one egg plus two egg whites (the other ingredients remain the same). But when I use the reduced-fat Bisquick mix I also use only 1 egg, no oil (instead of the 2 Tbsp. they call for,) and 1 percent extra light low-fat milk. In both cases, I don't need to add any fat to the waffle iron because I generously coat my waffle iron with no-stick cooking spray, and it always works out great.

When you follow these fat-fighting steps, they both have around 350 calories per whole square waffle, 7 or 8 gm. of fat (homemade had 7.6 and the Bisquick had 8,) and 75 mg. of cholesterol. As you might expect, the Bisquick mix waffle did contain more sodium (958 mg. per waffle).

Not that we should all toss out our breakfast cookbooks, but certainly we shouldn't feel like we are compromising taste or health on those occasions when we pull out the box of Reduced-fat Bisquick instead.

Nutrition listing per whole square waffle:

Homemade Recipe:
   1 egg, 2 egg whites
   1 cup plus 2 Tbsp. skim buttermilk
   1 1/2 cups flour
   1 Tbsp. oil
   3 tsp. baking powder
   2 tsp. sugar
   1/2 tsp. salt

Calories	Fat gm.	Percent of calories from fat	Cholesterol (mg.)	Sodium (mg.)
355	7.6	20 %	74	838

Reduced-Fat Bisquick® recipe:

2 cups mix
1 1/3 cup 1 percent low-fat milk
1 egg
   and no oil

Calories	Fat gm.	Percent of calories from fat	Cholesterol (mg.)	Sodium (mg.)
350	8	20 %	75	958

TIP #64 / MAKE SPECIAL CHOCOLATE CHIP PANCAKES.

As a child, I remember waking up to the smell of pancakes cooking on the camp stove. But what really put a smile on my face was knowing that each and every one of my pancakes would be chock-full of gooey chocolate chips. This was the only way my mother could get me to eat pancakes.

As an adult, I continued this breakfast ritual—and believe you me, I had to defend it all the way through college. I would rationalize to my friends and family, with all the confidence and scientific jargon I could muster, that adding chocolate chips actually added fewer calories and fat than using margarine and syrup.

I finally sat down and analyzed the caloric and fat contributions of the mere 1 tablespoon of chocolate chips (28 to 30 regular size chocolate chips to be exact) that I typically add to a batch of 4 pancakes. And guess what? I was actually right! Adding a tablespoon of chocolate chips does add

fewer calories and the same amount of fat as adding 1 teaspoon of butter or margarine and 2 Tbsp. of pancake syrup. See for yourself:

One tablespoon chocolate chips contains 54 calories, 3.8 gm. fat, no cholesterol, and 1.5 mg. sodium. On the other hand, 1 teaspoon of butter and 2 tablespoons syrup has 139 calories, 3.8 gm. fat, 10 mg. cholesterol, and 40 mg. sodium.

TIP #65 / LIGHTEN UP YOUR EGG DISHES.

All parts of the egg are not created equal. It's the egg yolk that contains all the fat and cholesterol that has given eggs a bad name.

Egg whites are mostly protein. So the trick with eggs is to capitalize on the white of the egg while pacing yourself on the yolk. Egg substitutes have come a long way. Several brands are fat free, primarily consisting of egg whites.

Omelette Tips

- For an unusually fluffy omelette, that will puff up in the pan, some of the white and yolks may be beaten separately before being folded together. Air is incorporated into the whites during the beating. So that the trapped air does not escape, blend whites with the yolk or egg-substitute mixture immediately and make omelettes without delay.

- Fresh herbs—marjoram, parsley, or a mixture with chervil, chives or tarragon—bring fragrance to an omelette without adding any fat or calories. Dried marjoram or oregano are good aromatic substitutes.

- Diced butter is usually beaten into the egg batter (with more butter used in the pan during cooking). You can cut out the butter completely from the omelette and reduce the butter in the pan to about 1/2 teaspoon per omelette. You can even use no-stick cooking spray in a nonstick pan if you'd rather.

- Preparation tips:
  —Use a heavy omelette or crepe pan.
  —Heat pan thoroughly before adding eggs.
  —Cook over medium-high heat to create firm exteriors with soft interiors.

Fluffy Omelette for Two

1/2 cup egg substitute
2 eggs, separated
Herbs and seasonings as desired
Low-fat fillings as desired

Blend egg substitute and egg yolks in a medium-sized bowl and set aside. Whip egg whites until stiff. Fold carefully into egg-yolk mixture. Heat omelette pan or small nonstick fry pan. Generously coat with nonstick spray (or use 1/2 tsp. margarine or butter). Spread half of mixture in pan. Heat until top looks firm (about 2 minutes). Fill with desired fillings or sprinkle with desired seasonings and fold. Remove to serving plate. Repeat with remaining egg mixture. Makes 2 fluffy omelettes. Serve with low-fat accompaniments to bring down the percentage of calories from fat for the meal.

Nutrition analysis per serving: 105 calories, 210 mg. cholesterol, 163 mg. sodium, 50 percent of calories from protein, 7 percent from carbohydrates, 43 percent from fat (5 gm. fat)

Matty's Scrambled Eggs Au Gratin

To lighten-up this wonderful egg dish, I reduced the butter and used low-fat milk in the white sauce. Then I used half real eggs and half low-fat egg substitute (which is mostly egg whites) for the scrambled egg part. I grated Cracker Barrel® Light Sharp Cheddar Cheese and switched to Louis Rich Turkey Bacon®. This dish turned out so well, even my egg-detesting husband ate it.

    1 Tbsp. butter or margarine
    3 Tbsp. flour
    1 1/2 cups 1% milk
    1/4 tsp. salt
    1/4 tsp. pepper
    2 1/2 cups sliced mushrooms
    3 Tbsp. chicken broth
    3 eggs
    3/4 cup low-fat egg substitute
    1/4 cup 1% milk
    6 strips Louis Rich Turkey Bacon, cooked and crumbled
    4 ounces reduced-fat sharp cheddar cheese, grated

Preheat oven to 325 degrees F. Melt 1 Tbsp. butter in small saucepan. Add 3 Tbsp. (from the 1 1/2 cups) of milk. Blend in flour until smooth. Slowly whisk in the remaining milk. Simmer, stirring constantly, until thickened. Season with salt and pepper. Set aside.

In medium, covered fry pan, simmer mushrooms in chicken broth until cooked (cover pan). Remove with slotted spoon. Beat eggs and egg substitute with milk. Coat frying pan with nonstick spray (or melt 1 tsp. butter to coat bottom). Pour in eggs, stirring over medium heat until set. In 2-quart casserole dish, combine turkey bacon, cheese, mushrooms, eggs, and white sauce. Stir to blend. Bake for 25-30 minutes. Serves 6.

Nutrition analysis per serving: 204 calories, 5 gm. fiber, 127 mg. cholesterol, 528 mg. sodium, 36 percent of calories from protein, 20 percent from carbohydrates, and 44 percent from fat (10 gm. fat)

NOTE: Because this dish is still pretty high in fat, it needs to be served with non- and low-fat side dishes like fruit, bread, and vegetables. The original recipe contains 317 calories, 25 gm. of fat, and 268 mg. cholesterol per serving.

TIP #66 / TREAT THEM TO SUGAR AND SPICE FRENCH TOAST.

1 egg, 2 egg whites (or 1/4 cup no-fat or low-fat egg substitute)
3 Tbsp. 1% milk
3/4 tsp. sugar
1/4 tsp. ground cinnamon
4 slices french, sourdough, or whole-wheat bread

In a shallow mixing bowl, blend egg and egg whites with milk. In a small cup, mix sugar with cinnamon. Sprinkle over egg mixture and blend in with fork. Heat nonstick fry pan over medium-low heat. Coat surface with nonstick spray. Briefly soak one slice of bread in egg mixture, turn over to soak other side. Let drip for a few seconds, then place in frying pan. Repeat with other slices to fill pan. If the pan will only hold two slices at a time, respray the non-stick coating and briefly soak the remaining two slices.

Nutrition analysis per serving: (2 slices): 233 calories, 1 gm. fiber (4 gm. if 100 percent whole-wheat or grain bread is used), 61 mg. cholesterol, 427 mg. sodium, 22 percent of calories from protein, 61 percent from carbohydrate, and 17 percent from fat (4 gm. of fat)

TIP #67 / MAKE EVEN BETTER BUTTERMILK BISCUITS.

2 cups all-purpose flour
I tablespoon baking powder
2 teaspoons sugar
1/2 teaspoon cream of tartar
1/4 teaspoon salt
1/4 teaspoon baking soda
1/4 cup butter-flavored shortening (butter or margarine can also be used)
1/4 cup Philadelphia Fat-Free Cream Cheese®
2/3 cup buttermilk

In mixing bowl, stir together first six ingredients. Using a pastry blender, cut in shortening and cream cheese till mixture resembles coarse crumbs. Make a well in the center and add buttermilk all at once. Stir with fork just till moistened. Turn dough onto lightly floured surface and knead gently (fold and press dough about 10 times.) Pat or roll dough to 1/2-inch thickness. Using 2 1/2-inch biscuit cutter, cut dough into 10 to 12 biscuits (dip cutter in flour between cuts). Place on baking sheet coated lightly with nonstick spray. Bake in 450-degree oven for 10 minutes or until biscuits are done. Serve hot.

Nutrition analysis per biscuit: 152 calories, 0.7 gm. fiber, 1.5 mg. cholesterol, 224 mg. sodium, 11 percent of calories from protein, 57 percent from carbohydrate, and 32 percent from fat (5.5 gm. fat)

NOTE: One serving of the original recipe, calling for 1/2 cup of shortening, contains 193 calories, with 11 gm. of fat (50 percent of calories from fat)

TIP #68 / CREATE HOMEMADE CINNAMON ROLLS.

Several months ago I came across a recipe for **"Best-Ever Cinnamon Rolls"** in a magazine. No disrespect for the title, but I was instantly inspired to make it "better still" by cutting out some of that nasty extra fat. Using the original recipe, each cinnamon rolls contains 744 calories, 28 gm. of fat, and 85 mg. of cholesterol.

Here's the recipe as it originally appeared.
Items with asterisks will be altered to lower the fat.

4 1/2 to 5 cups all-purpose flour
1 pkg. active dry yeast
1 cup whole milk*
1/3 cup margarine or butter*
1/3 cup sugar
1/2 tsp. salt
3 eggs*
3/4 cup packed brown sugar
1/4 cup all-purpose flour
1 Tbsp. ground cinnamon
1/2 cup margarine or butter*
1/2 cup raisins
1/2 cup chopped pecans*
1 Tbsp. half-and-half or light cream*
1 recipe powdered sugar glaze

Follow these steps to lower the fat.

Step #1. Use 1 cup of 1% (or skim) milk.

Step #2. Decrease the amount of butter or margarine added to make the dough from 1/3 cup to 2 Tbsp. To compensate for this loss in moisture, add 2 more Tbsp. of milk.

Step #3. Add 1 egg and 1/2 cup low-fat egg substitute (Egg Beaters® or Healthy Choice®) instead of 3 whole eggs.

Now for the filling. When you add melted margarine you only need 3 Tbsp. to blend the dry filling ingredients instead of cutting in the original 8 Tbsp. (a half a cup!) And if you bypass the pecans, the fat drops by almost 37 gm. and the calories by a whopping 360.

Ready for the **"Better Still" Cinnamon Rolls?** Here's the recipe:

> 5 cups all-purpose flour
> 1 pkg. active dry yeast
> 1 cup plus 2 Tbsp. 1% low-fat milk or skim
> 2 Tbsp. margarine or butter
> 1/3 cup sugar
> 1/2 tsp. salt
> 1 egg and 1/2 cup low-fat egg substitute
> 3/4 cup packed brown sugar
> 1/4 cup flour
> 1 Tbsp. ground cinnamon
> 3 Tbsp. butter or margarine
> 1/2 cup raisins (optional)
> 1/2 cup chopped pecans (optional)

In a large bowl, combine 2 1/4 cups flour with yeast. In a small saucepan, heat the milk, 2 Tbsp. margarine, 1/3 cup sugar, and salt until margarine is almost melted, stirring constantly. Add this to flour mixture. Add in egg and egg substitute. Beat with mixer on low speed for 30 seconds (scraping sides of bowl), then beat on high for 3 minutes. Stir in as much of the remaining flour as you can (reserve the rest for kneading).

Lay dough on floured surface, and knead in remaining flour until dough is smooth and elastic (about 3 minutes). Place dough ball in nonstick-sprayed or lightly greased bowl, turning once. Cover and let rise in warm place until double (about 45 minutes).

While waiting, combine filling ingredients (brown sugar, 1/4 cup flour, and cinnamon) in small bowl. Pour in melted margarine and stir (mixture will be sticky). Set aside.

Punch dough down on floured surface. Roll dough into a 12-inch square. Spread filling evenly over the dough and top with raisins and pecans if desired. Roll up jelly-roll style. Pinch the edges well to seal in the filling. Slice the roll into eight 1 1/2-inch thick pieces. Arrange slices, cut side up, in a nonstick sprayed or lightly greased 13- X 9-inch baking pan. Cover rolls and let them stand in warm place 45 minutes (or wrap with plastic and refrigerate 2 to 24 hours, then let stand 30 minutes at room temperature before baking).

Brush dough with 1% milk and bake in 375-degree oven until light brown (25 to 30 minutes). Remove from oven and brush rolls again with 1% milk. After rolls have cooled slightly, drizzle rolls with sugar glaze. Makes 8 large or 10 medium rolls.

Powdered Sugar Glaze:

In small bowl, stir together 1 cup powdered sugar, 1/2 tsp. vanilla extract, and about 1 Tbsp. 1% or skim milk until drizzling consistency.

Nutrition analysis per large roll (medium roll in parenthesis): 535 (428) calories, 2 gm. fiber, 46 mg. (37 mg.) cholesterol, 268 (240) mg. sodium, 9 percent of calories from protein , 76 percent from carbohydrate, and 15 percent from 8 1/2 gm. (7 gm.) fat.

TIP #69 / MAKE THESE ROLLS IN MINUTES.

What could be better than warm and wonderful cinnamon rolls fresh out of the oven first thing in the morning? Low-fat cinnamon rolls that taste great—but take only minutes to make!

Use low-fat, canned refrigerator dough for breadsticks or biscuits and add the cinnamon/brown sugar swirl yourself.

But aren't you adding in lots of butter this way? Not if you use apple juice to liquefy the cinnamon sugar mixture instead of butter or margarine. Add 1/4 teaspoon butter-flavored extract to the apple juice before mixing it with the cinnamon and sugar and you can even have the nice buttery flavor.

Minute Cinnamon Rolls

I can refrigerated Pillsbury® Soft Breadsticks
2 Tbsp. brown sugar, packed
I Tbsp. flour
2 tsp. ground cinnamon
I Tbsp. apple juice
1/4 tsp. butter-flavored extract

Preheat oven to 350 degrees. Open can and spread dough out to form a rectangle. In small bowl, blend sugar, flour, and cinnamon with a fork. In a cup, blend apple juice with butter extract. Pour apple juice into sugar mixture and stir with fork. Spread evenly over dough. Roll up gently, lifting and rolling so the filling stays spread on the dough. Roll along the longest portion of dough (so corrugated section of dough forms 8 cinnamon rolls when rolled up). Cut through corrugated areas with serrated knife and place on nonstick baking sheet sprayed with nonstick spray. Spoon any residual cinnamon-sugar mixture over the top of the rolls. Bake 12 to 15 minutes in center of oven until rolls are lightly brown. Makes 8 rolls.

Nutrition analysis per roll: 118 calories, 0 cholesterol, 271 mg. sodium, 11 percent of calories from protein, 66 percent from carbohydrates, and 23 percent from fat.

Better Bigger Meals

Moving on from breakfast, here are some ways to cut fat in main-dish favorites.

TIP #70 / CHOOSE MORE FISH.

Most of us eat far less fish than might be ideal. So let's start with fish as a main dish choice. Check out these ideas.

Traffic was all jammed up, so you were late picking up the kids. Now they're screaming for dinner. Even the dog's barking for some chow. Wouldn't it be nice if you could get dinner on the table in 15 minutes without turning to frozen food in a box? Sounds like a job for Super Fish!

Not only is fish a highly desirable protein source, low in fat, and rich in assorted nutrients (omega-3 polyunsaturated fatty acids, zinc, calcium, vitamin B^6 and B^{12}, to name a few), but one thing's for sure, fish can be a quick fix for the weekday dinner dilemma. When tossed under the broiler, the average fish fillet takes only about 6 minutes to cook.

Take it from one who knows. The one thing that can make or break your fish fillet is the broiling sauce, which is supposed to help keep the fish moist and complement it with subtle flavors. And when you don't have all the time in the world, you want a broiling sauce that can be whipped up just as quickly as the fish can be taken out of its wrappings, rinsed, and patted dry. Then just toss the sauce over the fish in a shallow baking dish and place it under the broiler. See how simple?

When it comes to quick fish you've got your higher-fat fishies (mackerel, herring, trout, salmon, which are also higher in omega-3's) and your lower-fat fishies. In either case, you don't want to pollute this fish with a sauce that's full of fat. So, the the broiling sauces should be made almost entirely from low- or no-fat ingredients, such as low-fat yogurt, lemon juice, or low-sodium soy sauce and chicken or beef broth.

Don't get stuck in the "fish is good for you, no matter how it's prepared" trap. Keep your fish low fat by staying away from oil or margarine for cooking.

To get you started on your quick fish fix, here are some low-fat broiling sauce recipes.

Honey Mustard Sauce (for 4 fish fillets)

1 Tbsp. honey
8 tsp. Dijon-style mustard
1 1/2 tsp. finely chopped parsley or parsley flakes
1 1/2 tsp. non-alcoholic beer
Black pepper to taste (about 1/16 tsp.)

Combine all ingredients, mixing well. Generously brush over 4 fish fillets in shallow baking dish. Broil until top surface changes color and is almost cooked (a few minutes or so depending on the thickness of the fish fillet). Flip fillets over and spoon any runoff sauce over the fillets. Continue broiling until fish flakes easily or is cooked throughout.

Nutrition analysis per serving of sauce: (4 servings per recipe): 25 calories, 0 cholesterol, 150 mg. sodium, 6 percent of calories from protein, 76 percent from carbohydrates, and 16 percent from fat (4 gm. fat)

Indonesian Saute Sauce (for 4 fish fillets)

1/4 cup low-sodium soy sauce
1/8 cup dark molasses
1/8 cup brown sugar
Chopped garlic (optional)
1/2 Tbsp. margarine or butter
Juice from 1/2 lemon

Over medium heat, stir first three ingredients until sugar dissolves. Add margarine and lemon juice and continue stirring and simmering until margarine has melted. Place fish fillets in shallow baking dish and brush with saute sauce. Broil until top surface changes color and is almost cooked (a few minutes or so, depending on the thickness of the fish fillet). Flip fillets over and spoon any runoff sauce over the fillets. Continue broiling until fish flakes easily or is cooked throughout.

Nutrition analysis per serving of sauce (4 servings per recipe): 60 calories, 0 cholesterol, 166 mg. sodium, 0 percent of calories from protein, 80 percent from carbohydrates, and 20 percent from fat (1.4 gm. fat)

Lemon-Dill Sauce
*Great broiling sauce for orange roughy, sole, or salmon.

1/2 lemon (or about 2 Tbsp. lemon juice)
2 Tbsp. low-fat lemon yogurt
1 tsp. cornstarch
1/4 tsp. dill weed
Black pepper to taste
2 5-oz. fish fillets

In a small bowl, blend yogurt with cornstarch, dill and pepper until smooth. Place fish fillets in a shallow baking dish. Squeeze juice of 1/2 lemon evenly over the top of the fillets. Broil until the top surface changes color and is almost cooked (a few minutes or so depending on the thickness of the fish fillet). Flip fillets over and spread evenly with yogurt-dill sauce. Continue broiling until fish easily flakes apart or is cooked throughout. Serves two.

Nutrition analysis per serving of sole (salmon values in parentheses): 129 (248) calories, 78 mg. (54 mg.) cholesterol, 146 mg. (134 mg.) sodium, 65 percent of calories from protein, 20 percent (8 percent) from carbohydrate, 15 percent (54 percent) of calories from fat (2 gm. for sole, 15 gm. for salmon)

TIP #71 / TAKE THE LEAN-MEAT COOKING CHALLENGE.

When it comes to cooking lean meat, preparation is the key to good taste. You just can't cook a London broil, with 4.2 gm. of fat per 3-oz. portion, the same way you cook a T-bone, with 10 to 18 gm. of fat, and expect to end up with the same succulent flavor.

The fat in the T-bone adds moisture, tenderness, and flavor. So, when you suddenly have a lot less fat to work with, you have to call on some special cooking techniques. An important one is tenderizing the cut beforehand with a marinade.

The more tender skinny cuts (top loin, sirloin, and tenderloin) can be broiled or grilled. The larger, thicker pieces of meat will maintain their moistness better than the smaller, thinner pieces. Avoid overcooking. The longer you cook the meat, the more moisture you lose and the tougher the meat becomes.

The leanest skinny cuts (top round, eye of round, and round tip) require tenderizing or adding moisture during cooking to produce a more tender product. You can tenderize these cuts with a high-acid marinade. (It's the acid in vinegar or citrus juice that tenderizes the beef muscle.) Keep in mind:

- Oil has no tenderizing capabilities whatsoever, so some or all of the oil in marinade recipes can be replaced with a nonfat liquid like low-sodium chicken broth, tomato juice, etc.

- When slicing cooked meat (or slicing raw meat for stir-frying), use a sharp knife and carve thin slices on the diagonal and, when possible, across (or perpendicular to) the natural grain of the beef.

TIP #72 / TRIM YOUR STEAKS.

After interviewing scads of elementary school children about their favorite foods, probably one of my biggest surprises was the popularity of steak. Steak can be a wonderfully lean protein source, as long as several rules are followed.

- Start with a lean cut of steak.

- Trim any visible fat from the steak.

- Refrain from adding fatty marinades or sauces.

- Serve moderate-sized portions (approx. 3 ounces of cooked steak).

There are more grams of saturated fat in 3 ounces of cooked untrimmed T-bone steak than there are total grams of fat in 3 ounces of trimmed sirloin. Three ounces of beef sirloin steak, trimmed of any visible fat and broiled, comes to: 171 calories, 6.8 gm. fat, 2.6 gm. saturated fat, and 76 mg. cholesterol. Even if you take a higher-fat cut of steak like T-bone but trim it of its visible fat and broil it instead of adding fat in the cooking, you still have a fairly lower-fat entree (3 ounces of T-bone trimmed of fat contains 181 calories, 8.8 gm. fat, 3.5 gm. saturated fat, 68 mg. cholesterol).

Compare that with 3 ounces of the untrimmed cooked T-bone steak, which has 253 calories, 18 gm. fat, 7.3 saturated fat, and 71 mg. cholesterol.

TIP #73 / PORK OUT
OCCASIONALLY.

Beef is not the only lean meat challenging cooks across America. The same goes for lean pork. Thanks to changes in breeding and feeding, hogs are literally skinnier today than in decades past (they have more lean muscle tissue and less fat). According to new data, fresh pork today contains an average of 31 percent less fat, 29 percent less saturated fat, 17 percent fewer calories, and 10 percent less cholesterol, after cooking and trimming, than the same pork cut in 1983.

The two leanest pork cuts are the tenderloin (133 calories, 4.1 gm. fat, 67 mg. cholesterol per 3-oz. cooked, trimmed portion) and the pork loin roast (160 calories, 6.4 gm. fat, 66 mg. cholesterol). The next two leanest cuts are the center loin chops and top loin chop.

Many of the pork cuts are indeed leaner, but are they lean enough to be considered "the other white meat"? I think it's fair to say three of the leanest pork cuts pass muster. But there are still plenty of cuts that don't. The following table will help you choose.

*3 oz. cooked fat trimmed	Calories	Fat (gm.)	Cholesterol (mg.)	Protein (gm.)	Iron (mg.)
Tuna canned in water	111	0.4	15	25	2.7
Turkey, white meat (roasted)	119	1	73	26	1.3
Chicken breast (skinless/roasted)	139	3	72	26	0.9

*3 oz. cooked fat trimmed	Calories	Fat (gm.)	Cholesterol (mg.)	Protein (gm.	Iron (mg.)
Pork tenderloin (roasted)	139	4	67	24	1.3
Pork sirloin chop boneless	156	5.7	78	27	0.8
Pork loin roast	160	6.4	66	25	1
Chicken thigh (skinless)	165	8.3	76.5	21	1.2
Pork rib roast boneless	175	8.6	71	24	0.9
Pork blade steak	187	10.6	80	27	1.7
Pork spare ribs	337	26	103	25	1.6

When it comes to grams of fat per 3-oz. serving, the three leanest pork cuts (tenderloin, sirloin chop, and loin roast) seem to be stuck in nutrition limbo between the real "white meats" (chicken and turkey breast) and the beginning of the "dark" poultry meats (chicken thigh). These three cuts seem to resemble the "other white meats" in terms of calories and cholesterol, protein and iron. So, yes, it seems we have found another "white meat" to add to our healthful shopping list, as long as we're talking about the three leanest cuts (tenderloin, sirloin chop, and pork loin roast).

TIP #74 / GO FOR THE BIRD.

The most respected "lean meat," the ever popular poultry breast, in case you haven't noticed, has this knack for drying up if not prepared with ample moisture. Now don't gasp, but leaving the skin on while cooking will also help keep the breast moist. I know, I know. You're wondering how dare I suggest leaving the skin ON!

Recent research looked at the problem of to-skin-or-not-to-skin. Apparently the fat content of the chicken breast meat is about the same whether the skin is peeled off before or after cooking, as long as the skin *is* removed before eating. The downside to leaving the skin on is you can kiss all that tasty sauce and nicely browned crust goodbye when you take the skin off. Personally, I still prefer to cook the breast without the skin.

Easy-As-Pie Turkey Pot Pie

2 red potatoes, cooked and cut into cubes
2 cups frozen mixed vegetables, lightly cooked
1/2 small yellow onion, chopped
1 1/4 cup chopped cooked turkey breast
1 cup Pepperidge Farm® Mushroom Gravy, 98 percent fat free
Parsley, pepper, garlic, and tarragon, if desired
1/2 of a 9-inch single pie crust, rolled out into a 7-inch circle
2 Tbsp. Parmesan cheese (optional)

In a medium bowl, stir together first five ingredients, plus any desired additional seasonings. Coat a 1 1/2-quart baking dish with nonstick spray. Spoon filling in baking dish. Top with pie crust. Poke crust with fork a few times. Sprinkle with Parmesan cheese if desired. Makes 4 servings

Nutrition Analysis per serving: 457 calories, 7 gm. fiber, 36 mg. cholesterol, 450 mg. sodium, 19 percent of calories from protein, 52 percent carbohydrate, 29 percent fat (14.5 gm. fat). Vitamin content will vary by which mixed vegetables are used. If a combination of broccoli, cauliflower, and carrots is used there will be 17 mg. of vitamin C per serving, 390 RE of vitamin A, 46 mg. of calcium, and 4 mg. of iron

TIP #75 / MODIFY THE PACKAGED STUFFING MIXES.

Every year, around Thanksgiving, I'm reminded of how yummy and savory stuffing is. Of course, on Thanksgiving many of us pull out all the stops—and make our stuffing from scratch (fresh parsley, celery, and all). So what do many of us do the other 364 days of the year? Turn to Stove Top® 15-minute stuffing mix, of course.

The serving on the package is 1/2 cup (6 servings per regular-sized box). Even my two year old eats more than that! So I reanalyzed the nutrition information based on four 3/4-cup servings. When prepared as directed on the package, a 3/4-cup serving contains 13.5 gm. of fat and 270 calories. The directions call for half a stick of butter or margarine (1/4 cup), which comes to an entire tablespoon of margarine per serving!

There is something very simple you can do about this without changing the taste or convenience of Stove Top Stuffing. Just use 1 tablespoon of margarine instead of 4. (If you like your stuffing on the moist side, add a few more tablespoons of chicken broth or water). This one step makes a great difference in fat and calorie totals.

Stove Top Stuffing® (Chicken Flavor)

*Per 3/4 cup serving	Calories	Fat (gm.)	% of Calories from fat	Sodium (mg.)
Stove Top with 1/2 stick of margarine	270	13.5	45%	750
Stove Top with 1 Tbsp. of margarine	190	4	19%	683
Savings per serving	80	9.5	26%	67

TIP #76 / NEVER SAY NEVER
TO NOODLE RONI®.

The idea of making pasta from a mix might not go over too well with Italian grandmothers and grandfathers, but Noodle Roni packaged mixes offer quick and fancy noodle dishes for the rest of us. No boiling and draining noodles. No searching for the Parmesan cheese and grater. No thickening a white sauce or measuring herbs and spices. Trouble is, the directions on the box ask you to add lots of butter and some whole milk.

You don't really need to add as much butter as they say. Trust me. I've been noshing noodles for years now. You just need to add enough butter or margarine to carry off the desirable taste and texture of the sauce and use 1%, 2%, or skim in place of the whole milk.

You can usually cut the amount of butter or margarine in half without anyone noticing the difference. In fact, in most cases, you can get away with adding only a fourth of the amount called for on the box. This means adding 1 tablespoon of butter or margarine instead of 4 tablespoons.

Noodle Roni®

*For 1/2 package mix	Calories	Fat (gm.)	Percent of calories from fat	Sodium (mg.)
Fettuccine prepared as directed	230	12	47%	600
Fettuccine with 1 Tbsp. margarine & 1/2 cup 1% low-fat milk	168	6	32%	544
Parmesano prepared as directed	250	14	50%	520
Parmesano with 1 Tbsp. margarine & 1/2 cup 1% low-fat milk	168	5	28%	429
Herb & Butter prepared as directed	240	13	49%	640
Herb & Butter with 1 Tbsp. margarine & 1% low-fat milk	158	4	24%	539

TIP #77 / TAKE THE FAT OUT OF POTATO AND RICE MIXES.

Pretty good-tasting scalloped potatoes are mere minutes away—no cutting or peeling potatoes, no going to war with your grater to produce a small mound of shredded cheese, no white sauce to whip up. That's the beauty of the box.

The part that's not so beautiful is the cost in terms of fat, calories, and sodium. But we can do something about the calories and fat. Most of the potato and rice mixes call for 2 tablespoons butter or margarine and less than a cup of milk. I guarantee your potatoes and rice dishes will taste just as good if you cut the butter or margarine in half and use only low-fat milk. If you're so inclined, you could cut out the margarine and butter entirely, but you'll probably want to add a couple of tablespoons of nonfat or light sour cream to maintain a creamy texture. And if skim milk is all you have in your house, by all means use it.

There are a number of different types of potato mixes on the market. You can buy potato slices with the "skin-on" in various flavors. You can also buy potato slices with the skin off or potatoes cut into julienne strips. And you can buy mixes with rice that is sauced, sauteed, or pan-fried. Here are some comparisons.

*Per 1/2 cup serving:	Calories	Fat (gm.)	Percent of Calories from fat	Sodium (mg.)
Betty Crocker®				
Homestyle Cheddar				
Cheese Potatoes (as directed)				
—with 2 Tbsp. butter				
& 3/4 cup whole milk				
	150	6	36%	520
—with 1 Tbsp. butter				
or margarine &				
3/4 cup skim or 1%				
low-fat milk	120	3	24%	500
Hungry Jack®				
Cheesy Scalloped				
Potatoes (as directed)				
with 2 Tbsp.				
butter & 2/3 cup				
whole milk	140	6	39%	560
—with 1 Tbsp. butter				
or margarine &				
2/3 cup skim or				
1% low-fat milk	119	3	24%	540
Rice-A-Roni®				
Fried Rice with Almonds				
— 2 Tbsp. margarine				
	170	6	32%	760
—1/2 Tbsp. margarine				
	137	2	12%	709
Savory Classics®				
Broccoli Au Gratin				
— 2 Tbsp. margarine				
	170	9	48%	460
—1/2 Tbsp. margarine				
	128	4	28%	401

TIP #78 / MAKE A HEALTHIER MACARONI AND CHEESE—FROM A BOX.

No matter how your kids say it, "cheese and macaroni" or "macaroni and cheese," this mix scores pretty high in the fat department. The problems is, it also scores high in convenience and child acceptance. These are two very important considerations when you're a parent.

Most of the fat in this food comes from the butter or margarine you add during cooking. The directions call for 4 tablespoons, or a tablespoon of added fat per serving! But you don't have to add that much margarine to make the macaroni and cheese your kids know and love. Just add 1 1/2 Tbsp. (or at the most 2 Tbsp.) of margarine, and use a lower fat milk and you've cut the fat in half.

*Per serving 1/4 cup	Calories	Fat (gm.)	Percent of calories from fat	Sodium (mg.)
Kraft® **Macaroni & Cheese** –1/4 cup margarine 1/4 cup milk	290	13	40%	530

Modified
–Made with 1% milk
   1 1/2 Tbsp.
   margarine
	235	4	23%	485

Homemade Macaroni and Cheese

Now for those of you whose macaroni and cheese means grating cheese, boiling noodles, simmering up a white sauce, and *not* opening a box, there are still several ways to trim the fat. Start by buying a reduced fat cheese. An ounce of cheese will now add around 5 gm. of fat instead of 9 gm.

Now for the tricky part. When you're making that white sauce (which usually requires melting butter or margarine and mixing in flour to make a paste), don't use any butter or margarine. You heard me right, folks. Don't add any. So how do you make a paste? With milk and flour instead of margarine and flour. Your sauce won't be lumpy if you stir the milk in a little at a time. It will look almost the same and thicken up just as quickly. But will it taste the same without all that butter?

Cheese sauce is only as flavorful as the cheese that's in it. So use the sharpest reduced-fat cheddar cheese you can find. I like Cracker Barrel Light® Sharp Cheddar. If it's that zingy processed cheddar flavor you're after, then try using 4 ounces of the Cracker Barrel Light® Sharp Cheddar and 2 ounces of processed sharp cheddar cheese.

The Fannie Farmer's version of macaroni and cheese calls for:

9 oz. macaroni, cooked
2 cups cheese sauce:
4 Tbsp. butter
4 Tbsp. flour
2 cups whole milk
I cup (packed) cheddar cheese
1/2 cup grated cheddar cheese
1/2 cup buttered bread crumbs

We're going to take all of the butter out, replace the whole milk with 1% milk, replace the cheddar cheese with reduced-fat cheese, and we're going to forego the buttered bread crumbs. If crust is a must, then try mixing 2 tablespoons of Parmesan cheese with 3 tablespoons of cornflake crumbs sprinkled over the top before baking.

Let's compare a serving of the new and nutritionally improved macaroni and cheese with the original recipe:

*Per serving 1/4 cup	Calories	Fat (gm.)	Cholesterol (mg.)	Fiber (gm.)	% of calories from fat	Sodium (mg.)
As directed with butter, whole milk, & 1 cup cheese	621	31	92	3	45	442
Modified with 1% milk, low-fat cheese, etc.	437	9.5	27	3	20	278

Here are a couple recipes to help cut the fat.

Lighter Macaroni and Cheese

9 oz. macaroni, cooked and drained (about 5 cups cooked)
1/4 cup flour
1/4 tsp. dry mustard
Pepper to taste (1/4 to 1/2 tsp.)
1 2/3 cup 1% milk
4 oz. part-skim sharp cheddar cheese, grated (such as Kraft Natural® sharp cheddar)
1/4 cup (2 oz.) processed sharp cheddar "cheese food"

In a medium saucepan, mix flour, mustard, and pepper. Add 1/3 cup milk and stir to make a paste. Then add another 1/3 cup of milk and stir. Repeat with remaining milk, stirring after each 1/3 cup. Heat milk mixture over medium heat, stirring constantly until it thickens and begins to boil (2 to 3 minutes). Remove from heat. Stir in grated cheese and processed cheese. Mix the cheese sauce with the hot noodles and serve immediately, or bake in 350-degree oven for 20 minutes. Makes 4 large servings.

Nutrition analysis per serving. (These values are approximate; exact values depend on the cheese used): 437 calories, 3 gm. fiber, 27 mg. cholesterol, 278 mg. sodium, 22% of calories from protein, 58% from carbohydrate, 20% from fat (9.5 gm. fat)

Three-Cheese Sauce

This sauce can be used to make macaroni and cheese, scalloped potatoes, or cheese-topped broccoli potatoes.

2 Tbsp. flour
1 1/4 cup low-fat milk
2 oz. part-skim Jarlsberg (or reduced-fat Swiss) cheese, grated
2 1/2 ounces reduced-fat sharp cheddar cheese, grated
2 Tbsp. grated Parmesan cheese
1/4 tsp. garlic powder, 1/8 tsp. pepper

In a small saucepan, blend flour with 2 Tbsp. of milk to form a smooth paste. Using a wire whisk, slowly blend in remaining milk until smooth. Simmer over medium heat until nicely thickened. Reduce heat and add all three cheeses, garlic powder and pepper and stir until well blended and cheese has melted. Remove from heat and use as desired. Makes about 4 servings of sauce.

Nutrition Analysis per serving of sauce. (Numbers in parentheses are for sauce with 1 cup cooked macaroni): 150 (347), calories, 23 (23) mg. cholesterol, 266 (267) mg. sodium, 35% (23%) calories from protein, 21% (56%) from carbohydrate, 43% (21%) from fat (7 gm. or 8 gm. fat)

TIP #79 / TRY A LOW-FAT, QUICK PIZZA.

If you're the designated pizza maker at home, you can cut the fat by using reduced-fat cheeses. There is a Frigo Lite® mozzarella available with 2 gm. of fat per ounce (instead of 5 gm. with part-skim, or 8 to 9 gm. with whole milk mozzarella). And if you like to shed some color on your pizza with a little grated cheddar, Kraft Light 'N Naturals® and Cracker Barrel Light® make flavorful (easy-to-grate) reduced-fat sharp cheddars (with 5 gm. of fat per ounce instead of the usual 9 gm.).

You can also be more selective about what you top your pizza with. At home you can use leaner meats like lean ham slices, ground sirloin, chicken breast strips, smoked turkey sausage, or shrimp or crab. Cook the raw meats first and drain off any excess fat, so no unappetizing pools of grease form on your pizza!

And choose a lower-fat bottled spaghetti or marinara sauce that contains around 3 gm. of fat per 4-oz. serving.

Here's an example of a quick vegetarian pizza:

Garden Lover's Pizza

- Crust: Boxed hot roll mix (follow directions on box for pizza crust), refrigerated Pillsbury canned soft breadstick dough, Pillsbury canned pizza dough, or Boboli®

- Up to 1 1/2 cups low-fat bottled spaghetti sauce (with 3 gm. fat or less)

- Assorted veggies, such as onions, fresh tomatoes, zucchini slices, green pepper rings, etc.

- 5 oz. mixture of reduced-fat cheese (available in sharp cheddar and mozzarella)

- Parmesan cheese, chopped garlic, or dried hot red peppers (optional)

If using a hot roll mix, follow package directions for pizza crust. Spread and shape refrigerated dough with rolling pin, and place on nonstick pizza pan or baking sheet that has been generously coated with no-stick olive-oil spray. Spread sauce over dough. Sprinkle grated cheese on top. Chop vegetables as desired and lay on top of cheese. Sprinkle with Parmesan if desired. Bake per directions on package or until cheese bubbles and crust is lightly browned (usually 15 minutes). Makes 8 slices.

Nutrition analysis per slice (using breadstick dough topped with zucchini, green peppers and onions): 185 calories 11 mg. cholesterol, 450 mg. sodium, 19% of calories from protein, 53% from carbohydrate, 28% from fat (5.7 gm. fat)

TIP #80 / BUILD A BETTER CHEESE ENCHILADA.

Enchilada sauce*

2 tsp. olive oil
1/2 cup chopped onion
1 clove minced garlic
2 tsp. chili powder (or more to taste)
1 1/2 cup tomato puree
1/2 cup hot water mixed with 2 envelopes or 2 cubes
    low-sodium chicken or beef broth powder
Pepper to taste
1 tsp. cumin
If you like a lot of enchilada sauce, double this recipe.

12 super-sized corn tortillas (one 14-oz. package)
1/2 cup chopped raw onion
8 oz. fat-free mozzarella cheese, grated (Healthy Choice®)
8 oz. reduced-fat sharp cheddar cheese, grated (Cracker Barrel Light®)

Preheat oven to 350 degrees. Generously coat baking pan with nonstick spray. In nonstick saucepan, heat oil and saute 1/2 cup onion and garlic until golden. Add chili powder, tomato puree, broth, pepper, and cumin and stir over heat until well blended. Remove from heat. Heat tortillas in microwave to soften (about 40 seconds on high, 3 at a time). Spread a little sauce along center of each tortilla. Fill center with equal quantities of onion and cheeses. Roll tortillas and place side by side in baking pan. Pour remaining sauce over the tops. Bake about 15 minutes. Makes 12 enchiladas.

Nutrition analysis per 2 enchiladas: 350 calories, 7 gm. fiber, 27 mg. cholesterol, 481 mg. sodium, 31 percent of calories from protein, 44 percent from carbohydrate, 25 percent from fat (10 gm. fat)

TIP #81 / MODIFY YOUR ALL-AMERICAN BURGER AND FRIES.

Most of us never outgrow our love for a good homemade burger and fries. And most of us think serving our children burgers and fries is a nutrition no-no. It's simply not so.

You can make a burger and fries combination with 27 percent of calories from fat, with around 426 calories and 13 gm. of fat—and I'm not even talking about using any fabricated soy-burger product. I'm not talking about a hamburger patty the size of a golf ball either.

Just start with a very lean ground sirloin hamburger (or ground-beef mixture with about 10 percent of calories from fat). Divide it into 4-ounce patties, broil it up, add a bun and some catsup (1 Tbsp.) and you've got a burger worth 316 calories, 9 gm. fat, and 76 mg. cholesterol, with 27 percent of calories from fat.

When you add a 3-oz.serving of Ore Ida Golden Crinkles® french fries (baked, not fried), the grand total is: 426 calories, 13 gm. fat, and 27 percent of calories from fat.

How does this compare to the traditional burger and fries combo? A 3-oz. cooked patty of regular ground beef with a bun and some catsup is 388 calories, 20 gm. fat, and 109 mg. cholesterol, with 48 percent of calories from fat. Add a tablespoon of mayonnaise and a slice of American cheese and you've got 593 calories, 40 gm. fat, and 61 percent of calories from fat. Then add a side of frozen french fries that have been fried in oil (3-oz. serving) and you'll end up with 860 calories and 54 gm. fat, with 57 percent of calories from fat.

TIP #82 / LET 'EM EAT SPAGHETTI.

Maybe it is because it has worm-shaped noodles to play with. Maybe it's the "fork-able" meatballs or ground beef. Or maybe it's the tangy bright red sauce that makes spaghetti such a childhood favorite.

Since tomato is the base ingredient in spaghetti sauce, it can be fairly low in fat, depending on how much olive oil is added. And since spaghetti sauce rarely tops pasta without a few meatballs, sausage links, or some sliced mushrooms, these ingredients also need to be factored into the equation.

To keep spaghetti sauce low in fat, stick with vegetables like onions and mushrooms and leaner meats such as ground sirloin or low-fat turkey sausage links.

And what a difference it can make. Compare the figures below:

	Calories	Fat (gm.)	% of Calories from fat	Cholesterol (mg.)
Traditional homemade recipe 1 1/2 cups spaghetti with meat sauce	495	18	32%	134
3/4 cup spaghetti noodles	148	.7	4%	0
6 Tbsp. plain spaghetti sauce	67	3.5	47%	0
2 oz. cooked sirloin	114	4.5	36%	50.5
Total 1 1/2 cups	329	9	25%	50.5

TIP #83 / PLEASE THEM WITH PASTA.

Pasta is always a favorite. When you combine a low-fat pasta recipe with low-fat meat choices, the results can be a true crowd pleaser. Here's an example.

Easy Oven Lasagna

    1 lb.(or less) very lean ground sirloin
    3/4 cup water
    32-oz. low-fat bottled marinara or spaghetti sauce
        (with 3 gm. of fat or less per 4-oz. serving)
    1 8-oz. package lasagna noodles, uncooked
    2 cups light or nonfat ricotta cheese
    1/4 cup grated Parmesan cheese
    12 oz reduced-fat mozzarella, grated

Preheat oven to 375 degrees. Coat skillet with nonstick spray. Brown very lean beef in skillet. Add water and marinara sauce. Bring to boil and remove from stove. Scoop out about 2/3 cup of sauce and spread on bottom of 13- X 9-inch pan.

Lay lasagna noodles over the top, leaving a little space between them. Spread half of cheese mixture over noodles. Sprinkle half of the mozzarella over the top and spread about 1 1/4 cup of meat sauce over it. Lay noodles over the top and spread rest of ricotta on them. Sprinkle with remaining mozzarella and another 1 1/4 cup of meat sauce.

Place remaining noodles over the top and spread with remaining meat sauce. Sprinkle some additional Parmesan cheese over the top if desired.

Cover pan tightly with foil and bake for 1 hour. Let stand 15 minutes before serving. Makes 12 servings

Nutrition analysis per serving (with ground sirloin, part-skim ricotta cheese and part-skim mozzarella and very low-fat marinara. Values would be less if nonfat products are used): 286 calories, 2 gm. fiber, 57 mg. cholesterol, 257 mg. sodium, 36% of calories from protein, 31% from carbohydrates, 33% from fat (10.5 gm. fat).

TIP #84 / LET THEM EAT LOWER-FAT CAKE!

There are a few things that the bright, bold lettering on the typical cake mix doesn't tell you—like the fact that the mix already has quite a bit of fat.

You don't need to add *any* of the 1/3 to 1/2 cup of oil they tell you to add on the mixing directions.

And, while we're at it, you don't have to add as many egg yolks as they say, either.

By making a few of these ingredient adjustments, you can transform what would have been a high-calorie, high-fat-and-cholesterol cake into a lower calorie, lower-fat-and-cholesterol cake that's just as delicious!

Confession #1—It's no joke, one yolk will do the job of three (in most cases). When a cake mix calls for two or more eggs, you really only have to add one (sometimes you can get away with none or just half a yolk) as long as you make up the difference with egg whites. If a cake mix, for example, calls for 3 eggs, just add 1 whole egg and 3 or 4 egg whites (add about 1 egg white for every yolk taken out). Egg substitutes work great too. Add 1/4 cup of liquid for each whole egg called for. So if a cake mix calls for 3 eggs, you can add just 1 whole egg and 1/2 cup egg substitute.

Confession #2—In most cases plenty of fat has already been added to the mix. To see for yourself, just check the list of ingredients. Some type of hydrogenated vegetable oil is usually the third ingredient (the first is usually sugar, and flour is second). Or better still, read the column marked "as packaged" on the nutrition information label and find out exactly how many grams of fat per serving are listed for just the mix ingredients, which is before you've added anything else. If there is already some fat added, in most cases you don't have to add a single drop of the oil they tell you to add.

But here's the catch. (You knew there would be one). With a cake or muffin mix, you will have to add some type of liquid to contribute the moisture that you need to make the cake work right and to replace the amount of oil that you are no longer adding. Among the liquids you could use are fruit juices, evaporated skim, or low-fat milk.

Confession #3—By substituting a mystery liquid for the oil normally called for on the mix directions, you are creating a new and exotic dessert. For example, by adding 1/4 cup whiskey and 1/4 cup water or evaporated skim milk to the mix instead of the 1/2 cup of oil normally called for, your standard chocolate cake becomes "Chocolate Whiskey Cake."

If you or your kids prefer the essence of fruit flavors with your cake, you could add crushed pineapple and pineapple juice (instead of oil) to your standard yellow cake mix or carrot cake and create a Hawaiian pineapple cake. Add apple juice or applesauce (instead of oil) to a spice cake and suddenly you're serving "Old-Fashioned Apple Spice Cake."

There's even an added nutrition bonus: These cakes will have so much flavor, you might not even mind skipping the frosting, which we all know is basically sweetened fat (butter or shortening and sugar). Bake these cakes in a Bundt® or tube cake pan (so you won't need to spread anything in the middle) and top them with sifted powdered sugar or flavored glazes or serve fresh fruit with each slice.

Is it worth it? Well, what would you say if I told you that by not adding the oil and cutting back on the yolks you could cut the grams of fat per serving (of just cake, no frosting) by two-thirds (from 11 to 13 gm. of fat per serving to 4 to 5 gm.) and cut calories by up to 100 per serving. You don't believe your ears? Well, maybe you'll believe your eyes. Here are a couple of examples.

*Per serving 3/4 cup	Calories	Fat (gm.)	Cholesterol (mg.)	% of Calories from fat

Duncan Hines Moist Deluxe® Swiss Cake Mix
Original recipe: 3 eggs and 1/2 cup oil are added to mix:

	280	15	65	48%

Modified recipe: 1 egg, 4 egg whites, and 1/2 cup evaporated skim milk:

	210	5.5	18	23%

Betty Crocker Super Moist® Carrot Cake Mix
Original recipe: 3 eggs and 1/3 cup oil are added to mix:

	250	11	55	40%

Modified recipe: 1 egg, 4 egg whites, and 1/3 cup pineapple juice are added:

	195	4.5	18	20%

TIP #85 / TRY THIS DEEP-
DISH APPLE CRISP.

Your neighbors just harvested their apples and dumped a bag full of the very ripe fruit on your doorstep. There are so many apples that even if you and every member of your immediate family ate an apple a day, you would still have apples well into the new year.

What to do with all those apples? Apple pie is too high in fat and it's too early for candied apples. How about deep-dish apple crisp. It has a nice ring to it doesn't it?

When it comes to crisps, all of the fat is in the crisp part. So the deeper the yummy apple filling, the lower the percentage of calories from fat.

When making a deep dish crisp, you can almost double the recipe for the filling part, but use just one recipe of crispy topping. On top of that, you can even add less fat when making the crisp topping. Now we're really getting somewhere!

A serving of the typical apple crisp recipe made with 4 to 5 cups of sliced apples and the topping ingredients (3/4 cup flour, 1 cup sugar, and 1/2 cup of butter) contains 281 calories, 12 gm. of fat (37 percent of calories from fat), and 31 mg. of cholesterol.

The first thing I do is double the apples to 8 to 10 cups . For the crisp topping, I used 3/4 cup of brown sugar (which I think adds more flavor than granulated), and 3/4 cup of flour and 1/4 tsp. salt. For additional flavor, add a teaspoon of ground cinnamon and half a teaspoon ground nutmeg. I then melt 4 tablespoons of diet margarine (I like Dairy Maid Challenge Light Spread®) and blend it into the flour mixture with a fork. Because the margarine was melted and is partially composed of water, less is needed to blend with the flour mixture.

The result? A great tasting deep dish apple crisp with less than half the grams of fat per serving (18 percent of calories from fat), 50 fewer calories (even though there is twice as much filling), and no cholesterol!

Serve it a-la-mode with low-fat frozen yogurt for a cool, summer treat.

Deep-Dish Apple Crisp

8 to 10 cups sliced apples
1/3 cup apple juice

Crumb topping:

3/4 cup flour
3/4 cup packed brown sugar
1 tsp. ground cinnamon
1/2 tsp. ground nutmeg
1/4 tsp. salt
4 Tbsp. diet margarine

Preheat oven to 350 degrees. Coat a 9- x 9-inch pan or 2-quart baking dish with nonstick spray. Spread the apples in the pan and sprinkle apple juice over the top. Combine the flour, sugar, cinnamon, nutmeg, and salt in a medium-sized bowl and pour in the melted margarine. Mix with fork. Spread evenly over the apples. Bake for 35 to 45 minutes or until the crust is lightly browned and apples tender. Makes 8 servings.

Nutrition analysis per serving: 235 calories, 3 gm. fiber, 0 cholesterol, 144 mg. sodium, 2% of calories from protein, 80% from carbohydrate, 18% from fat (5 gm. fat)

TIP #86 / RECREATE YOUR COOKIE CLASSICS.

To all those people who, since time began, have been making Toll House® cookies and the oatmeal cookies on the Quaker Oats® box, I confess I've done the unspeakable. I took a stab at lowering the fat and calories in these American cookie classics. What recipe is held in higher reverence by the American people than the Toll House cookie recipe on the package of Nestle® semi-sweet chocolate chips? Making these cookies has become a legacy passed from parent to child for generations.

It was a little scary, I admit—messing with perfection. But I got over it. I attacked these culinary masterpieces with my nutrition arsenal; my favorite diet margarine (Dairy Maid Light Spread® by Challenge) and the new fat-free ricotta cheese by Frigo®. I was as ruthless and unforgiving as they come—cutting the cooking fat in half, eliminating one of the yolks, lightening up a bit with the sugar, making chopped nuts optional. I even had the gall to use 1/3 fewer chocolate chips.

But do you know what? It worked. For some reason, though, I had to play a little bit more with the oatmeal cookie recipe to get it to the right taste and texture, a little more of this, a little less of that. In both cases, the lightened-up cookies looked and tasted more like the soft and chewy high-fat originals if they were slightly underbaked. If you, like my husband, prefer your oatmeal and chocolate chip cookies crisp and crunchy but lower fat too, I don't know what to tell you. According to my relentless cookie experimentation and much to my husband's chagrin, apparently, you can't have it both ways. It has something to do with the lower proportion of fat to flour and sugar.

Here is the original Toll House Cookie Recipe. Its Lightened-Up Bakery-Sized version follows.

Toll House Cookies
(Makes 60 small or 30 large cookies)

Original

    2 1/4 cups flour
    1 tsp. baking soda
    1 tsp. salt
    1 cup butter (softened)
    3/4 cup sugar
    3/4 cup brown sugar, packed
    1 tsp. vanilla extract
    2 eggs
    12 ounces (2 cups) semi-sweet
        chocolate morsels
    1 cup nuts

One of the golden rules for lower-fat baking is "if you cut out part of the fat that's originally called for, you have to replace that lost quantity with something of similar texture but preferably fat free." In the Toll House recipe that follows, I added fat-free cream cheese. These cookies are nice and big–and very satisfying.

Lightened-Up Version

Light Bakery-Sized Toll House Cookies

2 1/4 cup flour
1 tsp. baking soda
1 tsp. salt
1/2 cup butter or margarine
1/2 cup nonfat cream cheese (or fat-free ricotta cheese)
1/2 cup sugar
3/4 cup brown sugar, packed
1 1/2 tsp. vanilla
1/2 tsp. butter flavor extract
1 egg and 1 egg white
1 1/3 cups chocolate morsels
1/2 cup nuts (optional)

Preheat oven to 375 degrees. In a small bowl, combine flour, baking soda and salt; set aside. In large mixer bowl, blend butter with cream cheese. Add sugar, brown sugar, vanilla and butter extract; beat until creamy. Beat in egg and egg white. Gradually add flour mixture. Stir in the semi-sweet or milk chocolate morsels. Drop by cookie scoop or rounded measuring tablespoonfuls onto ungreased cookie sheets. For soft and chewy cookies, bake approximately 7 to 8 minutes. Makes about 30 bakery-sized large cookies.

Nutrition analysis per cookie, (original recipe in parenthesis): 138 (190) calories, 6 (11) gm. fat, 15 mg. (31 mg.) cholesterol, 160 mg. (169 mg.) sodium, 6% of calories from protein, 58% (48%) from carbohydrate, 36% (48%) from fat.

Soft Peanut Butter Cookies

2 cups all-purpose flour
1/2 tsp. baking soda
1/4 tsp. salt
1 1/4 cups dark brown sugar, firmly packed
3/4 cup white sugar
1/2 cup butter or margarine, softened
1/2 cup fat-free (or light) cream cheese
1 egg and 3 egg whites
1 cup creamy or chunky peanut butter
2 tsp. vanilla extract

Preheat oven to 350 degrees. In medium bowl, combine flour, soda, and salt. Set aside. In mixing bowl, blend sugars on medium speed. Add butter and cream cheese and mix (will look a bit grainy). Scrape sides of bowl and add eggs, peanut butter and vanilla. Mix until light and fluffy.

Add flour mixture on low speed, just until mixed (do not overmix). Drop by rounded tablespoonfuls (or use cookie scoop) on ungreased nonstick cookie sheet. With wet fork, press a crisscross pattern on top of cookies. Bake for 15 minutes or until cookies are slightly brown along the edges. Makes 3 1/2 dozen.

Nutrition analysis per large cookie: 120 calories, 11 mg. cholesterol, 98 mg. sodium, 10% of calories from protein, 52% from carbohydrate, 38% from fat (5 gm. fat)

NOTE: the original recipe contains 150 calories and 8 gm. of fat (46% of calories from fat)

Lower-Fat Oatmeal Raisin Cookies

2 1/4 cup flour
1/2 tsp. baking soda
1/4 tsp. salt
1 cup quick oats (not instant)
1 cup brown sugar
1/2 cup white sugar
1/2 cup butter or margarine
1/2 cup light sour cream
1 Tbsp. vanilla extract
1 egg and 2 egg whites
1 1/2 cup raisins

Preheat oven to 300 degrees. In a medium-sized bowl combine first four ingredients and set aside. In mixing bowl, blend sugars then add butter and sour cream and mix at medium speed. Scrape sides and add vanilla and eggs. Continue mixing until light and fluffy.

Turn mixer to low speed and add flour mixture. Stir in raisins. Do not overmix. Drop by rounded tablespoonfuls or cookie dough scoop onto cookie sheets lightly coated with nonstick spray. Bake about 15 minutes or until desired doneness. You may want to slightly undercook if you prefer your cookies chewy. Makes 36 cookies

Nutrition analysis per large cookie: 121 calories, 8 gm. fiber, 13 mg. cholesterol, 64 mg. sodium, 6% of calories from protein, 72% from carbohydrate, 22% from fat (3 gm. fat)

TIP #87 / MAKE A BETTER GERMAN CHOCOLATE CAKE.

Last month, I celebrated yet another birthday. And, like most people, I have made it a habit to enjoy at least one piece of my absolute favorite cake on this special day—and mine happens to be German chocolate cake.

So this year, I attacked my very own beloved cake with my fat-fighting furor. I know, it's sacrilege to make your own birthday cake—but who else would experiment with nonfat sour cream and ricotta and make coconut pecan frosting and chocolate cake batter with total disregard for the directions on the box?

This September my time was particularly stretched so I took the box route entirely, which I soon discovered gave me a nutrition advantage when it came to the obscenely high-fat coconut pecan frosting. Lucky for me, half the fat is added by us at home. So instead of adding 1/4 cup margarine or butter and 1/3 cup whole milk to the mix, like the manufacturer tells you to, I added 2 tablespoons of diet margarine plus 2 tablespoons of nonfat sour cream and 1/3 cup of 1% milk.

To the German chocolate cake mix, I added none of the fat called for in the box directions (1/3 cup oil) and used 1/3 cup of nonfat sour cream in its place. And instead of 3 eggs, I added 1 egg and 1/3 cup of low-fat egg substitute (Egg Beaters® or Healthy Choice®).

For the chocolate frosting, you can either use one of the light chocolate frostings in a plastic can (Lovin' Lights® or Betty Crocker®), which I have to admit taste pretty darn good, or follow my recipe for chocolate fudge frosting (page 141).

To make the lowest-fat frosting possible and still have the look and taste of a forbidden fudgey frosting, I use cocoa (de-fatted chocolate) for the flavoring. Instead of butter, margarine, or shortening, I used nonfat ricotta cheese blended with diet margarine. The consistency is definitely thinner than with butter, so I add less milk than called for in the regular recipe.

Every now and then I surprise even myself with how delicious lower-fat desserts can be—and this frosting recipe takes the cake!

What were the calorie and fat savings? A regular slice of German chocolate cake (1/12th of the cake) made with 1 cup pecan-coconut frosting on top and 1 1/2 cup chocolate fudge frosting in the middle and on the sides will cost you about 480 calories, at least 60 mg. of cholesterol, and 22 gm. of fat (41 percent of calories from fat).

A piece of my lower-fat, mouth-watering rendition of German chocolate cake will run you approximately 355 calories, 0 cholesterol, and 10.5 gm. of fat (26 percent of calories from fat).

Taste and compare:

One piece of German Chocolate Cake

	Before	After
Calories	480	355
Fat grams	22	10.5
Percent of calories from fat	41%	26%
Cholesterol	60 mg.	0

Chocolate Fudge Frosting

1/4 cup diet margarine
1/4 cup nonfat ricotta cheese (Frigo Truly Lite®)
1/2 cup cocoa
1 1/2 tsp. vanilla extract
2 1/2 Tbsp. 1% milk
3 cups powdered sugar

In a small mixing bowl, beat ricotta with diet margarine until blended. Add cocoa, vanilla extract, 2 Tbsp. milk, and 1 cup of powdered sugar and beat until creamy. Gradually add remaining powdered sugar. Beat until smooth. Add an extra teaspoon or two of milk if you desire a thinner consistency. Makes about 2 cups of frosting.

Nutrition analysis per 1/12th of recipe: 130 calories, 0 cholesterol, 75 mg. sodium, 23% of calories from fat (3.5 gm. fat)

Lunches: Making Them Healthier at School or at Home

Breakfast may be the meal recognized as the "most important meal of the day," but for my money, lunch holds that
honor for two reasons:

1. Lunch is conveniently located in the middle of the work
or school day. It provides the energy that gets you through.

2. Without lunch, people end up snacking or binging in a
big way when hunger hits in the afternoon. People also
tend to eat bigger dinners when they skip lunch. And one
of the healthiest eating habits is to eat light at night.

For our school-bound children, this important meal is eaten
away from home five days out of seven. But there are still
many things you can do to improve the quality of their noon
meal. We'll start with the old lunch standby, the sandwich.

TIP #88 / CHOOSE YOUR BREAD WITH CARE.

The average American ate a little less than a loaf of bread
each week last year. That's 50 pounds a year! So the type of
bread we choose can really add up in terms of fiber and
important nutrients. According to the U.S.Department of
Commerce, an estimated 55 percent of all these pounds of
bread eaten is balloon bread (regular white bread) and 45
percent is everything else

According to my calculations, the average person eating
approximately 800 slices of bread a year (16 slices per
week) can boost their fiber total by up to 1,120 gm. of fiber
a year simply by choosing a bread with at least 2 gm. of
fiber per slice (100 percent whole wheat, rye, pumpernickel, 100 percent whole multigrain) instead of white.

Types of Bread
I slice (weight)	Fiber (gm.)	Fat (gm.)
Rye, 32 gm.	2	1.1
Iron Kids® white, 28 gm.	2	1
Whole Wheat, 28 gm.	1.9	1.2
Pumpernickel, 32 gm.	1.9	1
Multigrain, 26 gm.	1.8	1
Oat bran, 30 gm.	1.4	1.3
"Wheat", 25 gm.	1.1	1
Sourdough, 28 gm.	0.8	0.6
White, 25 gm.	0.6	0.9

If you want to be a discriminating bread buyer, there are a few things you should know while you're strolling the aisles:

- Breads that sound wholesome and natural and full of fiber may be made primarily with the exact thing you're trying to avoid—refined white flour. The first ingredient in most oat bran and wheat breads is "wheat" flour, and "wheat" flour is the same as "white" flour.

- "Good source of fiber" can be used on products with 2.5 to 4.9 gm. per serving.

- Look for the "whole." The first ingredient listed on the label must be "whole-wheat" flour.

- What's in a name? There's no standard for ingredients of breads that are named everything from 4- to 12-grain to oat bran or wheat berry bread. So those names can literally mean almost anything.

- The advertising claim "high fiber" used to mean anything the bread company wanted it to mean. But as of November 1993 when the FDA's new food labeling law officially goes into effect, high fiber means there are 5 grams or more per serving. (Foods making high-fiber claims must meet the definition for low fat, or the level of total fat must appear next to the high-fiber claim.)

- Small amounts of sweeteners are added to bread dough to provide fuel for the yeast that makes bread rise and to make toast brown well.

- The salt content varies widely from bakery to bakery. It's added to toughen the protein in dough, to control fermentation of yeast, and, of course, for flavor.

- Experts on both sides of the fence agree that the scary-sounding additives in bread are generally harmless.

I have to admit this "light" bread thing bothers me because it helps perpetuate the myth that bread is fattening. The truth is, bread is relatively low in calories, with 65 to 75 percent of its calories coming from carbohydrates. Only a small amount of fat is usually added to help lubricate the dough and make it more expandable and fluffy.

A slice of most regular breads will cost you from 60 to 70 calories. (Some heartier types may hit the 90 calorie mark.) Most "light" breads run around 40 calories per slice. Where are these calorie savings coming from? There are basically two ways to cut calories in bread: You can reduce your serving size by making slices thinner, or you can add fiber (guar or vegetable gum, oat bran, wheat bran, cottonseed fiber or potato fiber are commonly used). The fiber adds nondigestible bulk to bread so it dilutes the calories per slice by taking up space without contributing calories.

Our Daily Bread

In the new food pyramid, **bread** is one of the items listed in the group we're encouraged to eat the **most** servings from. It's suggested every American eat 6 to 11 servings a day from the bread, cereal, rice, and pasta group. This is more servings than any other food group in the pyramid, which is why it's on the most spacious portion of the pyramid.

Bread is an important and delicious part of a low-fat diet. But don't take my word for it—see for yourself. Look at the list of ingredients for your basic loaf of bread, which are shown in order from the highest quantity by weight to the lowest. The first ingredient is usually flour, then water, then sugar. Vegetable fat and yeast tend to be low on the list.

GASP! Vegetable fat? Relax. They only add a smidgen of fat to help bind the dough better and to assist in even leavening (distribution of air bubbles).

How much more fiber do you get with whole-wheat bread than white bread? Each 35 gm. slice of 100 percent whole-wheat or 100 percent whole-grain bread contributes about 2 1/2 gm. to your daily fiber total. White flour bread contain about 1/2 gm. per 35 gm. slice. You also get several more vitamins and minerals that aren't added back when white flour is "enriched."

When they de-germ and de-bran the wheat kernel, for example, they also strip away many of the vitamins and minerals found in the bran and wheat germ. Food and flour companies do enrich the white flour with several, but not all, of these lost nutrients.

Anatomy of a Sandwich

Once upon a time I ordered a sandwich and found myself staring down, with enormous disappointment, at two anemic-looking thin slices of white bread with one lonely slice of turkey in the middle and margarine spread on both sides of the bread. I was, in a word, speechless. I had just paid top dollar for a "turkey sandwich," and I was not very happy about what I received.

Where was I? Of course, I wasn't in America! All it takes is one trip to Europe to discover what we consider a sandwich and what they consider a sandwich are two different things. I found myself exclaiming not only "Where's the beef?" but also "Where's the mustard, bread, tomato, lettuce, and onions?"

Most Americans like the kind of sandwich you need to hold with both hands—the kind where you have to open your mouth wide just to get a corner in. We have a lot of choices when it comes to ordering or fixing a sandwich—whole-wheat, rye or French roll, mustard or mayo, hot peppers, lettuce, onions, pickle or tomato? With cheese or without? And, of course, the grand finale is what type of meat to "sandwich" in?

But these big sandwiches can mean big trouble, depending mainly on what type of meat you choose and what spread you put on your bread. Let's go ahead and start our anatomy lesson for the day and take the typical American sandwich apart. Then we can see which fat and calorie sources are best left in the jar, deli counter, or supermarket shelf.

TIP #89 / USE THE BETTER
BREAD SPREADS.

No matter how much care you exercise selecting your bread and fillings, **what** and how much you spread on your bread, can make or break your sandwich, fatwise. A knife's worth of mayonnaise can send your sandwich into fat oblivion.

You are better off with mustard. True, mustard has 47 percent of calories from fat, but we're only talking about 4 measly calories and 65 mg. of sodium in a teaspoon. That's a whopping 0.2 gm. of fat, to be exact .

Regular mayonnaise has 100 calories per tablespoon, 98 percent of calories from fat and 78 mg. of sodium. Between the two, mustard starts looking pretty darn good in the calorie and fat departments. Light mayonnaise may have half the fat of regular mayonnaise but each tablespoon still contains 50 calories and 5 gm. of fat per tablespoon. Here are some ways to flavor your bread without fattening it up.

- At home, you might try adding a little salsa to spice up your sandwich.

- Catsup has 6 calories per teaspoon, 3 percent of calories from fat, and 59 mg. of sodium.

- Experiment with the wide variety of assorted mustards on the market. Mustard contains very little fat, while a tablespoon of mayonnaise has 10 gm. of fat.

- Spread jam or jelly on toast, bagels, or rolls instead of butter or margarine. This will save you almost 4 gm. of fat per teaspoon. A tablespoon of the lower-sugar jams only add about 24 calories (and all are fat-free calories).

- Fill your bagel with light or nonfat cream cheese. If you add 1 oz. of light cream cheese to your average bagel, it will add up to 240 calories and 6 gm. of fat, with 25 percent of calories from fat.

- If you like your sandwich bread with a little mayonnaise, try light, reduced-fat, or fat-free mayo instead. A teaspoon of light mayonnaise, on one side of your sandwich, adds 17 calories, 1.7 gm. of fat. The Kraft-Free® mayo adds 3 calories and no fat per teaspoon.

- Although peanut butter is high in fat, if you spread it thin, using 1/2 tablespoon per slice, you still have a reasonable combination (128 calories, 5.5 gm. of fat and 38% calories from fat).

- So what if adding margarine or butter to your toast is a habit you just don't want to break? As long as you add 1 tsp. of diet margarine or 1/2 teaspoon of stick margarine or butter your toast won't tip you over the fat and calorie edge (98 to 105 calories, 3.4 to 4.4 gm. of fat).

TIP #90 / BE FUSSY ABOUT FILLERS.

What you put between two slices of bread is a very personal thing. But you might have noticed the explosion of thinner choices in recent years. Not only are many cold cuts thinner on fat and calories, they're physically thinner. There are now several brands with "deli-thin" slices.

The better sandwich fillers have 2 gm. of fat per ounce. This distinguished group includes water-packed tuna, sliced fresh chicken or turkey breast, lean deli meats such as boiled ham and roast beef trimmed of visible fat.

TIP #91 / TRY THIS THINNER BLT.

One of my favorite sandwiches from a previous life (before I became a registered dietitian) was a bacon, lettuce, and tomato sandwich. I thought I had to bid them farewell for life. But, thanks to Louis Rich® turkey bacon, I can make a TBLT (turkey bacon, lettuce, and tomato) sandwich with about 30 percent of calories from fat. Use the following:

2 strips of Louis Rich®turkey bacon
2 slices of whole-wheat bread
Half a tomato
I tsp. of reduced-calorie mayo
Lots of lettuce

It has a total of 280 calories, 9 gm. of fat, 30 percent of calories from fat, and 820 mg. of sodium.

TIP #92 / BE CAREFUL WITH THE PEANUT BUTTER.

At 8 grams of fat per tablespoon, it's no wonder peanut butter has "butter" as a last name. Why is peanut butter such a fatty food? Well, first you crush the peanuts, which by themselves contain 18 gm. of fat per 1/4 cup. Then you add shortening (hydrogenated vegetable oil). Along with "creaminess," shortening adds 13 gm. of fat per tablespoon. Stir in some sugar and a pinch or two of salt for flavor and you have peanut butter.

Of course this peanut butter equation isn't set in stone. Some brands add honey instead of sugar. Some add mostly partially hydrogenated vegetable oil, while others add fully hydrogenated oil. And some add more or less of all these ingredients and some add none at all. Some even add air, creating whipped peanut butter.

I read all the peanut butter labels in my local grocery store recently and saw a few "nutty" differences.

- Some of the fancy types (Reese's® and Smuckers®) may have less fat than regular peanut butter, but they make up for it in calories by adding more sugar.
- Skippy® creamy advertises "less sugar than other brands". But they forgot to mention that they have more fat than other leading brands.
- The two "natural" brands I saw (Adams 100 percent Old Fashioned Natural Creamy®, Laura Scudder's Old Fashioned®) have a few more calories than the other commercial brands, especially Laura Scudder's. And although the ingredients were almost identical, the Adams peanut butter had 7 gm. of fat per tablespoon, while Laura Scudder's Natural had 8 gm.

In the new food pyramid, you'll find peanut butter, along with other nuts, stationed toward the top of the pyramid with the meat, fish, poultry, and egg group. It was probably placed there because peanut butter is a decent source of protein and contains a small amount of iron and some vitamins. And unlike the other meat group members, peanut butter (along with nuts in general) contains a bit of fiber.

But I haven't been talking about the most important part. Kids (and grown-ups alike) are "nuts" about peanut butter. According to one survey, a school-age child eats about 4.8 pounds of this creamy brown stuff every year. So what does a well-meaning parent do? Hide the peanut butter jar?

Switch to low-sugar, low-salt brands, get "whipped" or go "natural"?

Even if you choose the peanut butters with the least amount of fat per tablespoon (Peter Pan Whipped and Adams 100 percent Natural), we're still talking about 7 gm. of fat per tablespoon.

So you want to do two things:

#1. Since peanut butter looks a lot like butter when it comes to fat and calories, you'll want to spread it like you would butter—thin not thick! Try to keep it to a tablespoon or so. Making the jump to 2 tablespoon will push up the fat to at least 14 gm. and almost 200 calories—and that's not even counting the bread or crackers you're spreading it on.

#2. Add peanut butter to items that are low in fat and high in complex carbohydrates, such as bread, very low-fat crackers, or raw vegetables or fruits, so that the total snack or sandwich is lower in fat.

But don't take my word for it—see for yourself.

Example #1

- A peanut butter sandwich, with 1 tablespoon peanut butter and 1 tablespoon jam on 2 slices whole-wheat bread, contains 288 calories, 10.5 gm. fat, 31 percent of calories from fat, 5.6 gm. fiber...**compared with** 2 tablespoons peanut butter on 2 slices of whole-wheat bread, which contains 328 calories, 18.4 gm. fat, 47 percent of calories from fat, and 6.7 gm. fiber.

Example #2

- 1 tablespoon peanut butter spread on 3 celery stalks sprinkled with a total of 1 tablespoon of raisins contains 131 calories, 8 gm. fat, (51 percent of calories from fat), 2.5 gm. fiber. (The percentage of fat is high because celery is so low in calories)...**compared with** 2 tablespoons of peanut butter spread on an ounce of Ritz crackers, which contains 330 calories, 23.6 gm. fat, 61 percent of calories from fat, 2.8 gm. fiber.

TIP #93 / BUILD A BETTER HAM AND CHEESE SANDWICH.

One of the golden rules to low-fat eating is not to put two high-fat foods together in the same dish. For example, you can have cheese pizza, but put pepperoni on it and you get into trouble fatwise. Well, the same goes for sandwiches— you can have a ham sandwich or a cheese sandwich, but not a ham and cheese sandwich. Or can you?

If you start with 2 ounces of a very lean ham (such as Hillshire Farms Honey Ham) and then top it with an ounce and a half of reduced-fat cheese, you get a sandwich totaling 12 gm. fat, with 32 percent of calories from fat. It's close to dangerous, but it could be worse.

Why not just let the ham go solo on the bread and forget about the cheese? Some kids may only like the two together. And if you have a child like mine who decided milk would never again touch her lips, you may welcome the added calcium and high-quality protein that one small serving of reduced-fat cheese contributes.

Take a look at what this new and improved ham and cheese sandwich looks like nutritionally:

Ham & Cheese Sandwich

2 slices (28 gm. each) whole-wheat bread
2 oz. Hillshire Farms Honey Ham®
1 1/2 oz. reduced-fat cheese (5 gm. of fat per ounce)
1 tsp. mustard
Leaf lettuce
Tomato slices

Nutrition analysis: 334 calories, 12 gm. fat (32 percent of calories), 5 gm. fiber, 43 mg. cholesterol, 360 mg. calcium, 1250 mg. sodium.

Just-the-Ham Sandwich

2 oz. Hillshire Farms Honey Ham®
1 tsp. mustard
A leaf or two of lettuce
Tomato slices
2 slices (28 gm. each) whole-wheat bread

Nutrition analysis: 215 calories, 5 gm. fat (20 percent of calories from fat), 5 gm. fiber, 20 mg. cholesterol, 1031 mg. sodium.

TIP #94 / TEMPT 'EM
WITH TUNA.

I've made plenty a tuna salad sandwich, so trust me when I say half of a 6 1/2 oz. can mixed with a tablespoon of chopped green onions, celery, and a tablespoon of reduced-fat mayonnaise, makes one sandwich's worth of tuna salad. Dress it up with a couple slices of tomato and some lettuce and you have a great sandwich! And tuna canned in water is a good source of protein and iron without much fat.

Of course, you could always add your own personal touch by adding apple chunks or raisins or whatever. But here is the nutritional profile of your basic tuna salad sandwich:

Tuna Salad Sandwich

1/2 of a 6 1/2 oz. can of water-packed light tuna (drained)
1 Tbsp. reduced-fat mayonnaise (3 gm. fat per Tbsp.)
1 tsp. chopped green onions
1 Tbsp. chopped celery
2 slices whole-wheat bread (28 gm. each)
Tomato slices
Leaf lettuce

Nutrition analysis: 282 calories, 5 gm. fat (16 percent of calories from fat), 31 gm. protein, 5 gm. fiber, 22 mg. cholesterol, 683 mg. sodium, 69 mg. calcium, 5 mg. iron

TIP #95 / MAKE YOUR CHICKEN SALAD SANDWICH LOW IN FAT.

A chicken salad sandwich is only as lean and low-fat as the chicken used to make it and the dressing used to wet it. So, if you start with the leanest part of the chicken—roasted chicken breast *without* skin—and dress it with a reduced-fat mayonnaise or salad dressing (about 3 gm. of fat per tablespoon) you're in business.

You want to make sure you don't go through all the effort to select and prepare wonderfully low-fat chicken breasts and then spoon in gobs of high-fat mayonnaise. Remember *one* tablespoon of regular mayonnaise contains 10 gm. of fat!

Take a look at what a lean and low-fat chicken salad sandwich adds up to nutritionally. You can always make it fancier by adding apple cubes, raisins, or a sprinkling of walnuts.

Chicken (Breast) Salad Sandwich

1 chicken breast, skinless, roasted, and chopped
1 tsp. green onions, chopped
1 Tbsp. celery, chopped
1/2 Tbsp. reduced-fat mayonnaise
2 slices whole-wheat bread (28 gm. each)
Sliced tomato
Leaf lettuce

Nutrition analysis: 315 calories, 7.6 gm. fat (21 percent of calories from fat), 33.5 gm. protein, 5 gm. fiber, 81 mg. cholesterol, 453 mg. sodium, 72 mg. calcium, 3.3 mg. iron

TIP #96 / INCLUDE THE TURKEY BREAST SANDWICH.

When we think of a low-fat sandwich, most of us picture a turkey or chicken-breast sandwich on wheat. And it's true. This is about as low in fat as it gets, especially if only mustard is spread on the bread (no mayonnaise). Even an avocado and alfalfa sprout sandwich has way more fat.

Turkey-Breast Sandwich

2 oz. Louis Rich® turkey breast slices (as an example)
2 slices whole-wheat bread (28 gm. each)
1 tsp. mustard
Leaf lettuce
Sliced tomato

Nutrition analysis: 215 calories, 4.8 gm. fat (20 percent of calories from fat), 5 gm. fiber, 20 mg. cholesterol, 1091 mg. sodium

Chicken-Breast Sandwich

2 oz. Hillshire Farms® smoked chicken breast (as an example)
2 slices whole-wheat bread (28 gm. each)
1 tsp. mustard
Leaf lettuce
Sliced tomato

Nutrition analysis: 205 calories, 3.8 gm. fat (17 percent of calories from fat), 5 gm. fiber, 20 mg. cholesterol, 1011 mg. sodium

TIP #97 / MAKE GRILLED CHEESE SANDWICHES THE LIGHT WAY.

As we tend to make them, yes, grilled cheese sandwiches are too high in fat. We squeeze as much regular, high-fat cheese in between two slices of white bread as we possibly can. Then we grease the pan with a chunk of butter or margarine. The end result? A possible 448-calorie sandwich with up to 28 gm. of fat (57 percent of calories from fat) and 80 mg. of cholesterol (when 2 oz. of regular cheddar are added to the bread and 2 tsp. of butter melted in the pan).

But if you make it my way, with an ounce of reduced-fat cheese (1/3 cup firmly packed grated reduced-fat cheese) on two slices of whole-wheat bread and lightly spread 1 tsp. of diet margarine on the top and bottom of the sandwich, you cut the calories to 239, fat to 9 gm. (33 percent of calories from fat), and cholesterol to 16 mg. while increasing the fiber from 1 to 4 gm. The best part is that kids love it just the same.

When served with fruit, vegetables, and pretzels, for example, this sandwich can be part of a low-fat lunch with less than 30 percent of calories from fat for the entire meal.

TIP #98 / LIGHTEN UP YOUR B-O-L-O-G-N-A.

Bologna lovers now have a reason to rejoice! There are not one but two lower-fat bologna options in your supermarket deli case. There's a beef bologna, made by Oscar Mayer,® with half the fat, and a turkey bologna, made by Louis Rich,® with two-thirds less fat.

Unfortunately you can't just look for any old turkey bologna and call it low-fat. Some are actually just as high in fat as their beef or pork counterparts. So check the nutrition information label to be sure.

* Per 1 oz. serving	Calories	Fat gm.	Cholesterol (mg.)	Sodium (mg.)
Regular beef bologna	88	8	16	274
Oscar Mayer Light Beef Bologna®	60	4	15	310
Louis Rich Slow-Roasted Turkey Bologna®	45	3	15	280

TIP #99 / SWITCH FROM SANDWICHES.

Even if a parent purposely practices packing a variety of sandwich fillers, spreads, and breads in their child's lunch box, sandwiches, five days a week, every week of school, can get a little ho-hum. Or maybe you've got one of those children who doesn't like sandwiches even one day a week, even with peanut butter and jelly on top.

Exercise your creativity a little, Mom and Dad! Think about how you would feel eating sandwich after sandwich at every single lunch. Something new and different, like a taco salad, starts sounding pretty good.

You might want to go through the list of suggestions below with your children to select some items they think would make a great lunch—for a change. Remember, two slices of vegetarian pizza can be wrapped up and put in a lunch box faster than you can say "sandwich"

In consideration of the standard school set-up where lunch sacks and boxes sit on a shelf in the back of the room for three hours or more, most of these noontime suggestions taste great at room temperature or slightly chilled.

To keep these items chilled, pack a carton of frozen fruit juice next to the perishable food, such as meat, poultry, or dairy products. These foods should never be out at room temperature for longer than two hours. By lunch time, the item will still be cold and the fruit juice should be perfect for drinking!

TIP #100 / CHECK THESE SANDWICH-LESS SUGGESTIONS.

- Leftover pizza —A thick crust topped with vegetables is best nutritionally.

- Taco salad —Pack the reduced-fat dressing separately, so the lettuce and chips stay fresh.

- Pasta Salad—Dress the pasta salad with reduced-fat mayonnaise or a reduced-fat vinaigrette available in envelope packets or bottles. And add chunks of lean meat, chicken or tuna.

- Turkey breast or lean ham slices— Serve with reduced-fat cheese and fat-free or low-fat crackers.

- Turkey (and vegetable) roll-ups—Pack thinly sliced turkey breast cold cuts with an ounce or so of flavored spreadable cheese (like Philadelphia Light Cream Cheese® Kraft Spreadery Mild Cheddar®, or Vermont White Cheddar®) raw vegetable strips (zucchini, carrot, or celery, cut into 3-inch strips), and a plastic knife. Then at lunch, the kids can spread a little cheese on each slice of turkey, place a raw vegetable stick in the middle and roll it up! Add some bread by wrapping each roll up in a flour tortilla. "Light" flour tortillas made with all vegetable oil or 100 percent whole-wheat flour are now available in many supermarkets.

- Chicken fried rice —You can make this at home or use leftover chicken fried rice from a restaurant. Ask the restaurant to prepare it with as little oil as possible and with no MSG, please.

- Chef's salad—Pack the reduced-fat dressing of your child's choice separately.

- Oven "fried" chicken—Pack a boneless and skinless breast or thigh that has been oven-fried on a lightly oiled nonstick cookie sheet.
- Deviled eggs—Pack them with a roll, breadsticks, or low-fat crackers. Make lower-fat-and-cholesterol deviled eggs by throwing away half the yolks, adding some low- or nonfat cream cheese or cottage cheese in their place, and blending with your usual seasonings and reduced- or nonfat mayonnaise.
- Put it in a pita pocket—Leftover stir-fry mixtures, as well as shredded cold cuts, tuna, or chicken salad mixtures (made with reduced-fat mayonnaise) can fill a pita pocket for a nice change.

TIP #101 / WINTERTIME THERMOS® IDEAS.

Some schools have microwaves available in their cafeterias. In this case, you could freeze portions of the following in microwave-safe containers.

- Hearty, chunky soups or stews with roll, breadsticks, or low-fat crackers.
- Vegetarian or lean meat chili with cornbread or a roll.
- Leftover macaroni and cheese. You can make this low fat by adding just 1 Tbsp. of margarine and low-fat milk when making the standard size box of Kraft® Macaroni and Cheese. Or make it low-fat from scratch.
- Spaghetti can be made with a lower-fat bottled spaghetti sauce and a lower-fat ground beef (Healthy Choice® or any ground sirloin).

TIP #102 / DON'T FORGET THE RICE CAKE OPTION.

I've never been a big rice cake fan. I guess I still think about the olden days when there were only two types of rice cakes—plain and lightly salted. Back then many of my fellow nutrition majors were chomping on them by the bagful, but I thought they tasted like a mouthful of styrofoam.

So, I went on with my life, never looking back. Recently, though, after seeing a magazine advertisement for a new caramel corn-flavored rice cake (by Quaker®), I went looking for rice cakes at my grocery store. I couldn't believe how this section had grown! I turned the corner and there it was—wall to wall puffed cereal cakes made from all sorts of flavors and puffed grains. I thought I had died and gone to snack-food heaven. There were popcorn cakes sprinkled with sweet apple cinnamon, white cheddar, and spicy nacho flavoring, to name a few.

And rice cakes aren't just for puffed rice anymore. A new puffed grain has emerged as the popular favorite—popcorn. Which makes sense doesn't it? We've been adding butter, caramel, and cheese flavoring to popcorn for years now. But there are also rice cakes with added puffed millet, sesame seeds, rye, and wheat.

Two major brands have cornered the rice cake market—Quaker® and Chico San®. Each company has a couple of nutrition quirks. Quaker's white cheddar popped corn cakes have 110 mg. of sodium per cake while the Chico San version has 65 mg. And the third ingredient listed for Chico San's white cheddar popcorn cakes is partially hydrogenated oil, with each cake containing a gram of fat, while Quaker's version doesn't list added oils and contains no fat, according to the label.

Most non-flavored rice, sesame, wheat, or rye cakes contain 35 calories per cake. The flavored varieties contain 40 calories, except caramel popcorn cakes, which reach the rice cake calorie ceiling with 50 calories each. I'm not surprised that these caramel corn flavored rice or corn cakes taste exceptionally good, since 40 percent of their calories come from sugar (56 percent of the calories come from complex carbohydrates). But at 50 calories a cake, they still make a pretty good snack alternative to cookies and chocolate.

All the rice cakes are virtually fat-free, containing 0.5 gm. of fat or less per serving. Remember the federal labeling guideline that products can be listed as containing no fat per serving if they in fact contain 0.5 gm. of fat or less? That's why you might see zero fat listed on the nutritional label of a rice cake where one or more of the ingredients contain fat, such as Quaker's nacho and white cheddar rice cakes, which contain a minimal amount of cheddar cheese and buttermilk. And the third ingredient listed in Chico San's butter and plain popcorn cakes is partially hydrogenated oil, but according to the label, the cakes contain no fat.

If fat is a concern of yours, watch out for Hain's® butter, BBQ, and ranch-flavored mini rice cakes. Almost 40 percent of their calories comes from fat.

TIP #103 / LOOK FOR BETTER LUNCH-BOX BEVERAGES.

Maybe your child doesn't mind buying a carton of milk at school. But, as I recall from my own school days, the milk is never cold enough. Maybe the school isn't selling low-fat milk, or maybe your child doesn't like milk. These are all reasons why you might be looking for better beverages to stick in your child's lunch box.

Your child could also be at the age where he or she wants to pull out something "cool" to drink. As a parent and a dietitian, I don't care how "in" those single-serving plastic bottles are, I'm not putting colored sugar water in my child's lunch box. And soda is not my idea of a healthy beverage, either.

So what healthful options does that leave? Fruit juice, fruit juice, and fruit juice. No, actually you still have quite a few options. There is, of course, fruit juice and variations thereof. There is mineral water with or without flavors and without sweeteners. And there is vegetable juice—namely tomato and V-8®. Some of the possibilities are listed below:

Natural 10 Oz., unsweetened	Calories	Fiber gm.	Vitamin C* (mg.)
Grape juice	173	1.4	0
Apple juice	133	0.3	2.5
Orange juice	128	0.6	110
Pineapple juice	159	0.9	30
Grapefruit juice	108	0.8	83
Tomato juice, unsalted	48	2.2	52
Sparkling mineral water with natural flavors	0	0.0	0.0

* Some fruit juices are fortified with vitamin C and therefore would have more than is listed here. *NOTE:* Low-fat milk is always a healthful lunch option.

TIP #104 / CHOOSE CHIPS CAREFULLY.

For all the potato chip people, who just gotta crunch potato chips on a weekly basis, there are finally some lower-fat
options. You won't find them with the other chips. You'll
find these potato chip-taste-alikes in the cracker aisle. They
are Mr. Phipp's Tator Crisps® and Keebler Munch 'Ems®.

They may look like a cracker, but they crunch like a chip.
And better still, they have less than half the fat of regular
potato chips. Nutritionally, they even put Ruffles Light®
potato chips to shame. Take a look:

Per 1 oz. of chips	Calories	Fat (gm.)	Sodium (mg.)
Regular Pringles®	160	11	170
Regular Ruffles® chips	150	10	135
Keebler Tato Skins®	150	8	160
Ruffles Light Choice®	130	6	140
Pringles Light Potato Crisps	130	6	100
Mr. Phipps Tater Crisps	120	4	320
Keebler Munch'ems (original and Nacho flavors only)	120	4	280

TIP #105 / CHOOSE SOME OTHER THINGS TO CRUNCH.

There are other things that *go crunch in the night* besides potato chips. Many of them are just as high in fat as potato chips—even when they are puffy and orange and look "baked" instead of deep fried, like Chee-Tos Puffs®. Sun Chips® are self described as "multigrain snacks." But I think you should know that although corn is the first ingredient, these chips have more vegetable oil in them than any of the other "multigrain" ingredients (whole-wheat, rice, and oat flour), adding up to 16 gm. of fat for a 2-oz. bag of Sun Chips®. And almost half of the calories come from fat.

One exception is pretzels. Pretzels have always been low in fat. They are made mostly from enriched flour with a little vegetable shortening, salt, yeast, and baking soda. Now there are the regular low-in-fat and fat-free pretzels to choose from. Mr. Phipps even made their pretzels look more like chips (Mr. Phipps Pretzel Chips®). But try to find pretzels that have 1/3 less or 50 percent less salt, like Granny Goose 50% Less Salt Butter Pretzel Twists® (285 mg. per oz.)

There are a couple more crunchy options for your child's lunch box that may or may not be available in your area: Ultra Slim Fast Cheese Puffs®, Guiltless Gourmet Baked Tortilla Chips®, and Crisp *Baked* Bugles Corn Snack®. The Ultra Slim Fast Cheese Puffs have 2/3 less fat than Chee-Tos Puffs. And as a bonus, each ounce contains 3 gm. of fiber, which comes from corn meal, the first ingredient, and corn bran, the third ingredient.

And then there is my personal favorite—Crisp *Baked* Bugles®. Both my husband and I fondly remember the higher fat version from our youth. These traditional Bugles contained 8 gm. of fat per 0.83 oz. serving. But the new (and I think much improved) Crisp Baked Bugles only contain 2 gm. of fat per 42 bugles or 0.83 oz. serving.

Per oz. of snacks or chips	Calories	Fat (gm.)	Sodium (mg.)
Chee-Tos Puffs®	160	9	330
Chee-Tos Crunch®	150	9	310
Tortilla Chips Sun Chips Multigrain Snacks®	150	8	100
Traditional Chex Mix®	1208	320	--
Crisp Baked Bugles Corn® Snacks (0.83 oz. serving)	90	2	300
Ultra Slim Fast Cheese Curls®	110	3	360
Regular Pretzels	113	1	450
Fat-Free Mister Salty Pretzels® with 1/3 less salt	100	0	380

TIP #106 / AVOID MOST SNACK CAKES.

In 1994, the world will know the true nutritional identity of all the assorted snack cakes. For years now we've been blindly eating Twinkies®, mini donuts, and Ding Dongs®, not to mention fruit pies and HoHo's®.

My generation grew up with Twinkies, Ding Dongs and HoHos in our lunch boxes. Of all the snack cakes, HoHos had to be my all time favorite—not because of any redeeming value in taste, but because of the whole HoHo eating ritual: First you peel and eat the outside coating. Then you carefully unwrap the chocolate cake and creme part, tearing and eating it piece by piece.

How bad are these age old lunch-box traditions? And are any snack cakes better than the rest? Well it took some long-distance phone calls and quite a bit of persistence (since most of these products do not have nutrition information labels yet), but I finally got the skinny on these popular lunch treats.

The heaviest hitters are by far the fruit pies. One pie totals 400 to 520 calories and a whopping 19 to 29 gm. of fat. And, for some strange reason, Dolly Madison pies have about 10 gm. more fat per pie than the Hostess® pies. At face value, the HoHo fairs better than the Ding Dong (6 gm. of fat and 120 calories versus 10 gm. of fat and 170 calories), but the HoHo is also one of the smallest snack cake servings. If you have to choose between a Twinkie and a Zinger® , the Twinkie has 4 gm. of fat and 140 calories compared to a chocolate Zinger with 5 gm. of fat and 140 calories or a raspberry coconut Zinger with 6 gm. of fat and 160 calories. And watch out for those mini donuts. The calorie and fat information doesn't sound too bad until you realize that only two mini donuts constitute a serving. Most older children eat the whole six-donut pack, which changes the numbers quite a bit. One six-pack of mini donuts will run you 12 to 24 gm. of fat and 300 to 400 calories, depending on the brand and flavor.

As you look at the table below, the percentage of calories from fat may very well be lower than you expected. This is because of the high sugar content in snack cakes, which increases the total calories (bringing down the percentage of calories from fat). The Sno Ball® has all the snack cakes beat hands down when it comes to fat (2 gm. per Sno Ball), but if I remember correctly from my youth, these are not unlike a mouthful of marshmallow.

But if you had to select a couple of the least-hazardous snack cakes it would probably have to be the light Twinkie and the orange Hostess cupcake and the Sno Ball.

Snack	Calories	Fat) (gm.)	Percent of calories from fat
Hostess:			
Orange Cupcake, 1	150	4	24%
Chocolate Cupcake, 1	180	6	30%
Ding Dong, 1	170	10	53%
Ho Ho, 1	120	6	45%
Light Twinkies, 1	130	2	14%
Twinkies, 1	160	6	34%
Sno Ball, 1	140	2	13%
Donut Gems,			
—Crunch, 6	300	12	36%
—Powdered Sugar, 6	330	18	49%
ChocoDile, 1	250	11	40%
Pies-Apple, 4.5 oz.	390	19	44%
—Chocolate, 4.5 oz.	490	19	35%
—Lemon, 4.5 oz.	400	20	45%
—Blueberry, 4.5 oz.	410	17	37%
Dolly Madison:			
Zingers			
—Chocolate, 1	140	5	32%
—Raspberry Coconut, 1	160	6	34%
Mini Donuts			
—Chocolate, 6	390	24	55%
—Powdered Sugar	360	18	45%
Pies			
—Apple, 1	520	29	50%
—Lemon, 1	510	26	46%

TIP #107 / SEARCH FOR THE BETTER COOKIES.

Not all cookies are created equal. There are quite a few that would fit into a lunch box nutrition plan just fine. But let me warn you up front, these probably aren't the same cookies your kids are coaxing into the shopping cart. One ounce (1/2 cup or 22 teddy bears) of Teddy Grahams®, which come in four flavors including chocolate, make a nice treat with 120 calories and 4 gm. of fat, 30 percent of calories from fat.

HoneyMaid® Cinnamon Graham Crackers will also add up to 120 calories, but just 2 gm. of fat and 15 percent of calories from fat. By the way, other brands of graham crackers are not so light on fat. Keebler® brand and Sunshine® cinnamon graham crackers have double the amount of fat of HoneyMaid. To be sure, check the label.

Some of the other "not-so-bad" cookies are Nabisco's Devil's Food Cakes® with 2 cookies adding up to 140 calories, 2 gm. of fat, and 13 percent of calories from fat, and Nabisco Fig Newtons®, with 2 bars having 120 calories, 2 gm. fat, 15 percent of calories from fat. It takes 13 Sunshine Animal Crackers® (3 gm. fat, 22 percent of calories from fat) and 7 Nabisco Nilla Wafers® (4 gm. fat, 30 percent of calories from fat) to add up to 120 calories.

A few companies making the more "dietetic" cookies offer a few more cookie options. Estee® makes an oatmeal raisin cookie with 120 calories, 4 gm. fat (30 percent of calories from fat) per 4 cookies. And the Stella D'Oro Biscuit Co.® makes some lower-fat cookies, such as:

Cookie	Serving size	Calories	Fat gm.	Percent of calories from fat
Almond Toast	2 cookies	120	2	15%
Anginetti	3 cookies	90	3	30%
Anisette Sponge	2 cookies	100	2	18%
Anisette Toast,	2 cookies	100	2	18%
Anisette Toast	1 piece	110	1	8%
Dutch Apple Bars,	1 cookie	110	3	24.5%
Egg Biscuits (sugar)	1 biscuit	80	1	11%
Egg Biscuits	2 biscuits	90	2	20%
Egg Jumbo	2 cookies	100	2	18%
Pfeffernusse	3 cookies	120	3	22.5%
Prune Pastry	1 cookie	90	3	30%

Better buy a box of the new bite-sized Snack Well® chocolate-chip cookies fast. They disappear from store shelves quickly. These reduced-fat chocolate chip cookies are one of several new cookies and crackers under the Snack Well name. I've tried almost all of the products, all of which are either reduced-fat or "fat-free," but it was the chocolate chip cookies that won my family's vote.

When you read the list of ingredients, added fat is a lowly fourth on the list. Chocolate chips are the second ingredient, however. But it's hard to argue with that—being that they are chocolate chip cookies!

A handful of six bite-sized chocolate chip cookies, which if you piece them all together look like the size of a regular-sized chocolate chip cookie, totals 60 calories and only 1 gm. of fat (15 percent of calories from fat). I will warn you, though. These seemingly innocent bite-sized wonders can be addictive. The first handful of six mini cookies can quickly lead to six more—and before you know it, that cute little green box is empty.

I suggest counting out a dozen bite-sized cookies onto your napkin or into the zip-lock bag that you or your family member is taking to school or work. This way you are guaranteed a snack worth 120 calories and only 2 gm. of fat.

TIP #108 / TAME THE COOKIE MONSTERS.

Cookies are like potato chips: You can never eat just one. The funny thing is, many of the cookies in grocery stores use one cookie as the serving size on their nutrition label. So when you gasp at the calories and grams of fat per serving, you'll need to multiply that by as many cookies as you or your child usually eat.

I recently went looking at labels in the cookie aisle. But for a switch, I tried to find the cookies with the highest amount of fat. The hardest part was not finding enough types to talk about, but making the appropriate serving calculations so I would be comparing a 1-oz. serving for each of them. I soon discovered that, for a cookie to qualify as a "cookie monster," it had to contain 5 or more grams of fat per ounce—which in many cases was only one cookie!

You see, some cookies list a half ounce as a serving. Some give the nutrition information per 0.75- or 1-ounce serving, and some even neglect to mention the weight of the serving. So you have to divide the total package weight by the number of servings they list per package. These serving sizes end up being anywhere in between (like 0.65 ounce or 0.83 ounce). So then you have to divide 1 ounce by the particular serving-size weight to get the fraction now needed to multiply the calories and grams of fat by. Needless to say, this exercise isn't as fun as sampling all the cookies would be. But alas, you needn't resort to such complicated calculations. I have listed the 15 worst cookies and their 1-ounce nutrition information for you. The following cookies have at least 10 gm. of fat per approximate 1 ounce serving: Avoid these cookies.

Snack	Calories	Fat (gm.)	Percent of calories from fat
Keebler®:			
Fudge covered Creme Wafers	200	10	45%
Heath English Toffee Cookies	180	10	50%
Mother's®:			
Flaky Flix	160	10	56%
Chocolate Chip Angel	160	10	56%
Chips Ahoy® Chunky Chocolate Chip, Heath Toffee Chunk, & White Fudge Chunk	180	10	50%
Chocolate Chunk Pecan	200	12	54%
Striped Chips Ahoy	180	10	50%
Nabisco®:			
Pecan Supremes	160	10	56%
Chocolate Middles	160	10	56%
Orleans	153	10	59%
Pecan Shortbread	152	11	64%
Hazel Nut	145	10	65%
Brownie Choc. Nut	157	10	56%

There are plenty of not-so-great options—like the Fudge Covered Oreos® and Mystic Mints®—that didn't make this list because they had 8 gm. of fat per 1-ounce serving.

TIP #109 / PICK FROM THE BEST COOKIES.

The chances are pretty good that you or someone in your family moonlights as the kitchen cookie monster. And you probably know a kid or two who is crazy about cookies as a lunch box snack.This could mean the cookie monster in your house (big or small) is actually consuming relatively large amounts of fat without even realizing it.

So how do you soothe the savage cookie monster(s) in your house without adding too much fat? Offer them the lower-fat packaged cookies. The list of the best cookies on the market represent a blend of old and new choices.

One of the most important things to look for is whether flour (not vegetable shortening and not sugar) is listed as the first ingredient . Then you want to look at the grams of fat per serving and consider the serving size listed on the package. For a 1-ounce serving, you're doing pretty well if you can find a cookie with 4 gm. of fat or less.

Here are the cookies in my supermarket that qualify. There are plenty to choose from, so happy cookie crunching!

Per I oz. serving	Calories	Fat (gm.)	Percent of calories from fat
Nabisco®:			
Snackwell's			
Chocolate Chip	120	2	15%
Creme Sandwich	100	2	18%
Oatmeal Raisin	120	2	15%
Social Tea Biscuits	140	4	26%
Ginger Snaps	120	2	15%
Newtons, Fig	120	2	15%

Per 1 oz. serving	Calories	Fat (gm.)	Percent of calories from fat
Raspberry	93	2.7	26%
Strawberry	93	2.7	26%
Fat-Free Fig Newtons	93	0	0
Fat-Free Apple Newtons	93	0	0
Nilla Wafers	120	4	30%
Chocolate Chip Snaps	140	4	26%
Chocolate Snaps	120	4	30%
Famous Chocolate Wafers	120	4	30%
Grahams	120	2	15%
Barnum's Animal Crackers	120	4	30%
Bugs Bunny Graham Cookies	120	4	30%
Teddy Grahams	120	4	30%

Mother's®:

Whole-wheat Fig Bars	90	2	20%
Fig Bars	100	2	18%

Sunshine®:

Lemon Cookies	120	4	30%
Golden Fruit Raisin Biscuits	105	1.5	13%
Apple Biscuits	105	3	26%
Ginger Snaps	120	4	30%
Animal Crackers	140	4	26%
Fig Bars	100	2	18%
School House Cookies	120	4	30%
Grahamy Bears	120	4	30%

TIP #110 / MAKE YOUR OWN GRANOLA BARS.

Most of us know how easy it is to make Rice Krispies® treats (you can even melt the marshmallows in the microwave). Well, making your own granola bars is almost as simple as that.

Start with some low-fat granola, add some dried cranberries or a chocolate chip or two. Maybe melt in a token teaspoon of peanut butter—and call it a granola bar! That's generally what food companies are doing when they make their chewy granola bars, except they add more sugar and fat than is nutritionally desirable. Some even go so far as to dip their already sugared and oil-slicked granola bars in chocolate! With calories around 200 and fat up to 12 gm. per bar, these start looking more like candy bars.

But even your basic crispy, no-coating granola bars, like the type Nature Valley® brand makes, contain 6 gm. of fat each. The calories appear to be modest, at 120 per bar, but this is only for a 0.83-ounce serving. The Quaker Chewy Granola Bars® contain 120 to 130 calories each, with 4 or 5 gm. of fat for a 1-ounce bar.

One of the problems with commercially made granola bars is their unrealistic serving sizes. Using the recipe below, your homemade granola bars are much more substantial and better tasting (according to my taste testers). You can still vary your flavors by adding whatever dried fruit suits your fancy, like dried pitted cherries or cranberries, or adding peanut butter in place of the margarine. If you really feel like splurging—try adding 1/3 cup of chocolate chips to the granola. If you do add chocolate chips, let the marshmallow mixture cool slightly before mixing with the cereals.

Homemade Granola Bars

4 cups miniature marshmallows
1 1/2 Tbsp. margarine or butter
4 cups Kellogg's® low-fat granola
2 cups Kellogg's Rice Krispies® cereal
•*Optional ideas:*
1/4 cup peanut butter in place of the margarine
1/3 cup chocolate chips mixed in with granola
1/3 cup additional chopped dried fruit mixed in with granola

For Microwave: Put marshmallows in a glass mixing bowl. Microwave on high for 45 seconds. Stir and add butter or margarine. Microwave 45 seconds longer and stir. If margarine or marshmallows are not melted completely, microwave 30 to 45 seconds more. Stir in granola and Rice Krispies. If you are adding chocolate chips, wait till marshmallow mixture has cooled slightly before adding cereals and chips. Spray 13 x 9 x 2-inch pan with nonstick spray. Using a large piece of wax paper, press granola mixture evenly into pan. Refrigerate. When ready to serve or separate into plastic bags, cut into 14 bars, about 4 1/2" long.

*NOTE: For peanut butter granola bars, add peanut butter to marshmallows instead of the margarine.

Nutritional analysis per serving (1 bar):

Without options: 175 calories, 2 gm. fiber, 132 mg. sodium, 6 percent of calories from protein, 80 percent from carbohydrates, 14 percent from fat (2.9 gm. fat)

Peanut butter granola bars: 191 calories, 2 gm. fiber, 99 mg. sodium, 8 percent of calories from protein, 84 percent from carbohydrate, 18 percent from fat (4 gm.)

With chocolate chips: 195 calories, 2 gm. fiber, 132 mg. sodium, 6 percent of calories from protein, 75 percent from carbohydrates, 19 percent from fat. (4 gm. fat)

TIP #111 / TRY THESE SURE-TO-PLEASE HOME-MADE TREATS.

Rice Krispies® Bars

    2 Tbsp. margarine or butter
    10 oz. regular marshmallows (4 cups miniature)
    6 to 7 cups Rice Krispies cereal

Microwave margarine and marshmallows on full power in a glass mixing bowl for about 1 minute. Stir and microwave for 1 more minute. Stir until smooth. Add cereal, stir until well coated. Coat a sheet of wax paper and 13 x 9 x 2-inch pan with nonstick spray. Press into pan with wax paper. When cool, cut into squares. Store in refrigerator if you like them crisp and crunchy. Makes 24 treats.

Nutrition analysis: 78 calories, 5 percent of calories from protein, 84 percent from carbohydrate, 11 percent from fat (1.0 gm. fat)

Neapolitan Angel Food Cake

    1 box angel food cake mix
        (Check instructions on box for ingredients needed for cake mix)
    4 tsp. cocoa
    2 Tbsp. strawberry or raspberry preserves
        (no- or reduced-sugar varieties)

Preheat oven as directed on cake box. Follow instructions on box for mixing batter. When soft peaks form and batter is ready to pour into ungreased angel food cake pan, just gently pour 1/3 of batter into bottom of pan and smooth top with spatula. Divide remaining batter into two bowls. In one bowl, sprinkle cocoa over the top and gently blend by hand or use the lowest mixer speed. Carefully pour cocoa-flavored mixture over mixture in cake pan and smooth top with spatula. To remaining batter, add preserves and gently blend by hand. Carefully pour it over chocolate layer in pan and smooth top with spatula. Bake according to instructions on mix box (do not undercook). Makes 10 dessert or snack servings.

Nutrition analysis per serving: 163 calories, 0 cholesterol, 209 mg. sodium, 9 percent of calories from protein, 91 percent from carbohydrate, 0 from fat.

TIP #112 / PACK A PUDDING.

I'm sure there is a whole contingent of kids out there who love to find a little pudding packed in their lunch box from time to time. Although the package of Hunt's® regular-calorie chocolate pudding announces it's "made with skim milk," they decline to shout from the rooftops that it is also made with partially hydrogenated vegetable oil. I guess that's where the 7 gm. of fat (per 4-ounce serving) comes from! But fortunately Hunt's makes a "light" version with 2 gm. of fat and 100 calories (18 percent of calories from fat) per 4 ounces. The first three items in its ingredient list are skim milk, water, and sugar.

School Lunches Often Earn Low Grades.

This is the biggest hypocrisy going. In the classroom, we teach our children the health benefits of eating a low-fat, low-sodium, low-sugar diet and we encourage them to do so at home—then we give them high-fat hot dogs, fried chicken nuggets, and other high-fat felons in the school cafeteria.

Here's the situation. The USDA, which oversees the school lunch program, sets no limits for such things as fat or sodium in school meals. This is not so surprising considering the National School Lunch Program's origin. The program was created in 1946 for the sole purpose of preventing malnutrition in Army volunteers and to dispose of farm food surpluses. Just take a gander at what some of those are: peanut butter, whole-milk cheese, butter, shortening, ground pork, frozen french fries, and so on.

But this is the 1990s. One-fourth of American children have undesirably high blood cholesterol levels. And, according to one research study (the Bogalusa Heart Study), three in four children's diets exceed American Heart Association guidelines for saturated fat.

When it comes to the American Heart Association and the American Cancer Society diet guidelines, school lunches have a lot of room to improve. The typical school lunch totals more than 40 percent of calories from fat and up to 1800 mg. of sodium, according to the Citizens' Commission on School Nutrition, which evaluated school lunches across the country. Consequently, in a just-released report summarizing their findings and recommendations, the Citizens' Commission is calling for school meals with much less fat and sodium and more fiber.

More specifically, the Commission's report recommends that schools:

- Limit lunches first to an average of 35 percent of calories from fat and ultimately to 30 percent. No more than one-third of the fat should be saturated fat.

- Serve fresh fruits and vegetables, whole grains, and legumes more frequently to increase fiber and vitamin intake. There is growing evidence that diets rich in fiber-containing foods can help prevent colon cancer. And foods rich in water-soluble fiber may help reduce the risk of heart disease by lowering blood cholesterol levels.

- Lower sodium first to an average of 1,000 mg. per lunch and then to 800 mg. The American diet contains too much sodium which can increase the risk of hypertension and therefore heart disease and stroke in millions of susceptible people. Recent evidence suggests that 50 percent of normal weight six-year-olds (and 90 percent of overweight six-year-olds), who have blood pressures at the upper end of normal, will develop hypertension later as adults.

- Do not permit sale of relatively non-nutritious foods, such as soft drinks, candy, and chips on campus during school hours.

- Reduce the levels of cholesterol, sugar, and certain food additives in school lunches. If schools meet the fat and saturated fat guidelines, school lunches will generally also be low in cholesterol. To help reduce cholesterol, schools can serve eggs less frequently, discard half the cholesterol-rich yolks when possible, or use low- or no-fat egg substitute products consisting mainly of pasteurized egg whites.

When diets contain 20 percent or more of calories from sugar, it becomes increasingly difficult for children to meet all their nutrition needs from the other diet components.

Breakfast programs can use cereals that contain no more than 20 percent of calories from sugar. And canned fruit packed in 100 percent fruit juice can be purchased and served instead of fruits canned in syrup.

If you don't think kids would eat some of these lower-fat, lower-cholesterol-and-sodium lunch items, look again.

- Make pizzas with lower-fat cheese and top it with mixed veggies.
- Make grilled cheese sandwiches with lower-fat cheese, whole-wheat bread and grilled on a nonstick or lightly greased surface.
- Top green or pasta salads with reduced-calorie and reduced-sodium salad dressings.
- Serve grilled chicken sandwich (not fried) on a whole-grain bun without mayonnaise-based sauces.
- Offer tacos in soft, not fried, tortillas. Add canned kidney or pinto beans to hamburger mixture and sprinkle with lower fat cheese.
- Buy less-fat turkey hot dogs and serve with mustard and catsup, not mayonnaise.
- Make lasagna with lower-fat cheese, ricotta cheese, and vegetables instead of meat.
- Use frozen yogurt or ice milk instead of ice cream.
- Oven bake chicken instead of deep frying.
- Serve 1%, 2%, or skim milk and use them in recipes.

Some Success Stories

Any major change requires courage, knowledge and motivation—and changing the nutritional wheels of established, institutional school food services is certainly no exception.

You might run across the following reasons why your child's school food service and others say they won't even attempt to lower the fat and increase the fiber in school meals:

- *"The kids won't like it or eat it if we do."* One health program in a school cafeteria *(American School Food Service Association,* Fall '89,Vol. 13 [2], pp. 137-145) reduced sugar and salt by 50 percent and fat by 30 percent and found no difference in the amount of plate waste (food left on the plate) between the more healthful and the traditional foods. These encouraging results have been repeated in many other similar studies.

- *"The reality is we have to serve the popular foods kids like and most of these are high in fat."* The list of lower-fat options above gives just some of the ways the most popular foods can be adapted to lower fat and still be appealing.

- *"Lower fat foods and ingredients cost more."* For a nutrition education program at the University of Nebraska (Food Management, May 1987 Vol. 22 [5] p. 48), the school food service prepared breakfasts and lunches that were low in fat, cholesterol, calories, and sodium. The costs were only slightly higher than the traditional meals served—but no higher than other theme-type meals served.

- *Parents are concerned about possible nutrition deficiencies with lower-fat foods.* Fat-modified menus were analyzed for 10 key nutrients (protein, vitamins A, C, B1, and B2, calcium, iron, and phosphorus). No significant differences were found.

- *Some schools receive national food commodities and many of these are by definition full of fat.* According to one source, only 20 percent of the food used in school meals comes from USDA commodities. Schools, on average, purchase the remaining 80 percent of foods themselves. And some of the USDA commodities are actually lower-fat alternatives like part-skim mozzarella cheese, nonfat dry milk powder, water-packed tuna, and lower-fat ground turkey meat.

And to those who say it still can't be done? For 5 months, a lower-fat and lower-sodium school lunch program was conducted in 34 elementary schools in Minnesota (*Journal of the American Dietetic Association,* 1992; 92:1087-1091).

Recipes were modified, food preparation techniques were altered, and alternative vendor products were purchased. The result. Mutiny? Mass hysteria? Not at all. Student participation was maintained throughout the five-month program. And plate waste (the amount of food left on plates) stayed about the same.

When the new menu was compared with the traditional higher-fat fare, there had been a significant decrease in total grams of fat (from a mean daily amount of 32 gm. to 20 gm.) and percentage of calories from fat decreased significantly (from 40% to 28% calories from fat).

What were some of the keys to their success? Favorite foods like pizza, tacos, chicken nuggets, french fries, and treats like brownies were kept on the menu—they were just modified to reduce the fat. And the reduction in fat and sodium was moderate (lowered to 30 percent of calories from fat and 1,000 mg. of sodium), not extreme.

TIP #113 / MAKE SCHOOL LUNCHES WORK FOR YOU.

Rather than getting out the turkey slices, washing lettuce, slicing tomato and spreading mustard and mayonnaise on a sandwich, wouldn't it be easier to take five or six quarters out of your wallet and give it to your child for a school lunch?

But you might be worried that the school cafeteria will butter-up your child with high-fat foods. According to recent national reports on school lunches, unfortunately your fears are warranted. But wait, don't put that dollar fifty back in your wallet just yet. Many school cafeterias are already making bold product or recipe changes to help trim the fat. And there are several things you can do at home and your child can do in the cafeteria to keep excess food fat in check!

TIP #114 / MANIPULATE THE MONTHLY MENU SCHEDULE.

- Use the monthly school lunch menu to help plan which days to "bag it." Make your child a lunch on the days when a lower-fat entree is not being offered (see special section below for suggestions).

- Encourage the same type of lower-fat food choices at home for consistency.

When you're looking at that monthly lunch menu, you will undoubtedly come across the fearsome five:

—hot dogs

—hamburgers or cheeseburgers

—fried chicken nuggets

—pizza

—tacos

Of these, hot dogs and hamburgers wouldn't be so bad if the lower-fat turkey franks and very lean ground beef are used and if mustard or catsup is dressing the dog or burger. Pizza can pass if topped with vegetables instead of fatty meat (especially if part-skim cheese is used). Tacos may even squeak by if the cafeteria or your child skips the sour cream (or uses low-fat plain yogurt or nonfat or light sour cream), passes on the guacamole, and goes light on the cheese (especially if a meat filling is featured, and the leaner the better).

Instead of lunch accompaniments like potato chips, macaroni salad, chocolate chip cookies, or ice-cream bars, look for lower-fat items like baked potatoes, fresh fruit, three-bean salad, and ice-milk cups.

TIP #115 / AVOID THE WORST CAFETERIA LUNCHES.

The higher-fat lunch entrees are usually:

- Fried chicken
- Macaroni and cheese
- Fish sticks
- Pork ribs
- Sausages
- Chicken patties or nuggets
- Grilled cheese
- Nachos
- Corn dogs
- Sausage or pepperoni pizza

TIP #116 / BUY INTO THE BEST SCHOOL LUNCHES.

The lower-fat entrees are usually:

- BBQ or baked chicken
- Chili with beans
- Chicken enchiladas
- Vegetable pizza
- Baked fish
- Turkey sandwich or slices
- Beef and bean burritos
- Sloppy Joes (lean ground beef)

TIP #117 / LET YOUR VOICE BE HEARD — A SAMPLE LETTER

What can you do to make a difference at your child's school?

- Get involved. Talk to your school food service director or school administrator.

- If vending machines are provided at school, encourage the school to offer some nutritious options like 100 percent fruit juice, fresh fruit, low-fat milk, and yogurt.

- Write a letter. Here is a sample you can adapt to get your point across.

Dear _____ ,

    (School Principal) and/or (Food Service Director)

My son/daughter is a_____grader currently attending _____(name of school). As a parent, I am concerned about the future health of my child and all young people

I want to express my strong support for a lower-fat school cafeteria menu. I fully understand many of the challenges and limitations of a school food service (mass production, student acceptance, government commodities), but I believe many steps can be taken to reduce the fat :

- *Purchase lower-fat products when available. Buy part-skim cheeses, lower-fat turkey hot dogs, very lean ground beef, lower-fat frozen french fries, etc.*

- *Offer low-fat (and nonfat) dairy items, condiments, and dressings*

- *Incorporate low-fat cooking techniques when possible*

- *Warm or steam tortillas instead of frying*

- *Do not add butter or margarine to cooked vegetables, breads, and grains*

- *Make baked products with at least half the fat taken out. For example, replace the fat in muffins with apple-sauce or yogurt.*

Making these changes can make quite a difference in the amount of fat our children are taking in on a daily basis.

One crucial component to a low-fat diet, as you know, is eating enough fruits and vegetables.

My family and I want you to know we appreciate any efforts you have been making to serve more fresh or frozen fruits (instead of canned), raw vegetables, and to incorporate vegetables into main dishes (lasagna, spaghetti, macaroni and cheese, etc.) when possible.

If the school is already doing any of the above items, please let parents know on the monthly menu so we can be sure to send our children to school with lunch money on those days. Furthermore, if I can be of any help in this matter, please feel free to contact me.

Lowering fat in the American diet was recently considered the No.1 diet priority by the U.S. Surgeon General and the National Academy of Sciences. Certainly it would be ideal if our schools, which are teaching children about such important matters, would reinforce these messages by serving more fruits, vegetables, and lower-fat foods. Best of health!

Sincerely,

TIP #118 / GET YOUR CHILD INVOLVED.

Even when items like burritos, pizza, cheeseburgers, and hot dogs are being served at school, there are a few things your child can do in the cafeteria to lower the fat a little further:

- Encourage your child to eat all of their lunch so the lower-fat items like fruit and vegetables are included.

- Don't add more fat to an already fatty entree. For example, don't add mayo or cheese to hot dogs or hamburgers, and skip the sour cream and guacamole at the taco or burrito bar. Take the sausage or pepperoni off the pizza.

- Make lowering fat a priority at home by teaching your child good habits. Does your child skin his chicken at home and in restaurants? Is he used to "no mayo" on his burger and sandwiches? Does she usually prefer pizza without meat or her burrito or taco without sour cream and guacamole? If so, your chances are better than most parents' that your child will perform these same lower-fat maneuvers in the school cafeteria.

Even a few of the higher-fat lunch entrees can be cleaned up a bit nutritionally:

Item	What your child can do to lower the fat
Fried chicken patty	Don't add mayonnaise or cheese to it.
Fried chicken nuggets	Don't dip them in any creamy dipping sauces. Choose barbecue type sauces or catsup.
Fish sticks	Don't dip them in tartar sauce or mayonnaise. Use catsup instead.
Pork ribs	Trim away and toss any visible fat.
Fried chicken	Ask for breast meat and take the skin off.
Sausage/pepperoni pizza	Pick off meat topping and use a napkin to dab off any grease collecting on top.

TIP #120 / TRAIN YOUR "FIVE-A-DAY" CAFETERIA KIDS.

Such a big part of eating a healthful low-fat and high-fiber diet is eating enough fruits and vegetables. There is now a program through the National Cancer Institute that is devoted simply to educating Americans on the importance of eating at least 5 servings of fruits and vegetables every day and to helping Americans accomplish this goal. This fruit and vegetable awareness "wave" is called **"Five a Day."**

Certainly there is much that we as parents can do in our own homes to make sure our children grow up eating their "Five a Day." But what can we do to reinforce this desirable habit in the school cafeteria? Encourage your kids to do the following:

- Bring packets of their favorite reduced-fat salad dressing on days when the cafeteria is serving salad or raw vegetables.

- If your child likes the way they served the fruits and vegetables that day, encourage him or her to to tell the food service workers they liked it and ask them to please serve it again.

- Encourage your child to mix the cooked vegetable with the main dish when possible—like mixing the broccoli in with the macaroni and cheese.

- Encourage your child to pick up plenty of fresh tomatoes, cucumber, carrot slices, etc., when the cafeteria is serving a salad or taco or burrito bar.

Fast Food
Doesn't Have
To Be
"Fat Food"

Which fast-food chain is the best nutritional bet? That's not an easy question to answer. In a pinch you usually go to the one that's closest. On a budget you may go to the one with the best deal. But all these things being equal, if I could choose which fast food to drive my kids to would I be looking for those golden arches, that Jack in the Box, a yellow and brown bell, or a red Wendy's sign?

I suppose I would choose the chain that had low-fat items that my children like to eat. While I can't guess which chains your family enjoys most, I call tell you which have the most low-fat fast-food items to choose from and which have items lowest in fat. The highly prestigious award for

"The Chain With the MOST Low-Fat Fast-Food Items"

Goes to...

WENDY'S and LONG JOHN SILVER'S.

Both offer approximately seven lower-fat entree items. After that, it's a draw among Arby's, Carl's Jr., Hardee's, and McDonald's, with each offering about five lower fat items.

Tied for second-to-last place are Burger King, Taco Bell, and Jack in the Box, each with only about two lower fat entree items.

Last place goes to Kentucky Fried Chicken with only one entree item eligible—rotisserie chicken breast with the skin and wing removed. But I have to say one thing about KFC. They have lots of low-fat side dishes to choose from.

The chains with the lowest-fat fast-food sandwich-type entrees are Arby's, Carl's Jr., and Hardee's.

Arby's:

- Light Roast Turkey Deluxe, 260 calories, 6 gm. fat, 21 percent of calories from fat.

Carl's Jr.:

- Charbroiler BBQ Chicken Sandwich, 6 gm. fat, 17 percent of calories from fat, 310 calories
- Teriyaki Chicken Sandwich, 6 gm., 16 percent of calories from fat, 330 calories

Hardee's:

- Roast Beef Sub, 5 gm. fat, 12 percent of calories from fat, 370 calories
- Combo Sub, 6 gm. fat, 14 percent of calories from fat, 380 calories

Here are some tips for helping you choose at your kids' favorite fast-food spots.

TIP #121 / ARBY'S: KNOW THE ATTRIBUTES.

This chain has one great big thing going for it right from the start—"roasting." When you roast beef, turkey, or chicken—instead of frying—you are more likely to make an entree that is lower in fat. Most of the items listed below are "roasted" and around or below 30 percent of calories from fat, so you and your child have a choice between roasted beef, chicken, or turkey.

	Calories	Fat (gm.)	% of Calories from fat	Saturated fat (gm.)	Cholesterol (mg.)	Sodium (mg.)
Grilled Chicken Sandwich	386	13	30.5%	3.6	43	1002
Roasted Chicken Salad	204	7	32%	3	43	508
Light Roast Beef Deluxe	260	10	31%	3.5	42	826
Light Roast Turkey Deluxe	294	6	21%	1.6	33	1262
Light Roast Chicken Deluxe	276	7	23%	1.7	33	777
Light Italian Dressing, 2 oz.	23	1	39%	0.1	0	1110
Chicken Noodle Soup, 8 oz.	99	1.8	16%	.5	25	929

TIP #122 / BURGER KING: MAKE THE BEST CHOICES.

I'm afraid the pickins are pretty slim when it comes to eating at the Burger King's Castle. Burger King didn't have information in their brochure on the calories and grams of fat in their ocean catch fish filet or chicken sandwich when it's made without mayonnaise or tartar sauce. I imagine if you did order either of these two sandwiches without the sauce (or took it off yourself), each would be in the ballpark of "thirtysomething" percent of calories from fat.

As for breakfast options, Burger King unfortunately puts most of their high-fat breakfast treats (bacon, egg, sausage, etc.) on a croissant. Croissants, by themselves, are high in fat. Stuff them with high-fat fillers and they're even higher. Even the blueberry mini muffins contain 43 percent of calories from fat (14 gm. of fat and 292 calories).

The nutrition information on the selections with about 30 percent or less of calories from fat is listed here.

	Calories	Fat (gm.)	% of Calories from fat	Saturated fat (gm.)	Cholesterol (mg.)	Sodium (mg.)
BK Broiler Chicken Sandwich	280	10	32%	2	50	770
Chunky Chicken Sandwich	142	4	25%	1	49	443
Lite Italian Dressing, 2 oz.	30	1	30%	0	0	710

TIP #123 / CARL'S JR.: WHAT TO FEED YOUR JUNIOR.

Carl's Jr. is the king of the low-fat chicken sandwiches. You and your child have three to choose from. There are other selections, too, that fall below or around the 30 percent of calories from fat mark. They are listed below.

	Calories	Fat (gm.)	% of Calories from fat	Saturated fat (gm.)	Cholesterol (mg.)	Sodium (mg.)
Charbroiler BBQ Chicken Sandwich	310	6	17%	2	30	680
Teriyaki Chicken Sandwich	330	6	16%	2	55	830
Santa Fe Chicken Sandwich	540	13	22%	3	40	1180
Lite Potato	290	1	3%	0	0	60
Chicken Salad to go	200	8	36%	4	70	300
Other Items						
English Muffin with margarine	190	5	24%	1	0	280
Blueberry muffin	340	9	24%	1	45	300
Bran muffin	310	7	20%	1	60	370
Reduced-calorie French Dressing	40	2	45%	0	0	290

TIP #124 / JACK IN THE BOX: JOIN HIM WITH GOOD INFO.

These choices work best.

	Calories	Fat (gm.)	% of Calories from fat	Saturated fat (gm.)	Cholesterol (mg.)	Sodium (mg.)
Chicken Fajita Pita	292	8	25%	3	34	703
Sesame Breadsticks	70	2	26%	0	0	110
* Chicken & Mushroom Sandwich	438	18	37%	5	61	1340
*Grilled Chicken Fillet	431	19	40%	4.7	65	1070
*Fish Supreme	510	27	48%	6	55	1040
*Hamburger	267	11	37%	4	26	556

* You could lower the grams of fat and percent of calories from fat in the Chicken & Mushroom Sandwich by ordering it without the "Swiss-style cheese" and in the Grilled Chicken Fillet by ordering it without the "mayo-onion sauce" and "Swiss-style cheese." The Fish Supreme would be lower in fat if you ask for the sandwich to be prepared *without* the tartar sauce or if you scrape it off yourself. The hamburger would be lower in fat if you asked them to add catsup or mustard instead of the "Secret Sauce," whose first ingredient, after water, is soybean oil!

TIP #125 / KFC: CAPITULATE WITH THE COLONEL

When it comes to ordering fried chicken at fast-food spots, you are better off asking for the breast. But you should know that one Hot & Spicy Chicken center breast (which is the highest fat KFC breast), contains 25 gm. of fat (59 percent of calories from fat). The "Extra Tasty Crispy" chicken center breast is also "extra fatty" with 1 breast adding 21 gm. of fat to your child's daily total.

	Calories	Fat (gm.)	% of Calories from fat	Saturated fat (gm.)	Cholesterol (mg.)	Sodium (mg.)
Mashed Potatoes & Gravy	70	I	13%	<I	<5	370
Rotisserie Gold Chicken White Quarter with skin and wing removed by customer	199	5.9	27%	1.7	97	667
Garden Rice	75	I	11%	0	0	576
Green Beans	36	I	28%	0	0	576
BBQ Baked Beans	132	2	14%	I	3	535
Red Beans and Rice	114	3	23%	I	4	315
Breadstick	110	3	24.5%	0	0	15
Sourdough roll	128	2	12.5%	0	0	236

TIP #126 / LONG JOHN SILVER'S: CHOOSE FROM THIS LIST.

Many of the entrees offered at Long John Silver's are "baked," not fried. And because of this simple cooking difference, quite a few of their items make the list as being lower in fat. Children may only be interested in their a la carte items, since their meals contain quite a bit of food by anyone's terms, especially for small children.

	Calories	Fat (gm.)	% of Calories from fat	Saturated fat (gm.)	Cholesterol (mg.)	Sodium (mg.)
Batter-Dipped Chicken Sandwich (w/out sauce)	280	8	26%	2.1	15	790
Fish with Lemon Crumb (meal includes rice, green beans, slaw & roll w/out margarine)	570	12	19%	2	125	1470
Light Portion Fish, Lemon Crumb (2 pieces fish with rice and small salad w/o dressing)	290	5	15.5%	0.8	75	690
Baked Chicken (includes rice, green beans, slaw, and a roll w/out margarine)	550	15	24.5%	3.2	75	1670
3-piece Fish, Lemon Crumb	150	1	6%	<0.6	110	370
Chicken-Light Herb	120	4	30%	1.2	60	570

TIP #127 / MCDONALD'S: WHAT'S UNDER THE GOLDEN ARCHES

If you like burgers and salads, you'll like McDonald's. They offer three lower-fat salads and a light dressing to boot. When it comes to burgers, the littlest people can order the small hamburger while the larger little people can choose the McLean Deluxe (the size of a Quarter Pounder).

I happen to love someone who is a fan of the McDonald's filet of fish sandwich—my daughter. Of course, she has never actually eaten the true filet of fish as served—with gobs of tartar sauce. Before it ever reaches her plate, I've scraped it all off. While you may be tempted to order the Chicken McNuggets, remember they are higher in fat than the fish sandwich, especially if the tartar sauce is removed.

	Calories	Fat (gm.)	% of Calories from fat	Saturated fat (gm.)	Cholesterol (mg.)	Sodium (mg.)
Hamburger	255	9	32%	3	37	490
McLean Hamburger	320	10	28%	4	60	670
Fish Filet w/out tarter sauce	330	11	34%	NA	NA	NA
Garden Salad	50	2	36%	.6	65	70
Side Salad	30	1	30%	.3	33	35
Chicken Salad	50	4	24%	1	78	230
Vinaigrette	48	2	37%	0.4	0	240
English Muffin	170	4	21%	1	0	285
Hot Cakes with Margarine or Syrup	440	12	25%	2	8	685

TIP 128 / TACO BELL: RING OUT THE FAT.

As your children get older, they may be game for a fast-food restaurant offering something other than the typical hamburger and fries. This is when Taco Bell comes to the rescue. Unfortunately there aren't many selections with 30 percent or fewer calories from fat. I hope your kids like bean or chicken burritos! The better options are listed below.

	Calories	Fat (gm.)	% of Calories from fat	Saturated fat (gm.)	Cholesterol (mg.)	Sodium (mg.)
Bean Burrito	387	14	32.5%	4	9	1148
Chicken Burrito	334	12	32%	4	52	880

These are the selections that didn't make the cut because their percent of calories from fat are too high. But these choices are made with soft tortillas that aren't fried:

	Calories	Fat (gm.)	% of Calories from fat	Saturated fat (gm.)	Cholesterol (mg.)	Sodium (mg.)
Soft Taco	225	12	48%	5	32	554
Chicken Soft Taco	213	10	42%	4	52	615

One of the best things about Taco Bell is its fat-free sauces! These may appeal to your teenager.

- Taco sauce
- Pico de Gallo
- Green sauce
- Salsa
- Red sauce

If you have to choose between adding sour cream or guacamole to a Taco Bell entree, choose the green stuff. It has about half the fat of sour cream.

TIP #129 / WENDY'S: WHAT'S WONDERFUL?

Wendy's has a wide variety of lower fat options: two types of potatoes, two types of chicken sandwiches (one fried, one grilled), even a hamburger and a dish of chili made the list.

	Calories	Fat (gm.)	% of Calories from fat	Saturated fat (gm.)	Cholesterol (mg.)	Sodium (mg.)
Hamburger Jr.	270	9	30%	3	35	590
Grilled Chicken Sandwich	290	7	22%	1	60	670
Breaded Chicken Sandwich with catsup (no mayo)	388	13	30%	3	55	695
Breaded Chicken Sandwich with reduced-calorie honey mustard (no mayo)	405	15	33%	3	55	740
Fish Sandwich w/out tartar sauce	330	11	30%	3	40	665
Potato Sour Cream & Chives	370	6	15%	4	15	35
Potato Broccoli & Cheese	450	14	28%	2	0	450
Small Chili	190	6	28%	2	0	670

TIP #130 / HAVE IT
YOUR WAY.

The best way to "have it your way" is to order your fast-food sandwich without the high-fat sauce, saving you and your family from loads of fat, not to mention extra calories.

Be aware, of course, that this may take a few extra minutes if the fast-food restaurant has to assemble your sandwich differently. You may even be told to move aside and wait while they serve the next customer in line.

If you can't spare the time, you can still "have it your way" in the privacy of your home, car, or fast-food booth. You just scrape off the high-fat sauce before handing it to your child. Then let him or her add some mustard or catsup.

Having it your way is not just a snappy advertising slogan and it's not just an assertiveness training exercise. It can make a huge difference in the nutrition profile of your child's fast-food meal. How huge? Here is the nutrition information on the six high-fat sauces and toppings commonly used in fast-food restaurants.

- Mayonnaise—One level tablespoon of mayonnaise contains 100 calories and around 11 gm. of fat, 8 mg. of cholesterol, and 78 mg. of sodium.

- Special Sauce/Thousand Island—One tablespoon of the thousand island dressing used at Wendy's will add 65 Calories, 6.5 gm. of fat, 7.5 mg. of cholesterol, and 100 mg. of sodium to your sandwich.

- Tartar Sauce—You can expect anywhere from one to two tablespoons of tartar sauce on your fried fish fillet sandwich. One tablespoon will add at least 75 calories, 8 gm. of fat, 7 mg. cholesterol, and 99 mg. sodium, depending on the brand used. Wendy's tartar sauce contains 130 calories and 14 gm. of fat per tablespoon.

- Sour Cream—One of those little plastic serving cups of sour cream (about 2 tablespoons) will top your fast-food entree with an extra 62 calories and 6 gm. of fat, 12 mg. of cholesterol, and 16 mg. sodium.
- Guacamole—One-eighth cup (2 tablespoons) will add about 50 calories and 4 gm. of fat.
- Cheese—One quarter cup of shredded cheddar cheese is worth about 114 calories and 9 gm. of fat, along with 30 mg. cholesterol and 175 mg. sodium.

The cheese in the "Broccoli & Cheese Baked Potato" at Wendy's contributes around 140 calories and 13 gm. of fat to its grand total.

So what do you ask them to put on instead? There are so many lower-fat sauces and spreads to choose from. Your child will probably choose the catsup option, but barbecue sauce and mustard are also normally available.

TIP #131 / WHEN THEY WON'T "DO" FAST FOOD WITHOUT FRIES.

French fries—the perfect finger food, golden, glistening, and crispy. The problem is, they're crisp and glistening because they're dunked like a skunk in a vat full of fat.

Some restaurants offer steak fries or wedge potatoes. These are usually a lower-fat option than their thinner cousins, shoestring potatoes. Why? No big secret here: the thicker the fries, the more potato inside and the less surface area per pound of potato absorbing the oil.

Obviously the larger the serving, the more fat. So, let's compare the small size fries from each fast-food chain and take a longer look at the percent of calories from fat too.

Most fast-food fries get 45 to 50 percent of their calories from fat. So the chain with the lowest-fat french fries is probably the one with the fewest fries in their small serving bag.

- Hardee's has the french fries lowest in percent of calories from fat (43 percent) and grams of fat (11 gm.), with a total of 230 calories per small serving. Jack-in-the-Box's small order of french fries also contains 11 gm. of fat but has a higher percentage of calories from fat (45 percent) with 219 calories.

- The next lowest in percent of calories from fat is Wendy's with 45 percent and 12 gm. of fat (240 calories).

- The third in line is McDonald's. Their small order of french fries also contain 12 gm. of fat, but because theirs contain 220 calories (20 less than Wendy's), the percent of calories from fat (49 percent) is a little higher than Wendy's.

TIP #132 / WHERE TO "SHAKE" IT UP.

It's hot. You're on the road, and the kids are screaming for a snack—but not just any old snack. They want something sweet and cool. Which fast-food chain offers the lowest-fat frozen treats?

You may have noticed that most of the fast-food chains now offer low-fat frozen yogurt cones, shakes, or frosties. Be careful about the low-fat part. A milk shake may be low-fat but still packs a powerful 350 calories.

When measuring fast-food frozen treats against each other, you need to consider the size of the item. Most fast-food shakes are about 350 calories and 10 grams of fat.

Of all the chains, McDonald's has been busiest skimming the fat from their shakes. Their new-and-improved versions have 83 percent less fat than the original. They are about the same calorie-wise as the other chains' shakes, but they lead the pack by far for the fewest grams of fat.

McDonald's also offers low-fat frozen yogurt cones with only 1 gram of fat per small serving.

	Calories	Fat (gm.)	Saturated fat (gm).	% of Calories from fat
McDonald's Shakes:				
Vanilla	290	1.3	0.6	4%
Chocolate	320	1.7	0.7	5%
Frozen Yogurt				
cone	105	1	0.5	9%

The next lowest-fat shakes are at Carl's Jr. and Jack in the Box. Carl's Jr. regular-sized shakes contain 350 calories, 7 gm. fat, and 18 percent of calories from fat. Jack in the Box chocolate and strawberry shakes contain 330 and 320 calories—7 gm. of fat, with 19 percent for a chocolate and 20 percent of calories from fat for a strawberry shake.

TIP #133 / PICK YOUR PIZZA WITH CARE.

If you have a child over the age of one, you will, whether you want to or not, come to love take-out pizza. It fills a certain unavoidable need perfectly, like those evenings when you are juggling five different activities or when you are home later than expected, leaving you little time to eat, let alone cook, dinner. Then there are those evenings when you can't move off the couch, except maybe when the pizza delivery person rings your door bell.

Take-out pizza has some unmistakable things going for it:

- Someone else is slaving over a hot oven.
- You can call ahead and pick it up or have it delivered.
- It won't cost you an arm and a leg for a family of four.
- And, probably most important, the kids love it!

So which pizza chain is best? We all have our favorite pizza parlors. The kids might like the sauce at one and the crust at another, or they might love going to a particular pizza parlor because "they add gobs of cheese" or "they have the best video games." But the bottom line is, kids love pizza, any pizza. So why not frequent the parlor with the lowest-fat pizza?

Of course, you're on your own when it comes to the family-owned "Luigi's Pizza" or "Mama's" type of eating establishments. But I was able to gather the nutrition information on three leading pizza chains—Pizza Hut, Round Table Pizza, and Little Caesar's.

Because each pizza chain uses its own serving sizes in its analysis (some use a medium slice and others a large slice as a serving), and each medium or large slice can differ drastically anyway (in terms of how many slices they slice per medium or large pizza), the percentage of calories from fat becomes a more valid indicator of fatness than calories or grams of fat.

Then there is the issue of toppings. Obviously each pizza parlor will add varying quantities of toppings. A slice of pepperoni pizza at one establishment might include four to six pepperoni rounds, while at another place, you'd be lucky if you found two. For this reason, and of course because meat toppings add too much fat to an already moderately high-fat cheese-topped entree, we will be using cheese pizza in our comparison.

This being the case, the lowest percent calories-from-fat cheese pizza comes from Little Caesar's, with the others following not so far behind.

While looking at the table below, you'll notice the thicker crust pizzas have the lower percent of calories from fat, compared with the thin and crispy crusts. This doesn't surprise me at all. Why wouldn't thicker crust pizza have a lower fat value? You're adding more crust (which in most cases is a high-carbohydrate, low-fat bread dough) per amount of topping.

Remember, thicker crust pizzas just have thicker crusts—not thicker layers of topping! And, usually, because your kids fill up faster with the thicker crusts, they eat fewer slices than they would if the crust were thin.

Cheese Pizza Comparison:

Chain	Calories	Fat (gm.)	% of Calories from fat	Saturated fat(gm.)
Little Ceasars, (I large slice)				
Square	188	6	29%	380
Round	169	6	32%	240
Round Table (I large slice)				
Pan	310	11	32%	631
Thin	166	7	38%	332
Pizza Hut (I medium slice)				
Pan Pizza	246	9	33%	470
Thin'n Crispy	199	8.5	38%	434

It doesn't really matter whether I'm eating pizza that originated from a frozen Weight Watchers® box, from a well-known pizza chain, or from a local pizzeria where they flip the pizza dough and the chef has an Italian accent. I confess, I love pizza! And so do most kids.

But we equate pizza with grease and fat and feel guilty feeding it to our families. I'm here to raise the reputation of pizza to new, more healthful heights. I have news for you. The pools of grease you see on the top of the pizza come mainly from the fatty meat toppings, not the actual pizza base (crust, sauce and cheese). So you can order your pizza with vegetable toppings and presto, the grease is gone.

Allow me to present exhibit A: two slices of thin-crust pizza (each being 1/8 of a 15-inch pizza) average around 575 calories, 27 percent from fat (18 gm. of fat), with 110 mg. of cholesterol. But with this you also get 30 gm. of quality protein, which meets half of your daily protein requirement if you're a medium-sized male, as well as close to half your daily requirement for niacin, thiamin, and selenium. You will also get half of your requirement for calcium, vitamin B_{12}, a third of riboflavin and about 3 1/2 mg. of iron.

TIP #134 / WHEN IN DOUBT, TRY THE THICK CRUST OUT!

If your children eat a fourth of a 10-inch thick-crust pizza (almost the same weight as two slices of thin crust), they will enjoy fewer calories, about 4 gm. less fat, more than 30 mg. less cholesterol and about 200 mg. less sodium. There is no fancy magical trick here. When you order thick crust you are simply getting more crust (carbohydrate) for the same amount of higher-fat cheese topping. And one slice of thick tends to fill you up more than a slice of thin.

Kids not pleased with "just cheese" on top? Adding 1/8 cup of onions, or 1/4 cup of green peppers, or mushrooms increases the totals by only 4 to 7 calories, with no more fat. So feel free to order heavy on the veggies! One-quarter cup of pineapple will add 49 calories but no fat. And just in case your kids can't imagine pizza without a representative from the meat group, Canadian-style bacon or ham is probably your best bet. Two ounces of Canadian-style bacon adds about 100 calories and 5 gm. of fat. In contrast, 1 ounce of pepperoni adds 140 calories and 12 gm. of fat.

The Best Kids Meals at Popular Fast-food Chains

TIP #135 / PICK THE LOWEST FAT BURGER.

If your child orders the Wendy's Jr. Hamburger, shares his or her small order of french fries, and drinks 8 ounces of lemonade or similar beverage, he or she will end up with 504 calories, with 15 gm. of fat (27 percent of calories from fat).

- **Wendy's Jr. Hamburger and McDonald's small hamburger** have the least fat (9 gm.). Wendy's has 30 percent of calories from fat, along with 270 calories, 35 mg. cholesterol, and 590 mg. of sodium. McDonald's has 32 percent of calories from fat and 255 calories, 37 mg. cholesterol, and 490 mg. sodium.

- **McDonald's McLean Deluxe** is the lowest in percentage of calories from fat (28 percent), with 10 gm. of fat, 320 calories, and 60 mg. cholesterol.

TIP #136 / CHOOSE THE LOWEST-FAT CHICKEN SANDWICH.

Take the lowest-fat chicken sandwich you can find (Carl's Jr. Teriyaki Chicken or Charbroiler BBQ chicken) and add 1/2 of a regular size order of french fries and a 10-ounce glass of 1% low-fat milk and you've got yourself a kids' meal totaling 690 calories,19 gm. of fat (25 percent of calories from fat).

- **Carl's Jr.** Teriyaki Chicken has 330 calories, 6 gm. fat, 16 percent of calories from fat.

- **Carl's Jr.** Charbroiler BBQ has 310 calories, 6 gm. fat, 17 percent of calories from fat.

- **Wendy's** Grilled Chicken Sandwich with Reduced-Calorie Honey Mustard Sauce has 290 calories, 7 gm. fat, 22 percent of calories from fat.

TIP #137 / FISH AROUND FOR THE LOWEST-FAT FISH.

If your child eats a McDonald's filet of fish *without* tartar sauce, drinks a glass of fruit juice and splits a small bag of french fries, the entire meal will come to 490 calories, 17 gm. fat, and 31 percent of calories from fat.

- Wendy's fish sandwich *without* tartar sauce has 330 calories, 11 gm. fat, and 30 percent of calories from fat. But, this sandwich is not available in all restaurants.

- McDonald's Filet-O-Fish *without* tartar sauce has 340 calories, 11 gm. fat, and 34 percent of calories from fat.

- Long John Silver's Batter Dipped Fish Sandwich without sauce has 340 calories, 13 gm. fat, and 34 percent of calories from fat.

TIP #138 / PICK THE LOWEST-FAT PIZZA.

As we said earlier, pizza actually is one of the better fast-food kids meals. If your kids eat two large slices of Little Caesar's cheese pizza, they will be eating a total of 376 calories, 12 gm. of fat, or 29 percent of calories from fat. Add a glass of 100 percent fruit juice or nonfat or 1 percent low-fat milk and now we're talking about 475 calories and up to 15 gm. of fat (no more than 28 percent of calories from fat).

TIP #139 / LOOK FOR THE LOWEST-FAT CHICKEN NUGGETS.

Chicken pieces made from chicken parts—it may not sound so wonderful to us but this might just be your child's favorite fast food. Nuggets could be the ticket if your children are too little to chew hamburgers well, if they don't like fish sandwiches, or if the chain doesn't serve fish or any other agreeable alternative.

So, if you are stuck with ordering chicken pieces for your kids, keep in mind some fast-food nuggets are fattier than others. The highest-fat ones weigh in at about 20 gm. of fat per six pieces (without dipping sauce). So the chicken tenders at Burger King, with 13 gm. of fat and the Chicken Sticks at Hardees with 9 gm. of fat, suddenly don't look so bad.

If your child has the Hardee's Chicken Sticks, along with a whole order of french fries and an orange juice, he or she will be eating a meal that actually comes quite close to the guidelines—580 calories and 20 gm. fat (31 percent of calories from fat).

Here are your options for better or worse:

Better:

- Hardee's Chicken Sticks, 6 pieces (210 calories, 9 gm. fat, 39 percent of calories from fat)

Worse:

- Burger King Chicken Tenders, 6 pieces (236 calories, 13 gm. fat, 50 percent of calories from fat)

- McDonald's McNuggets, 6 pieces (270 calories, 15 gm. fat, 50 percent of calories from fat)

*Fast food chains not listed here actually offer chicken pieces with **more** fat.*

TIP #140 / ENCOURAGE SOME NONTRADITIONAL CHOICES.

As a break from the usual fast food, your kids might be willing to try one of the following.

Hardee's

- Ham or turkey sub sandwich (370 to 390 calories, 12 gm. of fat each, 28 or 29 percent of calories from fat)
- Roast beef sub (390 calories, 5 gm. fat, 12 percent of calories from fat)
- Combo sub (380 calories, 6 gm. fat, 14 percent of calories from fat)

Wendy's

- Small bowl of chili and a sour cream and chive potato (560 calories and 12 gm. of fat, 19 percent of calories from fat)

TIP #141 / STAY AWAY FROM THESE FAT GUYS.

Try to steer your kids away from these choices. The following contain at least half of their calories from fat.

Arby's:

- Sausage Biscuit (460 calories, 32 gm. fat, 62 percent of calories from fat)
- Bacon/Egg Croissant (430 calories, 30 gm. fat, 63 percent of calories from fat)
- Mushroom/Cheese Croissant (493 calories, 38 gm. fat, 69 percent of calories from fat)
- Sausage/Egg Croissant (519 calories, 39 gm. fat, 68 percent of calories from fat)

Burger King:

- Double Whopper Sandwich (800 calories, 48 gm. fat, 54 percent of calories from fat)
- Double Whopper with Cheese (890 Calories, 55 gm. fat, 56 percent of calories from fat)
- Croissan-wich with sausage, egg, and cheese (534 calories, 40 gm. fat, 67 percent of calories from fat)

Carl's Jr.:

- Super Star Hamburger (820 Calories, 53 gm. of fat, 58 percent of calories from fat)
- Double Western Bacon Cheeseburger (1030 calories, 63 gm. fat, 55 percent of calories from fat)
- Bacon & Cheese Potato (730 calories, 43 gm. of fat, 53 percent of calories from fat)

Hardee's:

- Bacon Cheeseburger (610 Calories, 39 gm. of fat, 57.5 percent of calories from fat)
- Fried Chicken Thigh (370 calories, 26 gm. fat, 63 percent of calories from fat)

Jack In the Box:

- Sausage Crescent (584 calories, 43 gm. fat, 66 percent of calories from fat)

- Supreme Crescent (547 calories, 40 gm. fat, 66 percent of calories from fat)

- Jumbo Jack with Cheese (677 calories, 40 gm. fat, 53 percent of calories from fat)

- Bacon Cheeseburger (705 calories, 45 gm. fat, 57 percent of calories from fat)

- Chicken Supreme (641 calories, 39 gm. fat, 55 percent of calories from fat)

- Grilled Sourdough Burger (712 calories, 50 gm., 63 percent of calories from fat)

- Ultimate Cheeseburger (942 calories, 69 gm. fat, 66 percent of calories from fat)

- Egg Rolls, 5 pieces (753 calories, 41 gm. fat, 49 percent of calories from fat)

- Chicken Wings, 6 pieces (846 calories, 44 gm. fat, 47 percent of calories from fat)

- Mini Chimichangas, 6 pieces (856 calories, 42 gm. fat, 44 percent of calories from fat)

KFC (Kentucky Fried Chicken):

- Hot Wings, 6 pieces (471 calories, 33 gm. fat, 63 percent of calories from fat)

- Hot & Spicy Chicken

  Thigh (412 calories, 30 gm. fat, 66 percent of calories from fat)

  Drumstick (207 calories, 14 gm. fat, 61 percent of calories from fat)

- Extra-Tasty Crispy Chicken

  Thigh (414 calories, 31 gm. fat, 67 percent of calories from fat)

  Drumstick, 205 calories (14 gm. fat, 61 percent of calories from fat)

Little Caesar's:

- Veggie Sandwich (784 calories, 47 gm. fat, 54 percent of calories from fat)

McDonald's:

- Biscuit with Sausage (420 calories, 28 gm. fat, 60 percent of calories from fat)

Taco Bell:

- Taco Salad (905 calories, 61 gm. fat, 61 percent of calories from fat)
- Taco Supreme (230 calories, 15 gm. fat, 59 percent of calories from fat)
- Taco Salad (905 calories, 61 gm. fat, 61 percent of calories from fat)
- Nachos Supreme (367 calories, 27 gm. fat, 66 percent of calories from fat)
- Mexican Pizza (575 calories, 37 gm. fat, 58 percent of calories from fat)

Wendy's:

- Chicken Nuggets, 6 pieces (280 calories, 20 gm. fat, 64 percent of calories from fat)

The Golden Rules for Low-Fat Fast Food

Wherever you choose to eat, keep these tips in mind.

TIP #142 / KISS MR. MAYO GOODBYE.

That white, creamy goop manages to weave its way into many fast-food sandwiches, either posing as itself or as a major ingredient in sauces such as "secret sauce" or tartar sauce. Even a certain "honey-mustard" sauce I know of features mayo. (It's a bad sign if the "honey-mustard" sauce is more white than yellow.)

At 10 gm. of fat and 100 calories per tablespoon you can see why it's best to kiss mayonnaise goodbye. Why is it so high on both counts? Could it be because basically mayonnaise is composed of oil and egg yolk?

If you don't have time to order your fast-food item without the mayonnaise (and perhaps ordering it with mustard or catsup instead), you can always order it as is and scrape off the goop yourself. It's a messy job, but someone's got to do it. The best part about doing it this way is your bread still remains a little wet from the mayo or sauce you couldn't completely scrape off.

TIP #143 / FORGO THE FRENCH FRIES.

What's a simple way to cut about 15 gm. of fat from your child's fast-food meal? Forgo the french fries. Your kids may say "what's fast food without french fries?" If so, this may be a difficult golden rule for your family to follow.

Perhaps a compromise could be ordering one bag for two kids to split. Or if you're at a fast-food chain that offers a low-fat frozen dessert, encourage them to order that instead.

If your child is old enough to be significantly impressed (and "grossed out") by the grease in french fries, you can tell them how much oil is in each serving of french fries or show them the grease spots by blotting your french fries on a brown paper bag or even a napkin (it's easier to see the spots on something brown than on something white).

TIP #144 / DON'T WASH DOWN YOUR HIGH-FAT FOOD WITH A HIGH-FAT BEVERAGE.

Don't add insult to injury by washing down your higher-fat fast-food meal with a high-fat beverage. Pass up the whole milk and if the milk shakes at that particular fast-food chain are high in fat, pass them up, too.

Opt for a lower-fat milk or fruit juice. And depending on your preference for avoiding sugar, artificial sweeteners, or caffeine, there is also usually soda, diet soda and iced tea available. And remember, most fast-food chains will serve ice water for free, even at the drive-through window.

TIP #145 / THE SMALLER THE BURGER THE BETTER.

In general, you'll find the lower-fat burgers are usually the smaller ones, which works out great since these are the size marketed to kids. These smaller burgers come with catsup, onions, and pickles, instead of mayo, special sauce, bacon, or extra cheese. You'll notice that with the small burgers, you're getting more bun and less burger. Remember the bun contributes mostly carbohydrate calories—and that's good.

TIP #146 / FORGO THE FANCY BREADS, LIKE CROISSANTS AND BISCUITS, AND STICK TO BUNS, BAGELS, AND ENGLISH MUFFINS.

Going to a fast-food chain and ordering eggs and sausage, ham and cheese, or a burger is bad enough, but put them on fancy, high-fat breads (like biscuits or croissants) and the nutritional profile goes from bad to worse.

You are much better off with fast-food sandwiches that come with a bun, bagel, or English muffin. Like a loaf of bread, these are high in carbohydrates and low in fat. Why add more fat where it isn't needed?

TIP #147 / BROILED IS BETTER THAN BREADED OR FRIED.

There are instances when fast-food chains take a piece of chicken or fish and cover it with crumbs or batter and then dunk it in hot oil (also known as frying). But they could just as easily take the same piece of chicken or fish and broil, barbecue, bake, grill, or roast it. This way they wouldn't add extra fat or oil.

Some fast-food chains offer sandwiches with broiled or barbecued chicken or fish. These are usually the items that offer the most nutritionally for the least amount of fat.

TIP #148 / NO SKIN IS A NUTRITIONAL MUST.

Chicken items can come with the skin on or off. You can always tear the skin off yourself, but I find it is best to leave this delicate process to the professionals.

Some fast-food chains now offer skinless chicken items. One of my favorite chicken sandwiches actually comes breaded and fried (Wendy's Chicken Breast Sandwich). But because they use a chicken breast without the skin, and because I order it with catsup instead of mayonnaise, it's actually a lower-fat option.

You'll find that some of the lowest-fat chicken items are not only grilled rather than fried, but are also skinless. One exception is the new skinless line of Kentucky Fried Chicken. Although it is a little lower in fat than the extra crispy version, it is still darn high in fat. So if you find yourself visiting the Colonel, at least ask for a chicken breast and encourage your kids to peel as much of the crispy coating off as possible.

TIP #149 / CHOOSE STEAMED TORTILLAS INSTEAD OF FRIED.

Freshly made tortillas, whether made with flour or corn, are actually low in fat. The flour type has a bit more fat, but it is usually still not a prohibitive amount. Take either one though, and fry it in fat or oil and they both become crispy and high in fat.

So, when it comes to fast-food fajitas or tacos, you want to look for the ones with steamed tortillas. This means ordering the soft tacos and the fast-food fajitas that come with steamed tortillas. Taco salads usually come with fried tortilla chips or they are served in a fried tortilla shell. This is why taco salads, along with all the creamy dressings, are usually high in fat.

TIP #150 / CUT THE SOUR CREAM.

Many fast-food items come with sour cream. But it is also usually easy to order these same fast-food items without the sour cream. At Taco Bell this usually means passing up the "deluxe" or "supreme" versions in favor of the regular tacos or burritos. If the restaurant packs a little cup of sour cream or guacamole along with your items, try to pass it right back before you leave the counter.

TIP #151 / DON'T PUT TWO HIGH-FAT FOODS TOGETHER IN ONE ENTREE.

Try to limit the high-fat choices to one per meal. For example, choose a plain cheese pizza or a plain burger. Don't make it a cheese and pepperoni pizza or a beef, cheese, and bacon burger. Every little change from those old habits means a savings in fat grams.

At the Supermarket: Using Convenience Foods

TIP #152 / LEARN ABOUT THE LONG-OVERDUE NEW NUTRITION LABELING LAWS.

For a decade now, the food regulatory "game," so to speak, had been canceled. So some food companies took the ball and ran with it! This was the era when misleading terms like "no cholesterol," "80 percent fat-free" (which means 20 percent fat by weight!) and "lite" were invented. To say there has been mass nutrition-claim hysteria would be an understatement.

New labeling laws will change all that. Food companies accustomed to making their own rules and saying whatever they please on their product labels are going to have to fess up. I think the most noteworthy changes are coming in the area of nutrition claims. The FDA is about to engage in a massive clean-up mission—of nutrition labeling claims that is.

For example, as part of the new labeling laws, the government has established standard serving sizes for product categories based on the amount people actually eat. (Now there's a novel approach.) Currently, food companies are able to choose their own serving sizes—no matter how impractical or ridiculous. Because of this, we see 1/2 ounce as a serving size for crackers, 1 cookie as a serving size for cookies, 3 or 4 ounces (1/2 cup) as a serving size for ice creams and frozen yogurts, and 1 ounce as a serving size for chips—when we all know most of us eat twice that at least.

And claims relating certain foods or nutrients to common diseases will only be allowed for seven specific government approved food-disease relationships, with very stringent rules, statements, and symbols being applied by the government. The seven approved relationships are:

- Calcium and osteoporosis
- Fat and cancer
- Saturated fat, cholesterol, and coronary heart disease
- Fiber-containing grain products, fruits and vegetables, and cancer
- Fruits and vegetables and grain products with fiber and coronary heart disease
- Sodium and high blood pressure
- Fruits and vegetables and cancer

Before the new labeling laws, commonly used terms like "lite," "reduced fat," and so on, didn't have any standard definitions recognized by the government. And there were no guidelines for food companies using terms like "no cholesterol," "no tropical oils," or " percent fat free" on their products. So, not surprisingly, companies have been making up their own definitions as they go along. "Lite" might refer to a smaller serving size or a lighter texture or color, while "reduced-fat" could be anywhere from 20 to 50 percent less. And terms like "no cholesterol," "no tropical oils," or " percent fat free" have been applied to products that are still considered high in fat or saturated fat. But there is a happy ending to this story: The Food and Drug Administration will be enforcing their own specific definitions and usage guidelines for most of the common nutrition advertising terms.

Here are a few of the more interesting changes for you to chew on.

- **"Free"** will refer to none or negligible amounts of fat, saturated fat, cholesterol, sodium, sugar or calories.

- **"95 percent fat-free"** can only be used on foods that are either low in fat or fat-free.

- **"Low Fat"** can be used on foods with 3 gm. of fat or less per serving.

- **"Less"** and **"reduced"** will refer to a product having at least 25 percent less than the comparable food.

- **"Light"** can be used on foods with one-third less calories than the regular product, or half the fat of the regular product. And if the item is high in fat and calories but the term "light" refers to the reduction in sodium, the label must specify "light in sodium." Please be forewarned, however, that under the new labeling laws "light" can still be used to refer to the texture or color, but the label must spell it out. (In what sized letters?)

- **"No tropical oils"** can only be used on the packaging if the product is also considered low in saturated fat. (It may still be high in fat, however.)

- A product can be named as a **"good source"** of a particular nutrient (such as fiber) if it contains 10 to 19 percent of the daily recommended value for that nutrient.

- **Percent of fruit juice** must be listed on the package of every fruit "drink." If it's only 5 or 10 percent, the whole world's going to know.

TIP #153 / LEARN TO CALCU-
LATE CALORIES
FROM FAT.

New nutrition labels will also include grams of fat and calories from fat. This is not the *percentage* of calories from fat—but the actual total number of fat calories per serving.

Why couldn't they go one step further and include the percent of calories from fat? Good question—and one I asked the government when the proposed labeling guidelines were first publicized. Some products will voluntarily include the percent of calories from fat on their label.

So for those of you interested in calculating this percentage, here's how to do it.

Step #1. Take the calories from fat per serving and divide by the number of total calories per serving.

$$\frac{\text{Calories from fat}}{\text{Total calories}} = \underline{\quad}$$

Step #2. Then take this fraction and multiply by 100 to get the percentage.

_____ x 100 = percent of calories from fat.

Example #1: Orville Reddenbacher's Smart Pop® popping corn contains 9 calories from fat per serving as consumed and 50 total calories per serving.

> *Step #1.* 9 divided by 50 = 0.18
>
> *Step #2.* 0.18 X 100 = 18 percent of calories from fat.

Example #2: Klondike® Lite Ice Cream Sandwiches contain 18 calories from fat per serving and 90 total calories per serving.

   Step #1. 18 divided by 90 = 0.20

   Step #2. 0.20 X 100 = 20 percent of calories from fat!

TIP #154 / PREPARE FOR STRANGE ENCOUNTERS OF THE SUPERMARKET KIND.

What health horrors await you on the dark side of the supermarket aisle? What new products lurk about tempting you with nutrition terror? The stories you are about to hear are true, but some of the brand names have been deleted to protect the innocent. (In this case, that means me.)

What are we spooning into our children's mouths in the name of convenience? Are the "just for kids" frozen meals any better for them than the frozen chicken and TV dinners that fed us as kids? Some are and some aren't.

Since these entrees are targeting the tiny-tot taste buds, expect to find foods that these mini consumers crave—hot dogs and corn dogs, hamburgers, macaroni and cheese, and, of course, pizza, pizza, and more pizza.

Before I tell you which of the frozen entrees for kids are on the fat side, let me reassure you there is a happy ending to this story. There are quite a few that have 30 percent or less of calories from fat. One of the highest fat meals made for kids has 430 calories and 23 gm. of fat (48 percent of calories from fat). The next two highest fat choices both total 400 calories and 19 gm. of fat (43 percent of calories from fat).

Not unlike frozen entrees for big people, several of these meals top the charts in sodium. The highest has 380 calories and 1,000 mg. of sodium.

TIP #155 / ANALYZE THE "FOR KIDS ONLY" FROZEN DINNERS.

Kids today have their own lines of frozen entrees featuring foods kids like and are familiar with—complete with cartoon characters on the package and little goodies. And each of those items can be ready in minutes—thanks to the magic of the microwave. How can parent and child resist?

Well, just in case you can't, listed below are the items with 30 percent or less of calories from fat, along with some comments on how to make some of these more complete and balanced meal options. For example, you want to make sure each of these dinners provides at least one serving from four out of the five New Food Pyramid's food groups (one fruit, one vegetable, one bread, cereal, rice or pasta serving, and one serving of meat or meat alternative.)

I'm not so worried about working in a serving from the milk and dairy group since most kids are drinking at least a couple of glasses of milk every day which, in and of itself, fulfills the minimum servings recommended for this food group in the New Food Pyramid.

	Calories	Fat (gm.)	% of Calories from fat	Sodium mg.	Comments
Kid Cuisine®					
Macaroni & Cheese	340	8	21%	600	fairly complete
Beef Patty Sandwich with Cheese	290	9	28%	410	very complete
Cheese Pizza	380	12	29%	390	fairly complete
Chicken Nuggets	330	11	30%	270	needs fruit serving added; fairly high in sodium
Fish Sticks	360	12	30%	270	needs fruit serving added
Swanson Kids®:					
Macaroni & Cheese & Franks	300	8	25%	750	very complete fairly high in sodium
Chillin' Cheese Pizza	350	10	26%	380	fairly complete
Hoppin' Hot Dog	330	10	27%	740	needs a fruit serving added; fairly high in sodium
Slammin' Sloppy Joe	260	8	28%	520	needs a fruit serving added
Tyson Looney Tunes®:					
Daffy Duck Spaghetti & Meatballs	320	10	28%	570	needs a fruit serving
Yosemite Sam BBQ Glazed Chicken	240	8	30%	540	needs a grain and fruit serving

TIP #156 / "DINNERS" THAT DON'T MEASURE UP.

The following are the frozen kid's meals that have more than 30 percent of calories from fat. Although a couple of the Tyson Looney Tunes® contained only 11 gm. of fat per serving, because of the low level of total calories (290 to 300) the percent of calories from fat comes out as slightly over the 30 percent of calories from fat mark (33 and 34 percent).

	Calories	Fat (gm.)	% of Calories from fat	Sodium mg.	Comments
Kid Cuisine®					
Fried Chicken	470	20	38%	800	needs grain and fruit serving; fairly high sodium
Swanson Kids®					
Chompin Chicken Drumlets	530	26	44%	730	needs a vegetable serving; fairly high sodium
Frazzlin' Fried Chicken	690	34	44%	1170	very high sodium; needs fruit and grain serving
Beef Patty Sandwich with Cheese	440	19	39%	710	needs a fruit serving; fairly high sodium
Tyson Looney Tunes®:					
Bugs Bunny Chicken Chunks	290	11	34%	440	needs a grain serving
Road Runner Chicken Sandwich	300	11	33%	490	fairly complete

TIP #157 / CONSIDER A HEALTHY CHOICE® GROUND BEEF.

Ground beef, the meat hamburgers, spaghetti sauce, and meat loaves are made of. Just a year ago, buying ground sirloin (about 13 percent fat by weight) was about as lean as you could get and still be able to call it an "all-beef patty." I personally got in the habit of mixing ground turkey with ground sirloin, and that suited me (and everyone else who sits at my dinner table) just fine.

So I have to admit my nose was pointed skyward when I heard of this "revolutionary" lean beef made from very lean beef but with hydrolyzed oat flour added as an extender and binder and beef stock for moisture and flavor, and salt as a flavor enhancer. I mean, I put it to the test! First I mixed it with meat-loaf makings and shaped it into what turned out to be a tasty, perfectly formed meat loaf. But my skepticism was unwavering, "I bet it doesn't 'burger.'" So I sculpted it into patties and watched it broil to perfection. Well, all right, so it's soft and moist. It probably doesn't crumble and brown nicely for chili or spaghetti sauce. Three strikes and I was out—and Healthy Choice beef was in.

It's tender, tastes terrific, and even browns up nicely in a fry pan. What else could you want? Even if you asked the butcher to take a sirloin steak, trimmed of any visible fat, and grind it fresh for you, it would still have 40 more calories and over 2 gm. more fat per 3-oz. cooked portion than the Healthy Choice beef.

Because salt is added to the raw beef, each 3-ounce patty will contain 240 mg. of sodium before any extra salt or salt seasonings are added (about 180 mg. more sodium than your other ground beef options). So for heavens sake, don't touch that salt shaker. You don't need it; the beef tastes great as is. If you do need to satisfy that shaker reflex, reach for one of the many no-salt herb/seasoning blends.

You'll find Healthy Choice beef in the frozen meat section of your grocery store, packed in 16-ounce plastic tubes (like sausage). If you want to compare the various ground beefs for yourself, take a look at the table below:

	Regular hamburger	Ground round	Sirloin steak lean only	Healthy Choice ground beef
Calories	269	231	171	130
Fat (gm.)	18	16	7	4
% of calories from fat	63%	63%	37%	36%
Cholesterol	92 mg.	74 mg.	76 mg.	55 mg.
% fat by weight	18%	8%	NA	4%

TIP #158 / FACE THE HOT DOG—HEAD ON.

It's darn difficult to do anything distinctly American, like going to a baseball game or family picnic, without your kids coming nose to nose with a frankfurter. Every red-blooded American usually has his or her own style of dressing that dog, too. I couldn't help but notice this while standing in line at the condiment counter at a recent baseball game.

Some might drizzle catsup in a geometric pattern across the length of their bun. Some methodically spoon relish on one side of the bun and onions on the other. Some like their mayonnaise and mustard to run together in yellow and white swirls.

Whatever your pleasure, everyone holding a hot dog has one thing in common. They're all biting into a pretty high-fat frank. The old-fashioned hot dogs, bunless, weigh in at about 2 ounces each and donate about 185 calories, 17 gm. of fat (82 percent of calories from fat), and 600 mg. of sodium to your diet.

When you include the carbohydrate-rich bun and condiments that add little or no fat to the cause, we're still biting into an entree with most of its calories coming from fat. A hot dog with bun and 2 teaspoons of mustard has 310 calories, 19 gm. of fat (56 percent of calories), and 915 mg. sodium. A hot dog with bun and 1 tablespoon of catsup has 320 calories, 19 gm. of fat (53 percent of calories), and 960 mg sodium.

But parents of hot-dog lovers, have no fear! A new generation of frankfurters is finally here! Take your pick. You can reduce the fat by one-third with Harris Ranch® less fat beef franks or with turkey franks from Butterball, Louis Rich, or Mr. Turkey. You can cut the fat by two-thirds with Armour® 90 Percent Fat-Free, One-Third Less Salt Jumbo Beef Franks® or Hormel Light 'n Lean 90 Percent Fat-Free Beef/Pork Franks®.

After sampling my share of these slimmer dogs, I can honestly say there is little difference in taste between the one-third less-fat hot dogs and the old-fashioned higher-fat frank. So if you or your family are fairly finicky frankfurter eaters, then you should probably start off with these:

- Butterball Jumbo Turkey Franks®

- Louis Rich Turkey Franks®

- Harris Ranch Less Salt Beef Franks®

- Butterball Bun Size 80 percent fat free®

- Oscar Mayer Beef 80 percent fat free®

On average, these franks contain (per 2 ounces) about 130 calories and 10 to 11 gm. of fat (69 percent to 76 percent of calories from fat). Add a bun and some mustard or catsup and the percentage of calories from fat drops to 41 to 44 percent, with 255 to 265 total calories.

For the more motivated fat watcher who thinks a hot dog is a hot dog is a hot dog, you may want to move your children straight to the franks with the least amount of fat:

- Armour® 90 percent fat-free, 1/3 less salt jumbo beef (90 calories per 2-oz. frank, 5 gm. of fat, 510 mg. sodium)

- Hormel Light 'n Lean®, 90 percent fat-free franks (88 calories per 2-oz. frank, 6.25 gm. of fat, sodium information was not on package).

- Healthy Choice Jumbo Franks®, 97% fat-free (70 calories per 2-oz. frank, 2 gm. fat, 570 mg. sodium)

- Healthy Favorites® 97 percent fat-free, pork (50 calories per 2-oz. frank, 2 gm. of fat, 530 mg. sodium)

- Hormel Light & Lean® 97 percent fat-free, pork (45 calories per 1.6-oz. frank, 1 gm. fat, 390 mg. sodium)

Lay these babies in a bun and you have a dog that comes closer to the 30 percent of calories from fat guideline!

With hot dog bun and 1 Tbsp. catsup:

Armour—227 calories, 7 gm. fat (28 percent of calories from fat), 890 mg. sodium

Hormel—225 calories, 8.3 gm. fat (33 percent of calories from fat)

With hot dog bun and 2 tsp. mustard:

Armour—216 calories, 7.5 gm. fat (31 percent of calories from fat), 842 mg. sodium

Hormel—214 calories, 8.7 gm. fat (37 percent of calories from fat)

TIP #159 / FACE FACTS ABOUT FROZEN FRENCH FRIES.

As good as homemade oven french fries taste, let's face it, it's a whole lot easier to slit open a bag of frozen french fries and pop them in the oven for 20 minutes while you get the rest of dinner together. Likewise, it's a lot easier to open a bag of hash browns than to wash, peel, and grate potatoes from scratch (especially with two or three little ones screaming for breakfast). But aren't all the frozen potato products greased to the gills with fats and oil? Most are—but thankfully some aren't!

Some of the "full of fat" options are the toaster type hash-browns, "golden" patties, crispy type french fries and of course tator tots in any flavor, shape, or form (because they are basically small pieces of potato held together by bits of fat). All of these items have the fat baked right in them, for your convenience.

You're better off buying the shredded hashbrowns, so you can decide how much oil you prepare them with. You're also better off buying the lower-fat frozen french fries and baking them in your oven. (They already come slicked down with plenty of fat.) Avoid the tator tots altogether. Many of the Ore Ida® products come with very little sodium added. This way, you decide how much is added (as little as possible). Take a look below at the best and worst choices. The best choices are in bold.

Per 3-oz. portion:	Calories	Fat (gm.)	% of calories from fat
Ore Ida Southern Style Hash Browns	70	<1	<13%
Ore Ida Shredded Hash Browns	70	<1	<13%
Ore Ida Potato Wedges	110	2	16%
Ore Ida Country Style	110	2	16%
Lites Crinkle Cuts	90	2	20%
Ore Ida Golden Crinkles	110	4	33%
Ore Ida Golden Fries	120	3	22.5%
Ore Ida Shoestrings	150	6	36%
Ore Ida Golden Twirls	160	7	39%
Ore Ida Zesties	160	8	45%
Ore Ida Tater Tots, regular	160	8	45%
Ore Ida Toaster Hash Browns	171	8.6	45%
Ore Ida Golden Patties	156	8.4	48%
Ore Ida Crispy Crowns	190	11	52%
Ore Ida Crispers	220	13	53%

TIP #160 / RATE THE FROZEN PIZZAS.

For those times when you just want to reach inside your freezer and pull out a pizza, there are a few pretty good choices in the frozen-food section.

In general, buy the cheese selections and add your own vegetable or lean-meat toppings at home. (Leftover barbecued chicken works great!) Of the frozen cheese pizza selections, these are the better choices.

Per 6-oz. serving :	Calories	Fat (gm.)	% of calories from fat
Weight Watchers®			
Deluxe Combo	330	10	27%
Veal Sausage	310	8	23%
Pepperoni	320	10	28%
Stouffer's Lean Cuisine®			
French Bread			
Cheese Pizza	310	10	29%
Healthy Choice®			
French Bread Pizza, Cheese	300	3	9%
French Bread Pizza, Deluxe	330	8	22%
Healthy Slices®			
(McCain Ellio's)			
Garden Style,			
Mixed Vegetable	300	4	12%
Cheese	320	4	11%

TIP #161 / CHECK OUT THE NEW SOUPS.

Cans are not just for high-fat, high-salt soups anymore. There is a whole new generation of lighter, leaner soups on the supermarket shelves.

If you have poo-pooed canned soups in the past, you might want to give these new soups a second look, especially the newest family of low-fat, lower-sodium soups. And we're not just talking about the "clear" or broth-based soups either. Campbell's Healthy Request® 98 percent Fat-Free Cream of Mushroom, Cream of Broccoli or Celery, and Cream of Chicken soups work great in casseroles.

The original versions of the cream of mushroom and chicken soup (still available under the regular Campbell's® line) contain 40 more calories and 5 more grams of fat per 8-ounce prepared serving. And when it comes to the condensed creamy soups that call for added milk, remember you can always add skim or 1% milk to make sure you're adding the least amount of fat possible.

Soup is a creative way to use leftover pasta, rice, beans, vegetables, or meat. Just add bite-sized pieces to your canned soup, and no one will even notice there are leftovers in there. About the only food group you won't find in commercial soup is fruit. (You can add the dairy group in condensed canned cream soups).

Low-Fat Soups

Per 3-oz. portion:	Calories	Fat (gm.)	% of calories from fat	Sodium
Tomato Based:				
Campbell's Ready-to-Serve Healthy Request®				
Hearty Minestrone	90	2	20%	420
Healthy Choice Ready-to-Serve®				
(per 7.5 oz. serving)				
Tomato Garden	130	3	21%	510
Minestrone	160	1	6%	520
Campbell's Condensed Soup®				
Tomato Soup	90	2	20%	670
Progresso Healthy Classics®				
(per 9.5 oz. serving)				
Tomato	90	2	20%	1120
Hearty Minestrone	90	2	20%	760
Minestrone	120	3	22.5%	910
Broth Based:				
Progresso Healthy Classics®				
(per 9.5 oz. serving)				
Chicken Rice	80	2	22.5%	440
Chicken & Wild Rice	120	3	22.5%	850
Vegetable	90	1	10%	810
Chicken Noodle	90	2	20%	870
Chicken Barley	110	3	24.5%	790
Chicken Rice with Vegetables	120	3	22.5%	800
Tortellini in Chicken Broth	80	2	22.5%	870
Campbell's Ready-to-Serve Healthy Request®				
Hearty Chicken Noodle	120	2	15%	460
Hearty Chicken Vegetable	80	2	22.5%	470
Hearty Chicken Rice	110	3	24.5%	480
Hearty Vegetable Beef	120	2	15%	460
Vegetable	90	1	10%	480

Per 3-oz. portion:	Calories	Fat (gm.)	% of calories from fat	Sodium
Campbell's Condensed Healthy Request Soups®				
Vegetable Beef	90	2	20%	500
Chicken Rice	60	2	30%	480
Chicken Noodle	60	2	30%	460
Healthy Choice Ready to Serve®				
(per 7.5-oz. serving)				
Turkey Vegetable	110	3	25%	540
Chicken Pasta	100	2	18%	560
Garden Vegetable	100	1	9%	560
Country Vegetable	120	1	8%	540
Chicken Rice	90	1	10%	510
Chicken Noodle	90	2	20%	540
Beef and Potato	110	1	8%	550
Vegetable Beef	130	1	7%	530

Bean Soups:

	Calories	Fat (gm.)	% of calories from fat	Sodium
Healthy Choice Ready to Serve®				
Split Pea & Ham	170	3	16%	460
Bean and Ham	220	4	16%	480
Lentil	140	1	6%	480
Campbell's Condensed Soup®				
Split Pea	160	4	22.5%	780
Progresso Healthy Classics®				
(per 9.5-oz. serving)				
Hearty Black Bean	140	2	13%	820
Lentil	130	2	14%	840

Creamy Soups:

	Calories	Fat (gm.)	% of calories from fat	Sodium
Campbell's Ready to Serve Healthy Request®				
Clam Chowder	100	3	27%	490
Campbell's Condensed Healthy Request®				
Cream of Mushroom	60	2	30%	480
Cream of Chicken	70	2	26%	490
Campbell's Condensed Soup®				
Clam Chowder				
(prepared with 2% milk)	130	4	26%	940

TIP #162 / CUT THE CREAM IN CANNED SOUPS.

On a cold winter's day, there's something about creamy clam chowder, with a dash of freshly ground black pepper, that just hits the spot. You can easily cut the fat in cream soups that come in the can just by using skim or 1% milk, instead of whole milk. Take a look at the table below to see how the savings add up.

Creamy soup Per 3-oz. serving:	Calories	Fat (gm.)	% of calories from fat
New England Clam Chowder			
with whole milk	150	6	36%
with 2% milk	130	4	28%
with 1% milk	128	3	21%
with skim milk	122	2	15%

TIP #163 / MOOO-VE OVER TO LOWER-FAT MILK.

Take it from a veteran 1% milk drinker: Ease your little ones off the creamy thick stuff. You may want to pour half whole and half 2% milk for a week or so. Then bring them down to straight 2% milk. Then if you think you can take them down one or more fat notches, go ahead and use half 2% and half 1% for a week or two. Then graduate to straight 1% milk.

What can you save just by switching to a lower-fat milk if you typically drink about two 8-ounce glasses of milk every day? Look at the table below to compare the savings. You also gain a little more calcium and a wee bit more protein when you switch to the lower-fat milks. How can this be? When they remove fat, they lose volume, so it takes more of this de-fatted milk to equal one cup. This is the part that contains the calcium and protein.

Savings:* from whole to 2%, from whole to 1%, from whole to skim

	from whole to 2%	from whole to 1%	from whole to skim
Calories	50	90	117
Fat, gm.	6.6	11.2	14.8
Saturated fat	4	7	9
Cholesterol	29.6 mg.	46.8	56.4

Bonus Nutrients * (When you switch to lower-fat milks you actually get more of these nutrients.)

Calcium	+42 mg. more	+42 mg.	+50 mg.
Protein	+1 gm.	+1 gm.	+1.5 gm.
Sodium	+18 mg.	+18 mg.	+20 mg.

Savings and increases are for two 8-oz. glasses of milk.

How Low Are You Willing To Go?

1 cup	Whole	2% low-fat	1% low-fat	Skim with nonfat milk solids
Calories	149	124	104	90
Protein	8 gm.	8.5 gm.	8.5 gm.	8.75 gm.
Fat	8 gm.	4.7 gm.	2.4 gm.	0.6 gm.
Saturated Fat	5.0	2.9	1.5	0.4
Cholesterol	33.2 mg.	18.4 mg.	9.8 mg.	5 mg.
Calcium	291 mg.	312 mg.	312 mg..	316 mg.

I find 1% milk ideal because it isn't as thin and fluorescent as skim, but it has almost the same nutritional advantages. It looks, tastes, and feels like 2% milk while having half the fat. If you don't have 1% available in your state, you can make your own by mixing 2% milk with skim.

TIP #164 / DON'T GIVE YOUR KIDS CANDY FOR BREAKFAST.

You expect something like a Snickers® bar or Nestles Krunch® bar to be full of fat and sugar because it's "candy." But you don't expect it in a breakfast cereal—especially one with "oat bran," "with 8 essential vitamins and minerals," or "bran flakes" in its name.

When you start looking at the percent of calories from sugar, and sometimes the percent of calories from fat, in many of the most popular cereals, it's almost as if your children are eating candy for breakfast! This wouldn't be quite so horrific if our children didn't eat these cereals on a near daily basis—but many of them do.

Here are some of the cereals highest in sugar and fat:

1 ounce	% of calories from sugar	Calories	Fat (gm.)	% of calories from fat	Sodium (mg.)
Cap'N Crunch®	40%	120	2	15%	220
Trix®	44%	110	1	8%	140
Lucky Charms®	44%	110	1	8%	180
Cookie Crisp®	47%	110	1	8%	140
Fruit Loops®	47%	110	1	8%	125
Smacks®	55%	110	1	8%	70
Cracklin' Oat Bran®	25%	110	3	25%	140
Nature Valley Granola®	27%	120	5	38%	NA

Compare these with a candy bar:

| 1-oz. Snickers® | 51% | 134 | 7 | 43% | 79 |
| 1-oz. Almond Joy® | 48% | 151 | 8 | 47% | 48 |

TIP #165 / CHOOSE A LOW-FAT BREAKFAST IN A BOX.

With about 150 different types of breakfast cereal being sold, it's no small task to go about choosing one. Do you buy a cereal simply on its fiber merits? Do you forget about the grams of fat and surrender to sugar and sodium?

You would think with so many cereals on the market there would be at least a handful that measure up in the fiber department without exploiting sugar, fat, and sodium. Well, thank goodness there are—but you have to wade through quite a few boxes and nutrition labels to find them.

What you definitely do not want to do is choose a cereal simply because it looks or sounds like it's high in fiber. Believe me, it's worth taking it a step further and actually checking the nutrition label on the side panel for it's true fiber value (grams of fiber per serving). But don't stop there. Make sure you investigate the grams of fat and grams of "sucrose and other sugars" per serving. You may also want to check the sodium, especially if you or someone in your family has high blood pressure or is on a low-sodium diet.

I'm afraid in some cases a spoonful of sugar (or fat) is helping the medicine go down. In one wheat-bran cereal, 40 percent of the calories come from sugar. And while one popular oat-bran cereal contains a seemingly impressive amount of fiber (13 gm. per 1 1/2 cups), along with this fiber comes 13 gm. of fat. A well-known granola cereal contains a whopping 30 gm. of fat in a 1 1/2-cup serving!

But, luckily, you have two choices. You can either rummage through a hundred cereal box labels with pencil, paper, and calculator in hand (looking for a diamond in the rough), or you can save yourself the trouble and frustration, since I've already done that. Take a look at the first table below, where the cereals are listed from the highest in fiber to the lowest in fiber. The second table lists the low-fat cereals, with less than 4 gm. of fiber, from the lowest in added sugars to the highest. Cereals with more than 25 percent of calories from "sucrose and other sugars" or more than 5 gm. of fat are not listed, no matter what their fiber content.

Cereals with 4 gm. or more of fiber per 1 1/2-cup serving (unless otherwise noted)

Brand	Fiber (gm.)	Calories	Fat (gm.)	Sodium (mg.)	% of calories from sugar
All Bran® with extra fiber, 2/3 cup	28	100	0	280	0
Bran Chex®	13.5	234	2	681	18%
Fruit & Fibre®, Peaches/Almond	11	269	4.5	381	17%
Fruit & Fibre®, Dates/walnuts	11	269	4.5	381	20%
Most®	9.7	262	1	412	24%
Shredded Wheat® 'N Bran	9	202	1	0	0
Shredded Wheat® with Oat Bran	9	224	2.2	0	0
Kellogg's 40% Bran Flakes®	8	190	1	453	22%

Brand	Fiber (gm.)	Calories	Fat (gm.)	Sodium (mg.)	% of calories from sugar
Shredded Wheat®, small	7	228	1.4	6	3%
Frosted Mini-Wheats® (8-9 biscuits)	7	224	0	0	24%
Common Sense Oat Bran®	6	200	2	520	24%
Quaker Oat Bran®	6	200	4	250	16%
Quaker Oat Bran Squares®	6	300	3	405	24%
Muesli®, Apple/Almond 1 cup	6	300	4	280	13%
Muesli®, Almond/Date, 1 cup	6	280	4	190	14%
Post Raisin Bran®, 1.4 oz	6	120	1	200	23%
Wheat Chex®	5	252	1.7	462	7%
Wheaties®	4.5	152	0.7	414	11%
Just Right® with Fiber Nuggets	4.5	224	2.2	440	20%
Whole Wheat Total®	4.5	150	1.5	300	12%
Nutrigrain Wheat®	4.2	237	0.7	448	7%

Low-fat cereals with less than 4 gm. of fiber per 1 1/2-cup serving (unless otherwise noted)

Brand	Fiber (gm.)	Calories	Fat (gm.)	Sodium (mg.)	% of calories from sugar
Cheerios®	2	110	2	290	4%
Rice Chex®	NA	110	0	240	7%
Kellogg's Cornflakes®	1	100	0	290	8%
Triples®	NA	110	1	200	8%
Corn Chex®	NA	110	0	280	11%
Total Corn Flakes®	NA	110	<1	200	11%
Rice Krispies®	0	110	0	290	11%
Crispix®	1	110	0	220	11%
Kix®	NA	110	<1	260	11%
Wheat Chex®	3	100	1	230	12%
Multigrain Cheerios®	2	100	1	230	24%
Frosted Mini Wheats®	3	100	0	0	24%
Life®	2	100	2	150	24%

TIP #166 / GRAPPLE WITH GRANOLA.

In the early '70s, sometime between tofu and trail mix, granolas were born. Many folks considered granolas to be the most wholesome member of the breakfast-cereal family—what with all the whole oats, nuts, and dried fruit. Granola may have had its share of added oils and brown sugar, but by golly, at least it was "all natural." Besides, no one seemed to mind about such things as calories from fat back then.

After refined sugar became the nutritional villain of the '70s, a few companies started selling fruit-juice sweetened granolas (still available today). But the fats and oil remained unscathed—until now.

Now we have two lower-fat granolas on the supermarket shelf, Kellogg's Low-fat Granola® with Raisins and Quaker 100 Percent Natural Low-fat Granola®. They both taste as good (if not better) than their original high-fat versions. How did these companies accomplish such a feat? They simply used less oil and more nonfat milk when manufacturing these great-tasting, lower-fat granolas.

Instead of shoveling in 6 gm. of fat per ounce of cereal in the morning, you will be eating 2 gm. of fat. Instead of purchasing a 42-percent-of-calories-from-fat cereal, you will have the option of choosing a 15-percent-of-calories-from-fat cereal. Of course, brown sugar is still the third ingredient listed on the label, accounting for about 30 percent of the total calories.

TIP #167 / SORT OUT YOUR SAUSAGES.

What's better to pair with pancakes—bacon or sausage? Even though 78 percent of the calories in bacon comes from fat, bacon is better. What's better to top your pizza with, hamburger or pepperoni? Pepperoni is much higher in fat.

A measly 1-oz. sausage patty contains 105 calories, 9 gm. of fat, and 24 mg. of cholesterol. Obviously, if you usually eat two or three patties in a sitting, you will need to double or triple these numbers. And six puny pieces of pepperoni (weighing in at a little more than an ounce) total 164 calories, 14.5 gm. of fat, and 26 mg. of cholesterol.

We Americans don't stop there. We get into double trouble by pairing sausage with other food items also very high in fat, such as sausage and cheese on pizza, a sausage patty on a breakfast biscuit, or sausage links with eggs. We're better off linking sausage with low-fat, high-carbohydrate entrees like pancakes, pasta, and marinara sauce or a big french roll.

But that's not all. Today, we can do even better than that. We can now buy sausage products that have only half or one-third the fat. Keep in mind that the better-tasting reduced-fat sausages still contain a handsome amount of fat. If you are only up to taking a baby step toward low-fat eating, then try Jimmy Dean® Light turkey and pork sausage. One patty (1.2 oz. raw) of the light type contains 7 gm. of fat while the regular Jimmy Dean Sausage® contains 11 gm. per patty (1 ounce cooked).

If you are ready and willing to take it one giant step further, try a couple of the sausage products that contain 50 percent or two-thirds less fat:

2 oz. serving	Calories	Fat (gm.)	Cholesterol (mg.)	Sodium (mg.)
Regular pork sausage patty	210	18	48	??
Louis Rich®				
Turkey Smoked Sausage	80	6	40	500
Turkey Polska Kielbasa	90	6	40	500
Original Turkey Sausage	120	8	60	620
Hillshire Farms®				
Turkey Polska Kielbasa	90	5	N/A	N/A
Healthy Choice®				
Low-fat Polska Kielbasa	70	2	30	460
Low-fat Polska Links (2.3 oz.)	80	2	25	550
Low-fat Smoked Sausage	70	2	30	70
Armour Turkey Selects®				
Turkey Breakfast Sausage	120	8	NA	NA

TIP #168 / BRING HOME THE BACON—PROVIDED IT'S TURKEY.

In many homes, the word "breakfast" is synonymous with "bacon." Where would two eggs sunnyside up or three flap-jacks be without a couple of strips of bacon?

Believe it or not, in terms of fat and calories, you're better off with a side of bacon than sausage. Better still are the pseudo-bacons made from turkey. If you're used to the real pork-belly stuff, strips of light and dark turkey molded together might look kind of funny. But when each ounce of regular pork bacon (cooked) costs you 163 calories and 14 gm. of fat, it's no laughing matter.

I'm a bacon quiche and BLT lover from way back, so trust me when I tell you I've tried all the turkey bacons, some of which were as chewy as beef jerky and look like anything but bacon! There is only one, in my humble opinion, that comes close to mimicking not only the taste but the melt-in-your-mouth texture of real bacon; Louis Rich® Turkey Bacon. It crisps up and can crumble into pieces like the real thing. Here's how an ounce of each compares:

	Louis Rich Turkey Bacon 1 oz. (approx. 3 strips)	Pork Bacon 1 oz. (approx. 4 strips)
Calories	105	163
Fat	9 gm.	14 gm.
Cholesterol	30 mg.	24 mg.
Sodium	600 mg.	452 mg.

A BLT made with three strips of Louis Rich Turkey Bacon and a teaspoon of nonfat mayo (on two large slices of whole-wheat bread with a few slices of tomato and a couple leaves of lettuce) adds up to 296 calories, 11 gm. fat, 32 mg. cholesterol, 1,038 mg. sodium, 19 percent of calories from protein, 47 percent from carbohydrate, and 34 percent from fat.

Compare this with a BLT made with an ounce (four strips) of pork bacon and a teaspoon of real mayo; 365 calories, 18.5 gm. of fat (44 percent of calories from fat), and 805 mg. of sodium.

TIP #169 / TALK TURKEY— LIGHT AND DARK.

All poultry parts are not created equal—nutritionally speaking, that is. Generally, the dark meat parts contain more fat and cholesterol (and more iron) than the light meat parts. This is probably why the chicken breast became a national symbol of health and dieting.

	Calories	Fat (gm.)	Saturated fat, (gm.)	Cholesterol (mg.)	Iron (mg.)
1 Roasted Chicken Breast, no skin (3 oz., cooked)	139	3	0.9	72	0.9
1 Roasted Chicken Thigh, no skin (3 oz., cooked)	177	9.3	2.6	81	1.1

TIP #170 / TAKE IT OFF—THE
SKIN, THAT IS.

When in doubt, take it off—take it all off—because poultry skin (no matter how cooked and crispy) contributes fat and saturated fat. You skeptically wonder, "How much fat could I possibly cut by peeling off a thin layer of skin?" Try half! That's right. A chicken breast without the skin contains less than half the fat of a breast with skin. And a chicken thigh without the skin contains 4 gm. less fat than a chicken thigh with skin.

Take a look at the actual numbers below:

	Calories	Fat (gm.)	Saturated fat (mg.)	Cholesterol (mg.)
Roasted Chicken Breast with skin	193	7.6	2	82
Roasted Chicken Breast no skin	141	3	.9	73
Roasted Chicken Thigh with skin	153	9.6	2.7	58
Roasted Chicken Thigh no skin	108	5.7	1.6	49

TIP 171 / BEWARE OF "NINETY-SOMETHING" CLAIMS.

While "thirtysomething" is now out, "ninetysomething" has never been more popular. You see ninetysomething-percent fat-free plastered across everything from Hostess® Cupcakes to turkey bologna. When you see this advertising claim, STOP. Do not pass GO. Strike this statement from your cognitive memory. It doesn't mean what you probably think it means.

This percentage refers to the percentage of fat in weight, *not calories*. This has absolutely nothing to do with the percent of calories from fat—a much more useful measurement of the product's fat status.

One company recently released some new "light" frozen-food options. But according to the Washington, D.C., watchdog agency, Citizens of Science in the Public Interest, this company really didn't lighten-up anything. They simply computed the percent of fat by weight in the regular, non-light line to be 5 percent and then slid "95 percent fat-free" onto the corner of the new box. What will "95 percent fat-free" get you in terms of fat grams and percent of calories from fat? More than you think! Their lasagna still gets 39 percent of its 300 calories from fat (13 gm. fat) and the steak gets 45 percent of its 260 calories from fat (13 gm. fat)—frighteningly close to the amount of fat in their regular line of lasagna and Salisbury steak.

How can these companies get away with this? Simple. They're not lying. Because water accounts for much of the weight, the percent of fat by weight is misleadingly low.

Whole milk is a perfect example of how this deception can work. Whole milk is 4 percent milk fat by weight, right? This is because most of the weight in milk comes from water. So theoretically the claim "96 percent fat-free" could decorate this milk carton. But 1 cup of whole milk still has more than 9 gm. of fat, which computes to about 50 percent of calories from fat.

I can't resist giving you just one more ninetysomething example. Butterball's® 80 percent fat-free turkey bologna and 80 percent fat-free turkey pastrami certainly sound like healthful alternatives. They're made from turkey, for Pete's sake! Well, I'm sorry to report these two have just as much fat as their higher-fat mentors, bologna and pastrami made from beef and pork (about 6 gm. of fat per 1-ounce slice and 77 percent of calories from fat).

TIP #172 / CUT THE COLD-CUT CONFUSION.

Are you looking for some assistance to the "what to fill my family's sandwiches with" question? Well, you won't find relief in the cold-cut section of your supermarket. There are at least four times more choices today than there were 10 years ago.

Once you start venturing out from your usual sandwich selections, you might discover one-third-less-fat salami, turkey bologna, thinly sliced smoked turkey breast, lean honey ham—it's enough to make you dizzy with decisions.

But the good news is never before have we had so many lower-fat coldcuts to choose from, as you can see from some of the selections below:

2 oz. serving	Calories	Fat (gm.)	Cholesterol (mg.)	Sodium (mg.)
Hillshire Farms®				
Chicken Breast	50	<1	20	690
Smoked Chicken				
Breast	50	<1	20	580
Honey Ham	60	2	20	600
Smoked Ham	60	<2	30	660
Louis Rich®				
Deli Thin Turkey	60	2	25	625
Turkey Breast	60	2	20	660
Turkey Bologna	90	6	30	560
Turkey Pastrami	63	<2.5	37	650
Turkey Salami	90	6	40	580
Oscar Mayer—Healthy Favorites®				
Ham	54	<2	27	459
Deli Chicken	57	2	23.5	470
Deli Turkey	57	2	23.5	470
*Beef Light Bologna	140	10	30	640
Gallo®				
*Light Salami				
12 slices/2 oz.	165	11.8	NA	708

These products still have a substantial amount of fat.

TIP #173 / KEEP AN EYE ON THE KIDS' CONDIMENT QUIRKS.

We all can be a little quirky when it comes to condiments, insisting on mustard for our hot dog but catsup for our burger, or spreading Dijon mustard on one side of our sandwich and mayo on the other. Some of us may even relish relish!

But depending which condiments you choose and how heavy-handed you are, you can transform your lunch into the sandwich from hell, nutritionally speaking. If you think a knifeful of mayo here and a spoonful of tartar sauce there isn't going to do too much dietary damage, don't bet on it.

Condiment Scenario #1—You go to the effort of selecting the new "light" breaded fish filets from Van de Kamp's with one-third fewer calories and less fat, but then you methodically spoon on a couple tablespoons of tartar sauce. With that wave of your hand, your fish filet jumped from 12 gm. of fat and 250 calories to 28 gm. of fat and 400 calories!

Condiment Scenario #2—As you make your sandwich you think to yourself, "I can't believe I finally found a brand of ham slices that are '96 percent fat-free' with 2 gm. of fat per ounce." But then you dip your knife into that habit-forming jar of mayonnaise. Adding just 1 tablespoon of mayonnaise to your ham sandwich (2 slices of bread, lettuce and tomato, and 3 ounces of lean ham) transforms your noontime nourishment into a high-fat food (from 285 calories and about 7 gm. of fat with 1 teaspoon mustard to 380 calories and 18 gm. of fat with 1 tablespoon mayonnaise).

As you can see from the following table listing all the condiments and their nutritional stats, when it comes to counting fat and calories there are four in particular to watch out for:

mayonnaise, tartar sauce, thousand island dressing, and light mayonnaise. Mayonnaise tops the chart with one measly tablespoon adding 11 gm. of fat and 100 calories.

There are people out there who buy mayonnaise by the gallon. I know because I've befriended a few myself. I call them mayo-holics because there are few foods they don't put mayonnaise on. I have to admit, it's a little difficult for me to understand the attraction to this egg yolk-oil emulsion. Switching to the "light" mayos will definitely make a difference, but at 5 gm. of fat and 50 calories per tablespoon you still have to take them "lightly."

If you're the type that won't miss the mayo but gets tempted by tartar sauce, you'll be happy to know there is now a fat-free tartar sauce (Kraft-Free® Nonfat Tartar Sauce). And you can always make you own by mixing one of the reduced-calorie or nonfat mayos with your choice of relish.

Concerning sodium, the six highest condiments are: soy sauce (1028 mg. per tablespoon), teriyaki sauce (689 mg. per tablespoon), A1 Steak Sauce (280 mg. per tablespoon) ,chili sauce-tomato (228 mg. per tablespoon), mustard (196 mg. per tablespoon), and catsup (182 mg. per tablespoon).

15 of the Most Common Condiments:

Per 1 Tbsp.	Calories	Fat (gm.)	Cholesterol (mg.)	Sodium (mg.)
Best Foods® Mayo	100	11	5	80
Tartar sauce	74	8	7	99
Thousand Island dressing	60	6	4	varies
Best Foods® "Light" Mayo	50	5	5	115

Low-cal Thousand Island	20	2	8	varies
Relish	21	0.1	0	109
Chili sauce-tomato	18	0	0	228
Catsup	16	0	0	182
Teriyaki sauce	15	0	0	689
BBQ sauce	12	0.3	0	127
A-1 Steak Sauce	12	0	0	280
Soy sauce	9.5	0	0	1028
Horseradish	6	0	0	15
Salsa (approximate)	6	0.4	0	varies
Chili sauce-hot red pepper	3	0	0	4

The Condiment Kids Love—Catsup

I recently watched my 20-month-old dip everything on her plate, including baby carrots, oven fries, turkey hot dogs, and her fingers into a pile of catsup. Kids love catsup. And why not? From a kid's point of view what's not to love—sugar, salt, and ripe tomatoes?

Catsup's high sugar and salt content has always bothered health professionals and parents alike. Personally, I have never been too concerned about catsup for two reasons:

#1. How much catsup are we really talking about here? Even my little catsup monger can only consume a tablespoon or two at a time.

#2. What are our alternatives for dipping, squirting, or spreading? Catsup is definitely the least of many evils, including mayonnaise, special sauce, Thousand Island dressing, and tartar sauce.

I know, there's always Colonel Mustard in the kitchen with 4 calories, 0.2 gm. fat, and 65 mg. sodium per teaspoon. Its nutritional profile isn't too bad, but I don't know many kids that go gah-gah over mustard. Let's just say it isn't exactly the kids' condiment of choice.

And to help sway you into the catsup camp, there's a new generation of lite catsups on the supermarket shelf that have less sugar and salt. They have half the calories and one-third less salt of regular catsup, to be specific. This brings it down to 8 calories and 115 mg. sodium per table-spoon. Catsup has always had zero fat and cholesterol.

Compare these condiments:

I Tbsp.	Calories	Fat (gm.)	Sodium (mg.)	Cholesterol (mg.)
Catsup	16	0	15	0
Heinz Lite Ketchup®	8	0	115	0
Mustard	12	0.6	19	0
Mayonnaise	99	11	78	8
Best Foods light mayo	50	5	115	5
Best Foods reduced-fat mayo	40	3	160	N/A

Kraft Free® mayo	8	0	125	0
Tartar sauce	74	8	99	7
Kraft Free® tartar sauce	10	0	120	0
Thousand Island dressing	59	5.5	109	4
Kraft Free® Thousand Island Dressing	16	0	130	0
Dijonnaise®	36	3	210	N/A

TIP #174 / CUT THE CHEESE.

There are really two ways to cut the fat in half when Mr. Cheese comes a' visiting: choose lower fat cheeses, or buy regular fat cheeses but use half as much. Being an over-achiever, I, of course, prefer doing both.

You can indeed get the flavor you want without all the fat when you buy lower-fat cheeses. The trick is buying the lower-fat cheeses that have been aged a little longer, which develops their flavors further. Reduced-calorie sharp cheddar or Swiss and Jarlsburg Light part-skim cheeses are good examples. There are at least two lower-fat sharp cheddars on the market: Cracker Barrel® Light Sharp Cheddar and Kraft Light Naturals Sharp Reduced-Fat Cheddar®.

Most regular fat cheeses, whether orange, white, processed, or aged, have around 106 calories, 25 mg. cholesterol, and 9 gm. of fat per ounce. But even the majority of the lower fat cheeses contain 80 to 90 calories, 20 mg. cholesterol, and 5 gm. of fat per ounce. The fat grams and calories can really add up in a dish composed primarily of melted, glistening cheese. So we need to teach our children (and ourselves) to sprinkle our food with cheese, not smother it. Slice it thin, not thick. Eat cheese with something, not alone.

Since even lower-fat cheese contains a handsome share of fat, the golden rule with cheese is to pair it with a food that's low in fat—like adding cheese to a potato, pile of pasta, or 2 slices of bread. We get into nutritional trouble when we add two high-fat foods together—like cheese to a hamburger or hot dog, or topping deep fried tortilla chips or high-fat crackers with cheese. If putting these two higher-fat foods together is inevitable in your house, then at least make sure you use the lower-fat cheeses as well as the lower-fat hot dogs, ground beef, chips, and crackers.

TIP #175 / PROMOTE 150-CALORIE SNACKS.

There comes a time in every child's morning or afternoon when they've just gotta have it! They have to have that snack. The munchies can strike without warning, hitting them right between the ears. You find yourself frantically reaching into that kitchen cabinet or diaper bag looking for something, anything to soothe the savage snack attack.

Don't get desperate. Get smart and plan ahead. Strategically place fairly harmless treats in your designated snack alert areas. How harmless is harmless? Well a 50- to 60-calorie snack may be fine for your furry feline friend, but it's a drop in the bucket for an older child's stomach. But 150 calories won't cause too much trouble, and if spent wisely on foods lower in fat and sugar, they're sure to satisfy.

What will 150 calories buy? That depends on whether your treat is loaded with fat and sugar. These two, especially the fat, can ring up the calories faster than you can spell S-n-i-c-k-e-r-s. For example, 150 calories will only buy you half of a 2.2-ounce Snickers® bar, while it is good for an entire NutriGrain® Cereal Bar.

The same 150 calories will also buy you 16 Pringles Light Potato Crisps, 20 Mr. Phipps Pretzel Chips, or more light butter-flavored microwave popping corn than you'll know what to do with (7 1/2 cups).

And, of course, you can't talk "snack" without mentioning the common cookie. Some cookies list fat as the first ingredient, others list sugar first. You want the ones that list flour first, then maybe sugar, then fat. The classic Oreo®, for example, lists sugar first. Cover it with fudge and the list reads, sugar, shortening, then finally flour. And while 150 calories will buy you three of the regular Oreos®, it won't even buy you 1 1/2 of the fudge-covered cookies.

There are some new cookies by Nabisco® and Pepperidge Farms® that are lower in fat (where the first ingredient is flour), but 150 calories still won't buy you a whole handful. You will get exactly 2 1/2 of the Pepperidge Farms Cranberry Honey® cookies or 1 2/3 of the Nabisco My Goodness Chocolate Chip Raisin Cookies® (although I admit this cookie is on the large size).

If a handful of snack food is what you're looking for, take a look at Nabisco Teddy Grahams®. (Flour is listed first, then sugar, then shortening.) Because they're bite-sized, for 150 calories you will end up holding 14 cute chocolate, honey, cinnamon, or vanilla teddy bears.

Of course, we all know we should be snacking on fruits and vegetables. Now here's where 150 calories can go the farthest! With 150 calories you can get more than four carrots, four cups raw zucchini sticks, 3 cups of watermelon, 2 cups apple slices, 1 1/2 cups of unsweetened canned peaches or applesauce, or 1 1/2 bananas. But at 3 o'clock in the afternoon, it's usually not an apple or celery sticks we're craving.

Here is a list of popular snack items. It may surprise you how much (or how little) 150 calories can buy of various snack products.

What will 150 calories buy? Items marked plus (+) have 30 percent or less of their calories from fat. Those marked minus (-) have more than 30 percent of calories from fat.

+ 1/2 bag of Butter Microwave Country Light Popping Corn® (30 percent of calories from fat, 4 gm. fat)

+ 30 animal cookies (21 percent of calories from fat, 3.5 gm. fat)

+ 20 Mr. Phipps Pretzel Chips® (15 percent of calories from fat, 2.5 gm. fat), lightly salted available

+ 16 Pringles Light Potato Crisps® (41 percent of calories from fat, 7 gm. fat)

+ 12 saltine crackers (25 percent of calories from fat, 4 gm. fat)

+ 6 large pretzel twists (3.25" X 2.25"), (8 percent of calories from fat, 1.2 gm. fat)

+ 4 breadsticks (7 percent of calories from fat, 1 gm. fat)

+ 3 Honey Maid® graham crackers (2 1/2" x 5"), 1 1/2 oz., 180 calories, (15 percent of calories from fat, 3 gm. fat)

- + 14 Nabisco Teddy Grahams® (30 percent of calories from fat, 5 gm. fat)

- + 1 Nutrigrain® Cereal Bar, 1.3 oz. each (30 percent of calories from fat, 5 gm. fat, and 29 percent of calories from sucrose and other sugars)

- + 3 fig bars (14 percent of calories from fat, 2.4 gm. fat)

- + 2 1/2 Pepperidge Farms Cranberry Honey® cookies, 1.3 oz., (25 percent of calories from fat, 5 gm. fat)

- + 1 1/2 Hostess® 97 Percent Fat Free Blueberry or Apple Streusel Muffin (about 9 percent of calories from fat, 1.5 gm. fat)

- + 1 slice of angel food cake, 1/12 of 10" tube pan (no fat)

- + 1 2/3 Nabisco My Goodness Chocolate Chip Raisin Cookies®, (30 percent of calories from fat, 5 gm. fat)

- + 2/3 of an Apple Cinnamon Pop-Tart® (26 percent of calories from fat, 4.3 gm. fat)

- - 11 Ruffle's® Potato Chips (60 percent of calories from fat, 10 gm. fat)

- - 10 Ritz® crackers (47 percent of calories from fat, 8 gm. fat)

- - 3 Tbsp. roasted cashews (68 percent of calories from fat, 12 gm. fat)

- - 2 1/2 Tbsp. macadamia nuts (88 percent of calories from fat, 16 gm. fat)

- - Less than 2 Keebler Chips Deluxe® cookies (56 percent of calories from fat, 9.4 gm.)

- - 1 1/3 Fudge Covered Oreo® Cookies (48 percent of calories from fat, 8 gm. fat)

- - 1/2 of a 2.2 oz. Snickers® bar (43 percent of calories from fat, 7 gm. fat)

TIP #176 / CRACK THE CRACKER CRUNCH.

There are almost as many varieties of crackers on the supermarket shelves as there are cookies! Now there are cheese crackers in the shape of fish and "wheat" crackers that are supposed to resemble vegetables. There are crackers with no salt, low salt, or high salt. You can buy your crackers with a little oat or wheat bran added.

When you're reading the nutrition information on the back of those cracker boxes, keep in mind that the information is usually based on a 1/2-oz. serving size. In my vast cracker experience, I have found 1 ounce is a much more realistic frame of reference.

Here is the nutrition information (per ounce) for the classic crackers, most of which are high in fat, followed by a list of low-fat crackers (containing 3 gm. of fat or less per ounce).

The Classic Crackers:
(from highest in fat *per ounce* to lowest)

	Calories	Fat (gm.)	% of calories from fat	Saturated fat (gm).	Sodium (mg.)
Ritz®	142	7.6	47%	1.8	230
Cheese crackers	136	6	40%	2.3	292
Thin wheat crackers	124	5	35%	1.8	245
Triscuits®	132	4.7	33%	1.3	158
Saltines	123	3.4	25%	0.8	312

The Low-Fat Crackers:

SnackWell's®
  Fat-free Cinnamon Graham Snack
* Reduced-fat Cheese Crackers
  Fat-free Wheat Crackers

Mister Salty®
* Fat-free Pretzel Twists and sticks

Mr. Phipps®
* Fat-free pretzel chips
* Lightly Salted pretzel chips
* Original pretzel chips

Nabisco®
* Premium Fat-free
* Zwieback

Natural Ry Krisp®
  Regular
  Seasoned

Old London® Melba Toast
  Rye
  White

Pepperidge Farms®
  English Water Biscuits

Sunshine
* **Krispy Unsalted Tops–Wasa**
  Hearty Rye
  Lite Rye
  Breakfast
  Golden Rye
  Extra Crisp

Kavli Norwegian
  Flatbread
  Thick Flat

* Crackers your child might be most likely to like.

Another little hint about buying crackers: Just because they claim to be low in saturated fat doesn't mean they're low in total fat. Be especially careful about the cheese-flavored options.

TIP #177 / BEWARE OF "BAKED, NOT FRIED."

Truckloads of snack products boast that they're "baked" not fried. Well, I've got news for them. You can bake in fat just as easily as you can fry it in. Case in point: the ever-popular chocolate chip cookie or flaky pie crust. They're "baked" and boy do they have oodles of fat. You might be interested to know that the "baked, not fried" Wheat Thin® family (Oat Thins®, Regular Wheat Thins®, and Nutty Wheat Thins®) all have at least 6 gm. of fat per 1-ounce serving (Nutty Wheat Thins have 8) and 39 percent of calories from fat (Nutty Wheat Thins have 51 percent).

The Nabisco® family came along with Better Cheddars, Vegetable Thins, and Chicken in a Biskit—advertised as "baked, not fried." Chicken in a Biskit tops the charts with 10 gm. of fat per 1-ounce serving, which is similar to an ounce of "fried" potato chips (56 percent of calories from fat).

Keebler® recently hopped on the "baked, not fried" bandwagon with their Keebler Munch'ems® line of potato chip-like crackers. Every flavor, except nacho and original flavor, contains 6 gm. of fat per 1-ounce serving (45 percent of calories from fat). The rather tasty nacho and original flavor Munch'ems shaved their fat down to 4 gm. per 1-ounce serving, with 30 percent of calories from fat.

TIP #178 / CHECK OUT THE GRAIN CLAIMS.

If these crackers are so "multigrain" that they were named after a particular whole grain, why is it that white flour is the first ingredient? In the case of Pepperidge Farm's® Pumpernickel Snack Sticks' list of ingredients, white flour is followed only by partially hydrogenated shortening. The third ingredient is finally rye meal; hence the name.

There is actually more shortening than there is whole wheat in Ritz Bits® with Whole Wheat. Although the whole-wheat Ritz® crackers do have 2 gm. less fat per 1-ounce serving than the regular Ritz, they are still pretty high in fat with 39 percent of the calories from fat.

When you read the front of the box of Pepperidge Farm's Wholesome Choice Multigrain Crackers® you picture at least three whole grains bursting from the seams. Although I was pleasantly surprised to find that these crackers have a moderate amount of fat (4 gm. per ounce, 26 percent of calories from fat), the first ingredient is flour, followed by whole-wheat flour then partially hydrogenated shortening. You don't find another "whole grain" until after you read sugar and cornstarch on the list of ingredients. Then finally you find barley flakes. Further down the list you find they add more invert syrup to make the crackers than they do the third type of "multigrain" and that's rice bran.

TIP #179 / KNOW WHAT THE SERVING SIZE IS.

Most cracker companies consider a serving to be 1/2 ounce of crackers. Almost every nutrition information label in the cracker section (including Mr. Phipp's Tater Crisps®) lists calories and grams of fat based on 1/2 ounce of crackers. Well, I sat and counted what half an ounce of crackers and Tater Crisps and Munch'ems would be, and if that's a serving—I'm Julia Childs! One ounce is a much more practical measurement.

So keep that in mind when you're reading labels for yourself.

TIP #180 / REMEMBER, SMALLER ISN'T ALWAYS BETTER.

When companies make "mini" versions of this and "bite-sized" renditions of that, something very interesting happens. With some products the down-sizing mysteriously adds a gram of fat or sugar (or both) per serving.

While an ounce of the regular-sized Frosted Mini-Wheats® cereal contains 6 gm. of sugar (24 percent of calories from sucrose and other sugars), the bite-sized version contains 7 gm. (28 percent of calories from sucrose and other sugars).

Nabisco tacked on a mighty 2 gm. of fat per ounce to make their Mini Chips Ahoy® cookies, compared with an ounce of the regular Chips Ahoy®. And in order to make their Cinnamon Graham Thin Bits® (bite-sized graham snacks),

Keebler also plopped on 2 gm. of fat per ounce compared with their regular-sized Cinnamon Crisp Grahams®. And Nabisco's Premium Bits® (mini Premium Crackers) contain 6 gm. of fat per ounce while the regular-sized Premium Crackers contain half that.

TIP #181 / DON'T BE FOOLED BY A HEALTHY NAME.

You don't have to look far in the cracker and cookie aisle to find products that refer to themselves as "oat bran" or "wheat." A little investigation into their true ingredient identity would call these items by another name.

Sunshine® Oat Bran Snack Crackers lists oat bran as its fifth ingredient. These crackers sure do look low in fat with "no cholesterol" listed on the front of the box. And for goodness sake these crackers are even shaped like hearts! But the second ingredient is none other than vegetable shortening, contributing 4 gm. of fat to each half ounce of crackers (45 percent of calories from fat).

Well at least Sunshine is consistent. Their Oat Bran Cookies with Nuts & Raisins lists oat bran (the fourth ingredient) after vegetable shortening and sugar. Each cookie (0.4 oz.) contains 60 calories, 3 gm. of fat, and 45 percent of calories from fat.

TIP 182 / CUT THE CREAM IN CREAM CHEESE.

For years now, I've been happily substituting Philadelphia Light Cream Cheese® (in tub) wherever the real thing was normally called for. But when you start adding it all up, 12 ounces of the light cream cheese, albeit half the fat of regular cream cheese, can still total a hefty sum of calories, fat, and cholesterol.

The 12-ounce portion equals 720 calories, 60 gm. of fat, and 120 mg. of cholesterol. That's about 60 gm. of fat I can do without. So when the fat-free version came out I was pleased as punch. But first, I had a couple of questions: How do they make this "no-fat" cream cheese and, probably more important, how does it taste?

Well, the fat-free Philadelphia® tasted better than I thought it would. In fact, I might even spread it on a bagel someday. But when used in a recipe, mixed with other flavorful ingredients, it works like a charm. So, how do they make it?

The fat-free cream cheese seems to be made by adding the cream cheese culture to protein-concentrated skim milk. Beyond skim milk it contains less than 2 percent of salt, sugar, cheese culture, artificial color, sodium tripolyphosphate, xanthan gum, carrageenan, potassium sorbate and calcium propionate (as preservatives), and finally vitamin A palmitate.

As a high-fat recipe modifier, I see Philadelphia® fat-free cream cheese not only as the beginning of a beautiful relationship with lower-fat cheesecake, but as a terrific substitute for some of the butter or margarine in cookies, spreads, and other rich and wonderful recipes. The fat-free cream cheese offers a similar texture to butter or margarine, a mild taste that won't compete with the other flavors in the recipe, and a creamy richness that is hard to duplicate with a bottle of applesauce or can of evaporated skim milk (commonly used fat substitutes).

	Calories	Fat (gm.)	Cholesterol (mg.)	Sodium (mg.)
Regular Philadelphia®	100	10	30	90
Philadelphia Light® (block)	70	6	20	115
Philadelphia Light® (in tub)	60	5	10	160
Healthy Choice® (in block)	30	0	5	200
Philadelphia-Free® (in tub)	25	0	5	170

TIP #183 / BEWARE OF "POPPING" PURE FAT IN MICRO-WAVE POPCORN.

Each generation of children seems to have its own "in" way of making popcorn. I'm of the foil-wrapped, stove-top, Jiffy-Pop®, generation. After that came the electric poppers with the plastic butter trays that never seemed to work quite right. And children today think popcorn is something you make in a microwave and eat from a bag, not a bowl.

Is this such a bad thing? Not if you grab the right bag. Some of the regular calorie microwave popping corns actually have 2 to 5 gm. more fat and up to 70 more calories (per 3 1/3 cup serving) than the now old-fashioned, oil-popped popcorn. Listed below are the lightest of the "lite" popcorns. In this table, I'm comparing "real" serving sizes—like half the bag. They say 4 2/3 servings per bag. That doesn't happen at my house.

Ironically, for many brands, the butter flavor has less sodium than the natural flavor. And for one popular brand, the butter flavor actually has less fat too. Go figure!

Brand per 1/2 bag	Calories	Fat (gm.)	Sodium (mg.)
Orville Reddenbacher's®			
Light Butter (50 percent less fat)	173	8.5	541
Light Natural (50 percent less)	173	8.5	628
Jolly Time®			
Light Butter	163	4.7	245
Light Natural	187	7	303
Pop Secret®			
Light Butter	180	8	320
Light Natural	180	8	400
Country Light®			
Butter	150	3.8	281
Natural	150	3.8	281
Jiffy®			
Light Butter	160	6	460

TIP #184 / CHECK OUT WHAT "LITE" REALLY MEANS.

Lite compared with what? A very important question when inspecting foods advertising this attribute. Ben & Jerry's® light vanilla ice cream (7 gm. fat per half cup) is indeed "lighter" in fat and calories than their regular, super rich and creamy premium ice creams (17 gm. fat per 1/2 cup). But the light version has just as many calories and fat as "regular" full fat ice creams (around 7 gm. fat per 1/2 cup). By the way, the tofu-based ice cream substitute called Toffuti® actually contains more fat than the regular ice creams (11 gm. fat per 1/2 cup).

TIP #185 / TRY SOMETHING COOL AFTER SCHOOL.

It never fails. Right about 3:30, after all the kids have returned home from school, you can hear the faint sound of the ice-cream truck weaving its way through every street where children play. It doesn't take long for children to become conditioned to the monotonous tune blasting from the ice-cream truck. Even my two-year-old will wake up from a sound nap as the truck passes, with visions of Push-Ups® and Popsicles® dancing in her head.

It seems to me, this whole business is based on the fact that most kids want something cool after school in spring or any time of day in summer. Which are the best choices? All of the items listed below are fairly low in fat and, therefore, usually calories, and none contain sugar as the first ingredient. If the ice-cream truck doesn't carry any of these, stock your freezer with a healthful variety of cool treats.

	Size	Calories	Fat (gm.)	% of calories from fat
Weight Watchers®				
Sugar Free Orange Vanilla Treats	1.75 oz	30	<1	<30%
Vanilla Sandwich Bar	2.75 oz	150	3	18%
Klondike Light®				
Sandwiches	2.8 oz	90	2	20%
Haagen-Dazs®				
Frozen Yogurt Bars	2.3 oz	100	1	9%
Strawberry Daiquiri, Peach, Pina Colada, Raspberry				
(generally water, fruit puree, sugar, and corn syrup for the sorbet and skim milk, fruit puree, sugar and corn syrup, cream for the yogurt part)				
Dole Fruit 'n Juice Bars®		70	<1	<13%
strawberry and raspberry				
Pine-Orange-Banana		60	<1	<15%
Kool-Aid Pumps®	2.75 oz	70	1	13%
(skim milk, water, sugar, corn syrup, cream, gelatin)				
JELL-O				
Pudding Pops®	1.75 oz	80	2	22.5%
(skim milk, sugar, corn syrup, hydrogenated coconut and palm oils)				
Fudgsicle® (ice-milk)				
Fudge Bars	2 1/2 oz	100	1	9%
(nonfat milk, sugar, corn syrup solids, whey, milk fat, cocoa..)				
Welch's®				
Fruit Juice Bars	1.75 oz	45	0	0
grape, strawberry, raspberry				
(water, grape juice concentrate (white or regular), sugar, fruit juice or fruit puree.)				

TIP #186 / PUT PUDDING IN ITS PROPER PLACE.

If you have a pudding lover in your house, I recommend the instant puddings in a box. They're a snap to make, and you can use whatever lower fat milk you like.

There are sugar-free versions available in almost all the flavors, too. This is probably more of an option if your child doesn't eat or drink many other artificially sweetened foods. I personally don't think it's a good idea to use so many artificially sweetened foods that artificial sweeteners become a major food group for our children.

Pudding has a few things going for it nutritionally. Milk is a major ingredient, so pudding is usually high in protein and calcium. (Half a cup contains about 150 mg. of calcium, more than 15 percent of the RDA). Also, because you can use low-fat or nonfat milk, you can cut the fat at least in half. Here are two types of puddings and their nutritional profiles with nonfat, 1% 2% , and whole milk:

	Calories	Fat (gm.)	% of calories from fat	Protein (gm.)	Sodium (mg.)
JELL-O® Sugar-Free Chocolate Instant Pudding					
•with skim milk	85	1	14%	5	383
•with 1% milk	92	2	21.5%	5	384
•with 2% milk	100	3	27%	5	380
JELL-O® Instant French Vanilla Pudding					
•with skim milk	135	.3	2%	4	350
•with 1% milk	142	1	8%	4	350
•with whole milk	160	4	22.5%	4	400

Prepared Pudding Packs

What could be simpler than opening a box and mixing its contents with milk? Buying pudding that is already made of course! Most of these come in individual serving cups, making them convenient for home or for stowing in a lunch box.

But many of these puddings contain 4 to 6 gm. of fat per serving (25 to 30 percent of calories from fat). And watch out for the pudding labels that read "made with skim milk" or "no tropical oils." Many of these puddings still contain partially hydrogenated oils in their ingredient lists and may not be low in fat.

These are the puddings that contain less than 10 percent of calories from fat and no more than 1 gm. of fat per serving:

4- or 4 1/2-oz. servings	Calories	Fat (gm.)	% of calories from fat
Hershey's Free Hershey's Kisses® Chocolate Pudding and Chocolate and Vanilla Swirl	100	0	0
JELL-O® Free Chocolate and Vanilla Swirls Pudding	100	0	0
Del Monte Snack Cups® Lite Chocolate and Vanilla Pudding	100	1	9%
Hunt's Snack Pack Light® Chocolate Pudding	100	1	9%
Swiss Miss® Light Vanilla Chocolate Parfait Pudding Snack	100	1	9%

TIP #187 / BUY ICE CREAM WISELY.

Where I come from (California), ice cream is a way of life. So this is an important food to skim the fat from.

Carefully choosing the ice cream to buy for your children can make a difference of 10 gm. of fat or more per half-cup scoop. And thank goodness the three-flavor ice milk of yesteryear (chocolate, vanilla, and strawberry) is gone and the age of fancy, assorted "light" ice creams is here to stay.

What do I mean by fancy? Try cookies-and-cream, marble fudge, pralines-and-cream, and strawberry swirl. But (you knew there had to be a "but") you have to be a cautious consumer because all ice creams labeled "light" aren't necessarily low in fat. And you need to check the fat content for each individual flavor within a particular brand.

The better choices in the ice cream section are the ones with:

- no more than 25 percent of calories from fat,

- 2 gm. or less of fat per 3-ounce serving or 3 gm. or less fat per 4-ounce serving (1/2 cup)

Also, find an ice cream that doesn't have sugar as the first ingredient. Milk should come first. After all, it's supposed to be a "dairy" product.

Here are the choices in my supermarket that met these guidelines and a few popular brand flavors that just missed them (with 4 gm. of fat per 1/2 cup serving):

Knudsen Nice 'N Light®, 4 oz. (Chocolate, Chocolate Marble, Neopolitan, Strawberry Swirl, Chocolate Chip, Cookies & Cream), 2 to 3 gm. fat, 100 to 120 calories, 18-22 percent of calories from fat

Stouffer's Lean Cuisine® Strawberry, 4 oz., 3 gm. fat, 120 calories, 22.5 percent of calories from fat

Dreyer's Grand Light Vanilla®, 4 oz., 4 gm. fat, 100 calories, 36 percent of calories from fat

Breyer's Light®, Vanilla, 1/2 cup, 4 gm. fat, 120 calories, 30 percent of calories from fat

Baskin Robbins 31®

- Fat-free Just Peachy, 0 fat, 100 calories, no calories from fat.
- Light Strawberry Royal , 3 gm. fat, 110 calories, 24.5 percent of calories from fat
- Light Double Chocolate, 3 gm. fat, 110 calories, 24.5 percent calories from fat

TIP #188 / STEER TOWARD FROZEN YOGURT.

Over the past few years, frozen yogurt has really come of age. There are almost as many brands and flavors of frozen yogurt as there are ice creams. Actually, when you read the ingredient list and nutrition information label on the packages of the lower-fat frozen yogurts and "light" ice creams, frozen yogurt starts looking more like a twin than a stepsister.

The first ingredient listed for the lower-fat frozen yogurts is usually nonfat milk or cultured skim milk, followed by some sweetener like sugar or a high-fructose corn sweetener. Breyer's frozen yogurt even lists "cream" as its second ingredient.

When buying frozen yogurt for your kids, always keep these two words in mind: Don't Assume! Don't assume that if it's frozen yogurt, it's better for your kids than ice cream. And don't assume if one or two flavors in the brand are low in fat that all the flavors will follow suit.

So what do you do? Three words—READ THE LABEL. Just as there are outrageously high-fat "gourmet" ice creams out there, there are "gourmet" frozen yogurts to be leery of, too.

To get you started, here are some of the better frozen yogurts. These products contain no more than 25 percent of calories from fat, 2 gm. or less of fat per 3-ounce serving or 3 gm. or less of fat per 4-ounce serving (1/2 cup). And they don't have sugar listed as the first ingredient.

- Honey Hill Farms Soft Style®, less than 1 gm. fat per half cup, 130 calories, less than 7 percent of calories from fat

- Colombo Shoppe Style®, Soft Low-fat Frozen Yogurt, most flavors (except Peanut Butter Twist) 3 oz., 1 gm. fat, 90 calories, 10 percent of calories from fat

- Dreyer's® Frozen Yogurt Inspirations, (Boysenberry, Vanilla Swirl, Marble Fudge, Orange, Vanilla Swirl, 4 oz., 3 gm. fat, 100 to 110 calories, 25 to 27 percent of calories from fat

- Dannon® Light Frozen Yogurt (Peach, Vanilla, Chocolate, Cherry Vanilla Swirl) 4 oz., less than 1 gm. fat, 80 to 90 calories, less than 10 percent of calories from fat (contains NutraSweet®)

Be Adventurous: Add Fruits & Vegetables to Everyday Recipes

When you're first learning to cut fat, it's tempting to stay with the most basic cooking. But you need not be afraid to move on to more adventurous ground. Here are a dozen recipes to get you started.

TIP #189 / DAZZLE 'EM WITH THIS PORK FRIED RICE.

1 1/2 cup diced barbecue-style pork
1 cup snow peas, slightly cooked
1 cup peas, slightly cooked
2 whole green onions, thinly sliced
1 egg and 2 egg whites, beaten
1 tsp. diet margarine
1 1/2 Tbsp. vegetable oil
4 cups cold cooked rice
2 Tbsp. soy sauce

Rub cooked rice with wet hands to separate the grains. Heat margarine in large nonstick fry pan. Pour in egg mixture to form large, thin omelette. Flip over when bottom side is lightly brown; cook other side. Remove and cut into shreds. Heat 1/4 cup low-sodium chicken broth in fry pan. Add pork, peas, and green onions. Stir-fry 2 minutes. Remove from pan and set aside. Heat oil in fry pan. Add rice and stir-fry for 2 minutes. Stir in soy sauce, egg strips, and pork mixture. Makes 4 large servings.

Nutritional analysis per serving: 497 calories, 3.5 gm. fiber, 105 mg. cholesterol, 394 mg. sodium, 24% of calories from protein, 55% from carbohydrate, 21% from fat (11.5 gm. fat), 62 mg. calcium, 4.2 mg. iron, 87 RE vitamin A, 8 mg. vitamin C.

For preparing barbecued pork: Cut a pork tenderloin (approx. 10 oz. raw) into bite-sized pieces and lay in 9 x 9-inch baking dish. In small pan, briefly heat 1 Tbsp. each of soy sauce and dry sherry, 2 tsp. each of honey and brown sugar, and 1/2 tsp. minced ginger until sugar is dissolved. Pour sauce over pork pieces and bake in 350-degree oven until cooked throughout. Turn pieces over after baking 10 minutes.

TIP #190 / CREATE KABOBS OF PORK TENDERLOIN TERIYAKI WITH VEGETABLES.

2 pork tenderloins (about 1 1/4 lb. total)
1/2 cup pineapple juice
1/4 cup low-sodium soy sauce
2 Tbsp. brown sugar
1 cup pineapple chunks (canned in juice)
10 cherry tomatoes (or button mushrooms)
1 large green pepper cut into large pieces (or 10 zucchini coins 1/2"-thick)

Cut tenderloins vertically into 1/4-inch thick medallions and set aside in medium bowl. In a small saucepan, heat juice with soy sauce and brown sugar until brown sugar dissolves. Pour over pork and let marinate in refrigerator for about an hour. Line your broiling pan with foil. String about 4 pieces of pork lengthwise onto 13-inch metal skewers while alternating with an assortment of the vegetables and pineapple chunks. Brush generously with remaining marinade. Lay on broiling pan and broil about 6 to 7 minutes on each side or until pork is cooked throughout. Makes 5 servings (2 skewers each). Serve with steamed rice if desired.

Nutrition analysis per serving: 272 calories, 1.3 gm. fiber, 83 mg. cholesterol, 480 mg. sodium, 22 mg. calcium, 1.4 mg. iron, 36 RE vitamin A, 28 mg. vitamin C, 42% of calories from protein, 28% from carbohydrate, 30% from fat (9 gm. fat)

TIP #191 / TREAT THE KIDS TO STRAWBERRY ALOHA SHAKE.

1/3 cup sliced strawberries (fresh or frozen)
1/4 cup crushed pineapple (canned in juice)
3/4 cup low-fat frozen yogurt (wild strawberry or strawberry cheesecake)
Optional topping:
1 Tbsp. flaked coconut, packaged
1 Tbsp. low-fat granola (i.e. Kellogg's)

Put ingredients in blender or food processor. Blend until smooth and well mixed. Spoon into serving glass. Sprinkle topping over the top (optional). Makes one large serving.

Nutrition analysis per serving: 232 calories, 2 gm. fiber, 10 mg. cholesterol, 71 mg. sodium, 8% of calories from protein, 84% from carbohydrate, 8% from fat (2 gm. fat)

TIP #192 / SERVE A SIDE OF SEASONED RICE.

1 cup uncooked brown rice
1 1/2 cup water
1 packet low-sodium chicken broth (or 1 cube)
1 cup chopped onion
1 1/2 cups vegetable pieces (grated carrots, broccoli, or a combination of others)
2 tsp. parsley flakes
1/2 lemon, sliced (used as garnish when serving, great squeezed on top of the rice)

Mix low-sodium chicken broth with water in a medium saucepan. Add the rice, onions, parsley, and mix. Spoon the vegetable pieces on top and cover saucepan. Let boil. Then reduce heat to simmer. Let simmer until rice is cooked and most of the water is absorbed (about 25 minutes). Stir vegetables into the rest of the rice mixture and serve. Makes four servings.

Nutrition analysis per serving: 195 calories, 6 gm. fiber, 0 cholesterol, 25 mg. sodium, 10% of calories from protein, 84% from carbohydrate, 6% from fat (1.5 gm. fat).

TIP #193 / ENJOY THESE BANANA COIN PANCAKES.

1 cup incomplete pancake mix
   (i.e., Aunt Jemima Buttermilk)
1 cup 1% low-fat milk
1/4 cup low-fat egg substitute
   (Egg Beaters or Healthy Choice) or 1 egg or 2 egg whites
3 tsp. diet margarine
2 small bananas, cut into 1/4-inch thick coins

In medium bowl, mix pancake mix with milk and egg. Melt 1 tsp. of diet margarine over medium heat in small nonstick fry pan (about 6 inches wide at bottom). Lay 1/3 of banana coins in pan. Pour 1/3 of batter over banana coins covering bottom of pan. When bottom side is nicely brown, carefully flip pancake over and cook until done. Repeat steps, making 2 more pancakes with rest of ingredients. Serves 2 (1 1/2 pancakes per person).

Nutrition analysis per serving: 305 calories, 1.5 gm. fiber, 6 mg. cholesterol, 890 mg. sodium, 285 mg. calcium, 1.14 mg. iron, 150 RE vitamin A, 9 mg. vitamin C, 13% of calories from protein, 67% from carbohydrates, 20% from fat (6.9 gm. fat)

TIP #194 / MAKE A HEARTY CREAM OF BROCCOLI SOUP.

1 cup raw carrot slices
3 cups raw broccoli pieces and florets
1 cup 1% milk
1/2 Tbsp. butter or margarine
3/4 cup chopped sweet or yellow onion
2 cloves garlic, finely chopped
1 cup chicken broth
2 Tbsp. flour
1 Tbsp. Molly McButter® butter sprinkles (or similar)

Layer carrot slices then broccoli pieces in microwave-safe dish with 1/4 cup water. Microwave on high for 6 minutes or until cooked throughout. Remove broccoli with slotted spoon and place in food processor with 1/2 cup of the milk. Puree for just a few seconds. Melt butter over medium heat in large saucepan, add onion and garlic, and let brown slightly, stirring frequently. Add broccoli mixture and stir to blend. Blend 3 Tbsp. of the broth with the flour and add to broccoli mixture and stir. Blend in remaining broth. Sprinkle butter sprinkles over the top and stir. Let soup boil gently until desired thickness. Add a little more milk for thinner soup. Makes four 1-cup servings.

Nutrition analysis per serving: 127 calories, 4.5 gm. fiber, 6 mg. cholesterol, 428 mg. sodium, 1142 RE vitamin A, 76 mg. vitamin C, 147 mg. calcium, 1.5 mg. iron, 23% of calories from protein, 57% from carbohydrate, 20% from fat (3 gm. fat)

TIP #195 / WARM THEM WITH A QUESADILLA SURPRISE.

I thick homestyle flour tortilla
I Tbsp. salsa (or bottled spaghetti sauce)
I 1/2 oz. reduced-fat Monterey Jack (Kraft Light Naturals,
   Weight Watchers), grated
1/2 cup finely diced zucchini
1/4 cup finely chopped red pepper (or green or yellow pepper)
3 Tbsp. cooked pinto beans (may use canned pinto beans, drained)

Over medium heat, add flour tortilla to nonstick fry pan. Once bottom of tortilla is hot and lightly browned, flip to other side. Spread salsa over one half, sprinkle cheese evenly over the tortilla, and top with diced and chopped vegetables and beans. Continue heating until bottom is lightly brown. Fold one side over the other and serve.

Makes 1 serving

Nutrition analysis per serving: 316 calories, 5.4 gm. fiber, 23 mg. cholesterol, 392 mg. sodium, 369 mg. calcium, 2.3 mg. iron, 220 RE vitamin A, 45 mg. vitamin C, 23% of calories from protein, 47% from carbohydrate, 30% from fat (11 gm. fat)

TIP #196 / MAKE A HEALTHY RAISIN TAPIOCA PUDDING.

3 Tbsp. Minute® tapioca
1/4 cup sugar
2 3/4 cup 1% milk
1 egg
1 cup raisins or currants
1 tsp. vanilla or 1/2 tsp. almond extract

Combine sugar, tapioca, milk, and egg in saucepan. Let stand 5 minutes. Stir in raisins. Cook and stir over medium heat until mixture comes to a full boil (it will thicken as it cools). Remove from heat and stir in vanilla. Cool 20 to 30 minutes. Stir and spoon into serving cups. Serve warm or chilled. Makes 4 large servings.

Nutrition analysis per serving: 285 calories, 2.3 gm. fiber, 60 mg. cholesterol, 105 mg. sodium, 234 mg. calcium, 1.25 mg. iron, 123 RE vitamin a, 3 mg. vitamin C, 11% of calories from protein, 79% from carbohydrate, 10% from fat (3 gm. fat)

TIP #197 / FOR A HEARTY TREAT, MAKE THIS QUICK PEA SOUP

1/2 cup chopped onion
1 Tbsp. diet margarine
2 cups frozen green peas
1/4 cup finely chopped celery
1 cup warm water mixed with 2 packets low-sodium chicken broth
  (or 1 cup chicken broth)
1 garlic clove, minced (or 1/4 tsp. garlic powder)
1/2 tsp. sugar
Pinch or two cayenne pepper
2 Tbsp. flour
2 cups 1% milk
1/2 cup diced cooked carrots
4 strips Louis Rich® Turkey bacon, cooked and torn into pieces

In large saucepan, melt margarine over medium-low heat. Add onions and let brown lightly, stirring frequently (about 3 minutes). Stir in green peas, celery, and chicken broth. Continue cooking until peas are tender and chicken broth almost evaporates (about 8 minutes; peas will gently boil). Let cool a few minutes. Spoon into blender or food processor. Sprinkle garlic, sugar, and cayenne over the top. Puree until fairly smooth. Spoon back into saucepan. Add 2 Tbsp. of flour to measuring cup. Stir in 4 Tbsp. milk. Pour in remaining milk and stir until blended. Add to saucepan along with cooked carrot and bacon pieces. Cover and let simmer 10 minutes on low heat, stirring frequently. Makes about four 1-cup servings.

Nutrition analysis per serving: 190 calories, 5 gm. fiber, 20 mg. cholesterol, 420 mg. sodium, 186 mg. calcium, 2 mg. iron, 640 RE vitamin A, 17 mg. vitamin C, 23% of calories from protein, 51% from carbohydrate, 26% from fat (5.5 gm. fat)

TIP #198 / GIVE THE FAMILY MACARONI & CHEESE IN A BROCCOLI FOREST

9 oz. macaroni, cooked and drained (about 5 cups cooked)
1/4 cup flour
1/4 tsp. dry mustard
Pepper to taste (1/4 to 1/2 tsp.)
1 2/3 cup 1% milk
4 ounces part-skim sharp cheddar cheese, grated
   (i.e., KRAFT Light 'N Natural sharp cheddar)
1/4 tsp. dry mustard
Pepper to taste (1/4 to 1/2 tsp.)
1 2/3 cup 1% milk
4 ounces part-skim cheddar cheese, grated
   (i.e., KRAFT Light 'N Natural sharp cheddar)
1/4 cup (2 oz.) processed sharp cheddar "cheese food"
2 cups broccoli florets, lightly steamed or micro-cooked

In medium saucepan, mix flour, mustard, and pepper. Add 1/3 cup of the milk and stir to make a paste. Then add another 1/3 cup of milk and stir. Repeat with remaining milk, stirring after each 1/3 cup. Over medium heat, heat milk mixture, stirring constantly until it thickens and begins to boil (2 to 3 minutes). Remove from heat. Stir in the grated cheese and the 1/4 cup processed cheese. (Don't worry, the cheese will melt). Mix the cheese sauce with the hot noodles and broccoli and serve immediately or bake in 350 oven for 20 minutes.

Makes 4 large servings

Nutrition analysis per serving: (Values are approximate. Exact values depend on the cheese used.) 437 calories, 3 gm. fiber, 27 mg. cholesterol, 278 mg. sodium, 22% of calories from protein, 58% from carbohydrate, 20% from fat (9.5 gm. fat)

TIP #199 / ADD FRUIT WITH THIS FRUITY FROZEN TREAT

1 1/2 cups diced, mixed fruit such as;
  peaches, pears, banana, berries, or kiwi
1/4 tsp. cinnamon
3 cups low-fat or nonfat frozen dairy dessert, softened
16 graham cracker squares or 32 ginger snaps

Sprinkle cinnamon over fruit and toss to combine. Fold fruit into softened dairy dessert. Line cookie sheet with wax paper and place 8 cracker squares on sheet. Top each square with about 1/2 cup dairy dessert mixture. Top each with remaining crackers. Place in freezer on cookie sheet until firm, then wrap in plastic wrap until needed. Makes 4 servings. (With ginger snaps, make 16 treats or 4 per person).

Nutrition analysis per serving (using low-fat frozen yogurt with 2 gm. fat per 3-oz. serving): 306 calories, 2 gm. fiber, 10 mg. cholesterol, 268 mg. sodium, 7% of calories from protein, 73% from carbohydrate, 20% from fat (6.8 gm. fat)

TIP #200 / MAKE YOUR OWN HAWAIIAN PIZZA.

1 can Pillsbury All Ready Pizza Crust
1 tsp. olive oil
3/4 cup low-fat bottled spaghetti sauce (2 gm. of fat or less per 4 oz. serving)
2 oz. reduced-fat mozzarella
3 oz. reduced-fat sharp cheddar
2 cups pineapple chunks (canned in juice)
4 oz. Canadian bacon (or sliced lean ham)

Preheat oven to 425 degrees. Grease 13" x 9" pan with oil. Pop can of pizza dough, unroll, and press into pan. Top evenly with sauce. Sprinkle cheese over the top. Add Canadian bacon, then pineapple chunks. Bake for about 20 minutes. Serves 4.

Nutrition analysis per serving: 442 calories, 1.5 gm. fiber, 37 mg. cholesterol, 1535 mg. sodium, 331 mg. calcium, 1.5 mg. iron, 140 RE vitamin A, 23 mg. vitamin C, 23% of calories from protein, 47% from carbohydrate, 30% from fat (14.5 gm. fat)

Moving On

What could be more important than our children's health and happiness? (Well, maybe world peace.) But with all the complexities of life, it's so easy for parents to lose this focus.

Spending a little time with adults who are trying to change their self-destructive, life-long eating habits is all it takes to realize how much easier it would be to start with children. In my experience, food habits and preferences start the moment table food hits those little lips. To my daughters, reduced-fat turkey bacon and low-fat cheese are real bacon and real cheese. Less-fat hot dogs are the one-and-only hot dogs, and the only way to eat pizza is without meat on top.

Forming new, healthful habits in children is far more productive (and successful) than changing old, bad habits in adults. Even at the ripe old age of 18 months, my daughter started asking for "butter sprinkles" on her potato because that's what she saw Mommy do.

After reading through all these tips, I hope I've left you with two thoughts: "What could be more important than the health of my child?" and "What could be easier?" In most cases, I haven't reinvented the way most kids eat or what their favorite foods are. I've just changed some of the choices within their framework.

Now that you've made it through the book, I'll let you in on a little secret. My goal was not only to inspire and educate you on lowering the fat in your child's diet. I was also aiming a little higher—at you, Mom and Dad. I'm secretly hoping you start shopping, cooking, and eating lighter for your own good health as well as your children's.

After all, a family that eats light together feels better (and probably lives longer) together, too.

Index

200 Kid-Tested Ways to Lower the Fat in Your Child's Favorite Foods by Elaine Moquette-Magee, M.P.H., R.D. For the first time ever, here's a much needed and asked for guide that gives easy, step-by-step instructions on cutting the fat in the most popular brand name and homemade foods kids eat every day–without them even noticing.

004231,   ISBN 1-56561-034-2 $12.95

How Should I Feed My Child? From Pregnancy to Preschool by Sandra Nissenberg, M.S., R.D., Margaret Bogle, Ph.D., R.D., Edna Langholz, M.S., R.D., and Audrey Wright, M.S., R.D. Addressing real issues and parents' most common concerns, this guide tells how to start your child off to a lifetime of good eating habits. Includes over 50 recipes.

"From four nutrition experts with impressive credentials, the book offers easy-to-read, practical advice."
-USA Today
* A Doubleday Health Book Club Selection

004232,   ISBN 1-56561-035-0 $12.95

Emergency Medical Treatment: Infants, Children, Adults, Revised and Expanded Edition by Stephen Vogel, M.D., and David Manhoff, produced in cooperation with the National Safety Council. With over 1.5 million copies sold, the #1-selling guide of its kind has saved countless lives and is now totally updated with the newest safety guidelines. Written especially for people untrained in emergency medical procedures, this indispensable, step-by-step guide tells exactly what to do during the most common, life-threatening situations you might encounter for infants, children, and adults.

004627,   ISBN 0-916363-10-4 $12.95

The Healthy Eater's Guide to Family & Chain Restaurants by Hope S. Warshaw, M.M.Sc., R.D. Here's the only guide that tells you how to eat healthier in over 100 of America's most popular family and chain restaurants. It offers complete and up-to-date nutrition information and suggests which items to choose and avoid.

004214,   ISBN 1-56561-017-2 $9.95

Fast Food Facts by Marion Franz, R.D., M.S. This revised and up-to-date best-seller shows how to make smart nutrition choices at fast food restaurants—and tells what to avoid. Includes complete nutrition information on more than 1,000 menu offerings from the 32 largest fast food chains.

Standard-size edition   004068,   ISBN 0-937721-67-0 $6.95
Pocket edition   004073,   ISBN 0-937721-69-7 $4.95

Convenience Food Facts by Arlene Monk, R.D., C.D.E., with introduction by Marion Franz, R.D., M.S. C.D.E. Includes complete nutrition information, tips, and exchange values on more than 1,500 popular name-brand processed foods commonly found in grocery store freezers and shelves. Helps you plan easy-to-prepare, nutritious meals.

004081,   ISBN 0-937721-77-8 $10.95

60 Days of Low-Fat, Low-Cost Meals in Minutes by M.J. Smith, R.D., L.D., M.A. Following the path of the best-seller *All American Low-Fat Meals in Minutes,* here are more than 150 quick and sumptuous recipes complete with the latest exchange values and nutrition facts for lowering calories, fat, salt, and cholesterol. This book contains complete menus for 60 days and recipes that use ingredients found in virtually any grocery store—most for a total cost of less than $10.

004205,   ISBN 1-56561-010-5 $12.95

One Year of Healthy, Hearty, and Simple One-Dish Meals by Pam Spaude and Jan Owan-McMenamin, R.D., is a collection of 365 easy-to-make healthy and tasty family favorites and unique creations that are meals in themselves. Most of the dishes take under 30 minutes to prepare.

004217,   ISBN 1-56561-019-9 $12.95

Let Them Eat Cake by Virginia N. White with Rosa A. Mo, R.D. If you're looking for delicious and healthy pies, cookies, puddings, and cakes, this book will give you your just desserts. With easy, step-by-step instructions, this innovative cookbook features complete nutrition information, the latest exchange values, and tips on making your favorite snacks more healthful.

004206,   ISBN 1-56561-011-3 $12.95

All-American Low-Fat Meals in Minutes by M.J. Smith, M.A., R.D., L.D. Filled with tantalizing recipes and valuable tips, this cookbook makes great-tasting, low-fat foods a snap for holidays, special occasions, or everyday. Most recipes take only minutes to prepare.

004079,   ISBN 0-937721-73-5 $12.95

The Joy of Snacks by Nancy Cooper, R.D. Offers more than 200 delicious recipes and nutrition information for hearty snacks, including sandwiches, appetizers, soups, spreads, cookies, muffins, and treats especially for kids. The book also suggests guidelines for selecting convenience snacks and interpreting information on food labels.

004086,   ISBN 0-937721-82-4 $12.95

The Guiltless Gourmet by Judy Gilliard and Joy Kirkpatrick, R.D. A perfect fusion of sound nutrition and creative cooking, this book is loaded with delicious recipes high in flavor and low in fat, sugar, calories, cholesterol, and salt.

004021,   ISBN 0-937721-23-9 $9.95

The Guiltless Gourmet Goes Ethnic by Judy Gilliard and Joy Kirkpatrick, R.D. More than a cookbook, this sequel to *The Guiltless Gourmet* shows how easy it is to lower the sugar, calories, sodium, and fat in your favorite ethnic dishes—without sacrificing taste.

004072, ISBN 0-937721-68-9 $11.95

European Cuisine from the Guiltless Gourmet by Judy Gilliard and Joy Kirkpatrick, R.D. This book shows you how to lower the sugar, salt, cholesterol, total fat, and calories in delicious Greek, English, German, Russian, and Scandinavian dishes. Plus, it features complete nutrition information and the latest exchange values.

004085, ISBN 0-937721-81-6 $11.95

Beyond Alfalfa Sprouts and Cheese: The Healthy Meatless Cookbook by Judy Gilliard and Joy Kirkpatrick, R.D., includes creative and savory meatless dishes using ingredients found in just about every grocery store. It also contains helpful cooking tips, complete nutrition information, and the latest exchange values.

004218, ISBN 1-56561-020-2 $12.95

CHRONIMED Publishing
P.O. Box 47945
Minneapolis, MN 55447-9727

Circle the book (s) you would like sent. Enclosed is $_____.
(Please add $3.00 to this order to cover postage and handling. Minnesota residents add 6.5% sales tax.) Send check or money order, no cash or C.O.D.'s. Prices are subject to change without notice.

Name _____

Address _____

City _____ State_____Zip_____

Allow 4 to 6 weeks for delivery.
Quantity discounts available upon request.

Or order by phone: 1-800-848-2793,
612-546-1146 (Minneapolis/St. Paul metro area).
Please have your credit card number ready.